ADVERTISING INTERNATIONAL

The advertising industry has changed out of all recognition over the past twenty years. The map of global communications has been redrawn by a flood of mergers and takeovers, and the media industry is now dominated by a handful of transnational conglomerates. Advertising companies have diversified into television production, public relations, media buying and marketing services. In the gap created by the crisis in public service provision, advertising has stepped in, forming a network which enervates media, economies, cultures, politics and international relations. Armand Mattelart's outstanding survey assesses the development and future prospects of this 'industry of public noise', and examines the implications for democracy of the seemingly irresistible rise of the communications society.

Armand Mattelart is Professor of Information and Communication Sciences at the University of Haute-Bretagne (Rennes-France). From 1962 to 1973, he taught at the University of Santiago, Chile. He is the author of several books, including *How to Read Donald Duck* (with Ariel Dorfman) (1975), *Multinational Corporations and the Control of Culture* (1979), *International Image Markets* (with Michèle Mattelart and Xavier Delcourt) (1984) and *The Carnival of Images: Brazilian Television Fiction* (with Michèle Mattelart) (1990). He has carried out missions relating to communications policy for the governments of Belgium, France, Mozambique and Nicaragua.

Michael Chanan, the translator, is Senior Lecturer in Film and Video at the London College of Printing; he is also an independent film-maker and author.

COMEDIA
Series editor: David Morley

ADVERTISING INTERNATIONAL

The privatisation of public space

Armand Mattelart

Translated by Michael Chanan

A Comedia book
published by Routledge
London and New York

A Comedia book

First published in 1989 as *L'Internationale publicitaire* by
Editions La Découverte, 1 Place Paul-Painlevé, 75005 Paris

Revised English language edition first published 1991
by Routledge
11 New Fetter Lane, London EC4P 4EE

Simultaneously published in the USA and Canada
by Routledge
a division of Routledge, Chapman and Hall, Inc.
29 West 35th Street, New York, NY 10001

© 1991 Armand Mattelart

Translation © 1991 Michael Chanan

Set in 10/12pt Baskerville by Witwell Ltd, Southport
Printed and bound in Great Britain by Clays Ltd, St Ives

British Library Cataloguing in Publication Data
Mattelart, Armand
Advertising international: the privatisation of public
space. – (A Comedia book)
1. Advertising industries. Management
I. Title   II. L'Internationale publicitaire
338.47659.1

Library of Congress Cataloging in Publication Data
Mattelart, Armand.
[Internationale publicitaire. English]
Advertising international: the privatisation of public space
/Armand Mattelart: translated by Michael Chanan. – Rev. English language
ed.
p.   cm. – (Comedia)
Translation of: L'Internationale publicitaire.
Includes index.
1. Advertising.   2. Advertising agencies.   3. International
business enterprises.   4. Advertising–Social aspects.
5. Communication, International.   6. Intercultural communication.
I. Title.   II. Series.
HF5821.M3213   1991
659.1–dc20   90-24146
ISBN 0-415-05063-4
0-415-05064-2 pbk

'Come on, Mitz! There were five hundred Veenies out there!' And so there had been – maybe more – at the time, I could have sworn half of Venus was silently parading around our embassy with their stupid signs – 'No Advertising!' and 'Take Your Filth Back Where It Belongs!' I didn't mind the picketing so much – but, oh, the pathetic amateurishness of their slogan writers! 'They're crazy,' I said – a complicated shorthand that didn't mean 'crazy' for thinking we would use advertising techniques on them, but 'crazy' because they were getting upset about it – as though there were any possibility that, given a chance, we wouldn't.

I also meant crazy in the specific context of incompetent copysmithing . . . .

All the same I came up with some beauties. I called Dixmeister in to see them, all beautifully calligraphed and ornamented by Art, with theme music and multisensual background by Production. He gaped at the monitor, puzzled. 'Hands Off Hyperion' ? That's truly superb, Mr Tarb,' he said by reflex, and then, hesitating, 'but isn't it really kind of the other way around? I mean, we don't want to let go of Hyperion as a market, do we?'

'Not *our* hands off, Dixmeister,' I said kindly.

'*Veenies*' hands off. We want them left alone by Veenies.'

His expression cleared. 'A masterpiece, Mr Tarb,' he said raptly. 'And this one. "Freedom of Information." That means no attempts at censoring advertising, right? And "Get Government Off the Backs of the People"?'

'Means abolishing the requirement to post warnings at Campbell areas,' I explained. [Thus named after Dr H.J. Campbell, celebrated pioneer of psychology during the heroic epoch, inventor of limbic pleasure therapy.]

Frederick Pohl,
one of the craftsmen of American science fiction,
The Merchant's War, St Martin's Press, New York, 1984.

CONTENTS

AUTHOR'S PREFACE

No media without advertising. This is what most television clearly demonstrates. Some would hasten to add, no creation, no national production, no preservation of cultural identity without the manna of the advertisers, whilst others speak of the collapse of national cinema, the asphyxiation of creation, the degradation of programme quality. One of the objects of this study is to analyse the multiple forms taken by the growing overlap of the advertising industry and the media.

The question of advertising has long ceased to be a national question, and indeed its transnational dimension constitutes its history as a network and a network of networks. This book analyses the trajectory of this network which today – with varying intensity – forges ever-stronger links between the economy and a universalised culture. It presents numerous realities which this network comprises, which it both unites and separates in this era of the abolition of frontiers. For this epoch of ours is rich in contradictions. When everything in the evolution of technology and the economy seems to lead to the homogenisation of taste and behaviour, when this complex world of interrelations and interpenetration favours concentration and gigantism, one has never felt with so much force the tensions which mark the encounter between the universal and the particular, between external logic and territorial communities of understanding, which in their own way are sources of universality. Like all networks, this one has its own splits and discontinuities.

Advertising has become an essential actor within public space. It has overflowed the cramped frame of the commercial break in order to constitute itself as a mode of communication. From the isolated and isolable product, it has become a diffuse environment, pregnant and present in the everyday. Yesterday a simple instrument, today a central feature. Its field of competence is so diversified and branching, that it forms a social network which enervates media, economies, cultures, political and civil society, international relations. Network of networks, these systems of connection regulate the relations between individuals and groups. The so-called communications society chases the so-called consumer society. We must therefore examine this essential change which provokes a whole cascade of mutations and redefinitions in the practice of democracy.

This book is also a book about intellectuals. Not about those who not so long ago defined themselves through the exercise of the critical function, but these new mediators and bearers of knowledge and know-how who run this institution and this industry of public noise.

Lastly, the issues examined in this book concerning the networks' progress are unfolding in a particularly volatile international environment. Uncertainty governs the strategies of the big groups and the flow of capital released by the new world economy. If the golden Eighties of megamergers, takeovers and unmediated globalisation were able to sustain the illusion of the limitless (and exponential) growth of advertising markets, the Nineties have begun by planting seeds of doubt. The combined effect of the first post-Cold War international conflict in the Persian Gulf and the recession in the leading industrialised countries like the USA and Britain, comes as a sharp reminder: on a planet where a geo-economic logic increasingly prevails, geopolitics is far from losing its rights. And this remains the case, even if the new conditions of international competition and the realignment of the relations of power between nations, regions and blocs, radically change their nature.

A.M., Paris

TRANSLATOR'S PREFACE

Translating a book about advertising from French into English makes one singularly aware of language differences – not only between French and English but also within English itself, between English and American usage. While the original sources have been used for all direct quotations which originated in English, one still has to match up French neologisms with Anglo-Saxon jargon (thus 'feedback' has become *rétroalimentation*, the latter a word not found in the translator's dictionary), or else find English words for a kind of discourse on advertising that is foreign to Madison Avenue and the Harvard Business School. Then again, one finds at times an English phrase like 'television commercials' has been translated into French – doubtless without the approval of the Académie Française – as *des spots*. In short, one discovers that the world of advertising and the media has induced in late twentieth-century speech a certain polyglot element, of a kind which inevitably offends purists.

Occasionally it has been necessary to coin a new word to translate a neologism of the author. French and Spanish are often more graceful in this respect: handy English words are often lacking. I hope the results are not too ugly. An important word in this regard is *médiatique*. In some instances – like *des compagnies médiatiques* – I have left it as 'media companies'. In other cases I translate it as 'mediatised'. What I have tried to capture here is Mattelart's sense of an idea or a concept becoming transformed by being taken up in and through the media. What Woody Allen meant when he said, 'I've got an idea for a film, and I think I know where I can get the money to turn it into a concept.'

Another crucial word in the book is *réseau*. This translates quite straightforwardly as 'network', and the whole book is about the networks which comprise global advertising, global media, global telecommunications, global conglomerates, global finance operations and supposedly global audiences. But Mattelart uses the term, from the outset, to indicate the characteristic form of interrelationship between units of production not just in the advertising industry but in the mediatised culture industry as a whole. As we read his analysis, we begin to realise what this means in real historical terms: the media have grown by networking; and the concept of the network represents a new paradigm of the social order which sits above the real world, so to speak, and throws its web over it. Above all, it is not a state of existence but an active and continuing process.

Another feature of the difference between English and American English in the field of advertising is the use of language within the advertising copy itself: the verbal originality of English advertising compared to American, which many an observant American visiting England notices quite rapidly. It's not much to write home about, but they notice a quality of playfulness in the written language which written American – apart from its literary authors – tends to lack. (The reverse is true of spoken English. In the States, though academic speech is often full of circumlocutions, the street rap is much more inventive than in the Old World, where except for youth culture, speech is more stilted.)

The ascent of British advertising, the British agencies' 'creative' pre-eminence in the 1970s and 1980s, is probably not unconnected. At any rate, in English (as opposed to American) advertising, punning, *double entendre* and constructed ambiguity are ubiquitous (from pre-war slogans like 'Players please' to British Telecom's 'It's you we answer to'). What has happened in the 1970s and 1980s is the translation of this unsubtle subtlety into the visual domain, where American advertising is also more stilted and trite, and with it the predominance of the new technical wizardry of computer graphics that has been nurtured in Soho – London's, not New York's. The whole process is strongly mediatised. As Mattelart shows, Saatchis built itself on hype, advancing its own media image in order to persuade a reticent stock market of the speculative value of the advertising business. But the tide has recently turned and the company finds itself hoist with its own petard: it has been replaced as the world's largest advertising network by WPP, a group built up by Martin Sorrell, who was once their own man. And now WPP is in trouble too.

This word 'creative', as a term of vocabulary in advertising discourse, has very little to do with what a poet, a philosopher, a psychologist or even a neuro-psychologist might mean by it. For all the differences which divide such experts, the word has in each case a real and plastic meaning which links it intimately with the faculty of imagination. 'Creativity' and 'creative staff' in the advertising world are fetishistic terms. To borrow the aesthetic terminology of the poet Coleridge, there is never any *imagination* in advertising, only the work of *fancy*, which produces nothing original, but merely recycles and recombines existing material. What Stravinsky admired in composers of jingles was not their originality but their economy of means. The only possible originality advertising could claim is in technique, and even then this is doubtful;

certainly never in content, which consists entirely in pseudo-speech, Orwellian non-speak. The latter part of this book is concerned with exposing the pseudo-discourse which the advertising industry has constructed to mask this non-speak, which only robs us of the deeper meaning of our words.

The Spanish translator of this book elucidated various language matters by adding a number of elegant footnotes. I have occasionally borrowed from these, and also added a few footnotes of my own. These are found on the page with the text. The author's references are found at the end of the book, together with an index specially prepared for this edition. The English edition incorporates new material from the Spanish edition, and has been further updated in consultation with the author to reflect some of the most important new developments in the field.

M.C., London

1

THE GEOSTRATEGY OF
THE NETWORKS

The rise of the global agencies

THE FALL OF A SYMBOL

'You cannot be a global communications business if you're not big in the United States', confided the British magnate Robert Maxwell to *Newsweek* in November 1987.[1]

Everyone has thought this and many have tried it. Indeed, the second half of the 1980s has seen the arrival of big firms of European, Japanese and Australian provenance on the American scene. Maxwell himself launched no less than three fabulous public takeover bids – two of them shortlived – for three major publishers, and finally carried off Macmillan. The German Bertelsmann has taken over the publisher Doubleday and the record company RCA-Ariola. The Japanese company Sony made a successful bid for the prestigious CBS Records, and has since acquired the Hollywood film company Columbia. The foremost French publisher, the Hachette group, has purchased shares in Grolier (world number one in encyclopaedias) and the magazine publisher Diamandis. As for the Australian Rupert Murdoch, proprietor of News Corporation, he is so convinced that the United States represent the obligatory step in building up a multimedia conglomerate of global vocation that he swapped his own nationality for that of his new properties Twentieth Century Fox and *TV Guide*. The American reply to this foreign offensive was not long in coming: in 1989, the *rapprochement* between Time-Warner Communications and the reorientation towards communications of the conglomerate Gulf & Western, owner of Paramount Pictures and the publisher Simon & Schuster, sparked off manoeuvres aimed at a restructuring of the publishing and entertainments industry in the threatened fiefdom.

Advance guard of the media industry, the advertising sector, has shown candidates who wish to capture the New World the way to proceed. In July 1987, the British group Wire & Plastic Products (WPP) spent $566m to absorb the world's fifth-largest advertising firm, the American company J. Walter Thompson. The deal gave them a diversified group: an

1

advertising enterprise which employs 7,700 people; a public relations firm – the world's foremost company in this specialisation – Hill & Knowlton, with 1,600 employees; a research company, Market Research Bureau (MRB), which occupies eighth position in commercial research; a specialist agency, namely Lord, Geller, Federico, Einstein, devoted exclusively to up-market products of which the most prestigious are those of IBM. By symbolic coincidence, in that same month of July, the British press and publications group Reed International purchased the American journal *Variety*, bible of the world of spectacle and audiovisual production, created eighty-two years earlier and widely read outside the US.

The previous year, the agency Saatchi & Saatchi, also British, hoisted itself to top place among large international holdings in the advertising industry through the purchase, for $450m, of the American firm Ted Bates, fourth-largest network in the world. Indeed in three years, Saatchi & Saatchi enriched itself with three large agencies and two public relations firms, all American.

In short, a race was launched in the second half of the 1980s to form a global advertising enterprise. 'Between now and the year 2000, there will be ten or twelve large global communications groups. In the advertising sector, there will be fewer still . . . perhaps six', was the prognostication in 1987 of a financial representative of Saatchis.

Even if a single takeover doesn't make a summer, the cliché of British decline has been superseded. Stimulated by the deregulation of the London markets which reached its climax with the 'Big Bang' of 1986, British investment on American soil has reached a historical record: nearly $32b*, more than six times that of 1984. The same year, Japan invested $15b.[2]

'Reversal of history', 'Rebellion of British agencies', commented the City newspapers, congratulating themselves on these assaults against the stronghold of American advertising, Madison Avenue. During the previous decades, Great Britain had seen the decimation of its own advertising industry. In a way, this dismantling was a symbol of the decline of its film industry which during the post-war years had fallen practically lock, stock and barrel into the hands of the Hollywood majors. This was a very different panorama to that of France, which during the same years succeeded in maintaining the independence of both its film industry and its advertising market. But by 1979, more than 70 per cent of the turnover of the twenty leading London agencies had ended up in the portfolios of American firms.

With control of J. Walter Thompson passing to British capital, that image was smashed. Although created in 1864, this agency cannot claim

---

* 'Billion' throughout this book denotes one thousand million. [Translator's note.]

to be the first. Such paternity is rather to be found in Volney B. Palmer, established in Philadelphia in 1840 – where Benjamin Franklin had become famous as a statesman, physician, philosopher and publicist – with subsidiaries later set up in Boston and New York. James Walter Thompson, however, fresh from the Marines where he served on the USS Saratoga, and proprietor of the homonymous agency from the 1870s, was the first to take a special interest in magazine advertising, especially women's magazines. From a small firm placing announcements mainly in religious publications with an ecumenical profile, he went on to construct by the end of the century one of the first modern agencies: the kind which thinks in terms of precise targets to aim at. In the portrait gallery of the 'ten men who shaped American advertising', he can be seen in his Marines' uniform, and the inscription underneath: 'He contributed importantly to awareness of the woman consumer and the efforts of media and advertisers to appeal to and sell to her'.[3] His pamphlet *Advertising as a Selling Force*, published in 1909, is still astonishingly up to date.

The first agency to plant itself on foreign soil, J. Walter Thompson, set up shop in London in 1899. At this time, when American capital was still far from boasting the industrial power of the major European countries, the objective of this first 'sales bureau' was 'to urge businessmen of the Old Continent to sell in America and advertise their products there'. In 1888, the American agency had already published the first bilingual (French-English) annual, 440 pages thick, in order to initiate Europeans into the mysteries of the US market and its press. It was also at this time that a 'Latin American Department' began to explore the markets and media of the subcontinent, while in 1923 JWT signed its first campaign in England for the account of its Chicago client, the food canners Libby, McNeill & Libby.

In 1927, the London office was transformed into a true subsidiary when General Motors invited JWT to represent them throughout the world and to install themselves in particular wherever they were in the process of constructing factories or automobile assembly plants. Thus the history of this first phase of the agency's internationalisation parallels more closely than any other the worldwide expansion of the great American enterprises: Chesebrough-Ponds, Eastman-Kodak, Kraft, Kellogg, IBM, Ford, RCA and all the others. Year by year, in step with its clients, JWT set up office in some forty countries: in Antwerp and Madrid in 1927; Paris and Berlin in 1928; Montreal, Bombay, São Paulo, Buenos Aires, Stockholm and Copenhagen in 1929; Sydney, Melbourne and the Cape in 1930; Toronto and Rio de Janeiro in 1931; Calcutta in 1935; Mexico in 1943; Santiago de Chile and New Delhi in 1944; Milan in 1951; Frankfurt in 1952; Madras and Puerto Rico in 1955; Tokyo, Karachi, Colombo and Manila in 1956; Lima, Porto Alegre and Recife in 1957; Amsterdam in

1958; Belo Horizonte in 1960; Osaka and Vienna in 1961; Vancouver and Caracas in 1964, etc.

The successive foundation of subsidiaries in the great regional capitals of India and Brazil indicates how intimately the American firm has been associated with the establishment of the apparatus of advertising in each of these environments. In countries like Brazil, which in those years did not possess a press, radio or television of national scale, the advertising network laid the foundations for the integration of the market. And by the late 1960s, by means of telecommunications, the technological network of commercial television was in place.

PATRIOTISM STARTLED

Of the founding firms of the modern advertising industry in the United States, the agency of JWT is one of the few to have celebrated its centenary under the same flag as its earliest days. An astonishingly stable company, in a hundred years JWT has only had three presidents. Since 1878, when James Walter Thompson acquired the firm which had engaged him ten years earlier, its growth has been achieved almost without incorporating any other agencies.

Proud of this historical tradition, JWT continued to defend the doctrine which had guided its expansion until just before its purchase by the British group WPP. Four months before the murderous takeover, in what would be its last annual report to its shareholders, the president of JWT reaffirmed:

> The year 1986 was peppered with news of megamergers. . . . What all this loses sight of is the essence of an advertising agency, which is a service business, a business that prospers or fails based on how effectively it services its clients. In all the megamerger frenzy and excitement, there is very little that is of benefit to clients. . . . In fact, megamergers have raised in many clients' minds profound questions about the loyalty and professional commitment of their agencies. . . . The Thompson Company has no intention of participating in this mating of giants. It doesn't need to. Thompson has grown over the course of 122 years, one account at a time, one office at a time, one country at a time. Today it operates full-service offices in 40 countries. In terms of geographic growth there's not a lot more you could ask for. Rather than attempting to grow via megamerger, we intend to maintain Thompson's identity as 'advertising's leading brand' with all that means in terms of a coherent professional philosophy and a distinct corporate culture.[4]

This founding code of the expansionist strategy of its advertising network allowed JWT to be considered by its peers as the paragon of the

4

'imperial model' of internationalisation, or according to a British advertising man, the 'colonial model'.

It is precisely this policy which in July 1987 was to founder with all hands. Victim of bad management and repeatedly poor performance, what London-based professionals nicknamed 'the university of advertising' and New Yorkers 'the old lady of Madison Avenue' became the subsidiary of a group with a history which dated back no further than June 1985. Nevertheless the founder of this group, Martin Sorrell, alumnus of Cambridge and Harvard, is not an unknown figure in the milieu. In scarcely ten years he had forged a solid reputation as a specialist in financial packaging – what the *Financial Times* baptised 'financial engineering' but a Wall Street expert, simultaneously irritated and fascinated by this new race of arrogant predators, preferred to call an 'exercise in trick-riding'.

Sorrell served his apprenticeship as financial director of acquisitions at Saatchi & Saatchi. He then put together his own group in a mere twenty-four months. The first enterprise he acquired was a manufacturer of supermarket trolleys, which cost him $600,000, followed by sixteen more companies, most of them linked with the highly fragmented sector of 'marketing services' and closely related to media and advertising (design, graphics, sales promotion).

One sector of the American business community took it badly that such a tiny European group should snap at their own legendary terrain. The negotiations which preceded the purchase of JWT show the tone. Scarcely a month before the merger, the American advertising weekly *Advertising Age* recognised that in moving against JWT, WPP 'has launched the first unfriendly takeover battle in advertising agency history, and it is likely to be a bloody one'.[5] This is a perfect example of what has come to be called a 'hostile takeover bid' or *raid*: an operation aimed at taking control of a target company, against the opposition of its directors, by offering shareholders a price for their shares higher than their market value.

Some of JWT's clients themselves took up battle-stations. At their heads were Kodak and Goodyear, who had been using JWT's services for fifty-six and twelve years respectively. Still smarting from an attempted takeover of Goodyear by the British businessman James Goldsmith a few months earlier, a spokesman for the tyre company went so far as to affirm publicly that Goodyear 'would not feel comfortable working with a firm controlled by interests outside this country'.[6]

In one last attempt by the business community to prevent the ancestor of advertising falling into the hands of British capital, the multimedia conglomerate MCA made a last-minute bid of its own. Proprietor of the film company Universal, a chain of television stations, a publishing house (Putnam), and also well established in the record industry, MCA saw the acquisition of JWT as a valuable complement to its cultural industries. But it was already too late and the bid was only a gesture. In 1990, MCA-Universal was taken over by the Japanese electronics group Matsushita. This, on top of Sony's merger with Columbia, gave the Japanese control of 25 per cent of the Hollywood industry.)

When WPP took possession of JWT, several big advertisers like Pepsi Cola, Burger King, and Goodyear cancelled their contracts with the new owners. The cost of restructuring the agency was the sack for 17.4 per cent of the personnel. In 1988 there was a rebellion in the up-market division of Lord, Geller, Federico, Einstein, when WPP was done out of one of its most prestigious accounts, IBM, by the American network Lintas. Sorrell took the rebels to court and accused them of conspiracy.

The following year, Sorrell again returned to the game of finance with the takeover of another giant American advertising agency, Ogilvy & Mather, founded in 1948. At a cost of $864m this was the largest sum ever paid for such a network. A leading company in the field of direct marketing and with a strong presence in Europe, Ogilvy brought to WPP-JWT an international network covering fifty-two countries (55 per cent of its total revenues were generated outside the US). This operation put the new group constituted by WPP, JWT and Ogilvy practically on a par with Saatchi & Saatchi, and in 1990, as Saatchis' fortunes failed, Sorrell's WPP overtook them as the world's largest advertising network.

DOUBLE NETWORKS

The process of merger-concentration and the construction of megagroups did not begin yesterday, and its first protagonists were not the British. The first such regrouping, which dates from 1978, was the merger of a Madison Avenue star, McCann-Erickson, and the London agency Lintas, under the umbrella of the American Interpublic Group.

Lintas, a flower of British pre-war advertising, was born to serve the old soaps and detergents giant Lever Bros, which subsequently became the Anglo-Dutch group Unilever. (In 1970, Lintas had already been partly taken over by another American agency, SSC & B, founded in New York in 1946.) McCann-Erickson made its debut back in 1912 in the shadow of the Standard Oil Company. It was only in 1930, however, that it got its full name through the merger of the two agencies of McCann and Erickson. It launched itself in London and Paris in 1927, and in 1928 in Berlin, in the service of a single brand-name: Esso. During the 1930s, subsidiaries multiplied. Latin America became its preferred terrain. The eternal rival of J. Walter Thompson, the two networks have long since shared the monopoly position of first and second places in the international market.

In fact it was in the 1960s when McCann-Erickson started restructuring, to result eighteen years later, thanks to the Lintas takeover, in the formation of the premier world advertising conglomerate. In 1960, Marion Harper, the youngest president in McCann-Erickson's history, decided to create a federation around Interpublic Group, with his own agency as the leading light and an ensemble of recent acquisitions of lesser brilliance; thus transforming the group into a diversified advertising enterprise, and reinforcing its presence abroad – especially in Asia (Japan, Hong Kong, Popular China and India).

Ten years later and thanks to a flood of acquisitions, Interpublic possessed a double network: the first centred on McCann-Erickson with New York as its general headquarters, the second based on a long-established London agency, Quadrant International. The purchase by Lintas completed what became a new model of organisation. All the candidates for megamergers in the 1980s adopted it. The double network makes it possible to anticipate eventual conflict between two competing clients who share the same agency. Partitioned off from each other, the two networks compete as if they belonged to two different proprietors, but their profits end up in the same account. If Interpublic can claim the credit for first applying this idea to the advertising industry, its invention cannot be attributed to them. In fact Marion Harper borrowed the form of organisation from the automobile manufacturers General Motors, who produced five different models with the same engine power, which they put on the market in artificial competition with each other.

Interpublic is a group of five companies, which offer the whole range of advertising services, with 12,000 employees divided between nearly 200 bureaux in more than 50 countries, and co-operative relations with local agencies in a couple of dozen more. Turnover in 1989: $8.5b. Profit margin: $1.28b. (An advertising agency's turnover, also called 'billings', is defined as the total of the bills to its clients, that is to say, the sum of the budgets which are entrusted to them, including the cost of the advertising space taken up in the media.) Of this turnover, McCann-Erickson brought Interpublic 55 per cent, and a third came from SSC & B: Lintas.

An index of the high degree of internationalisation of McCann-Erickson Worldwide: 60 per cent of its turnover comes from outside the United States. In 1968 the proportion was 46 per cent, ten years earlier 22 per cent.[7] Faithful to this transnational vocation, in 1986 McCann-Erickson founded Initiatives Media International in London, offering its clients the chance to plan and purchase advertising space on a pan-European level, a pan-Asiatic level, or if they preferred, a global scale. Foremost group in the world in 1978, the American Interpublic was dethroned in 1986 by the British company Saatchi & Saatchi.

SUCCESS STORY

If the rearrangements which went on at the end of the 1970s brought back on stage actors in the history of advertising going back to the 1920s, the megamergers of the second half of the 1980s belong to newcomers.

Saatchi & Saatchi only entered the advertising business in 1970. Eighteen years later they had a turnover of $13.5b and a profit margin of $2b. They employed 14,000 people in 150 bureaux of their own and were minority shareholders in twenty-one others. More than sixty of the hundred leading advertisers in the world were their clients. In nine national markets, including the United States and Great Britain, they occupied first place; in a dozen more, they were among the first five. The US provided 57 per cent of their turnover, Britain 22 per cent, and the rest of the world the remainder.

The founders of the group, Charles and Maurice Saatchi, are the oldest and youngest of five children of well-to-do Sephardi Jews of Iraqi origin. Charles gave up studying at the age of 18 and started out in advertising as a copy-writer. After a brief detour in an American agency, he experienced his first campaign in one of the most creative British agencies of the time, CDP (Collett Dickenson Pearce). Maurice is a graduate of the London School of Economics. Charles would become the architect and strategist of the group, Maurice, the organiser.[8]

Five years after setting up a small agency, they made their first big acquisition through the purchase of Compton UK Partners, a company twice as big as themselves in which Compton Advertising of New York were minority shareholders. These formed the first steps towards international expansion. At the start of the 1980s, things took off: the purchase of their American partner Compton Advertising and its network covering thirty countries, created in 1935 and long since known as the house of the big soap manufacturers Procter & Gamble; the acquisition of one of the foremost British agencies, Dorland, heir of an American agency founded in 1886; not to mention the acquisition of design studios and public relations offices. In 1985 the brothers paid out money for another American agency, Dancer Fitzgerald Sample, founded in Chicago in 1930; they also diversified their activities towards consultancy through the capture of the Hay Group of Philadelphia. In 1986 their designs fell on the most dynamic and creative of US agencies, Backer & Spielvogel, as well as Ted Bates, thirty years their senior.

By 1979 Saatchis had become the top agency in the UK, dethroning J. Walter Thompson in Europe two years later, and in 1986 making number one in the American and world markets. This spectacular growth was achieved in an economic climate which was particularly favourable towards the British advertising industry. In ten years the British advertising sector had grown by 70 per cent while the GNP had increased by only

22 per cent. However, this had not been accompanied by a growth in employment, since according to the *Financial Times*, 'the same numbers of staff were employed in 1986 as a decade earlier'.[9] What had changed was productivity.

In 1987 Saatchis reorganised itself into two networks along the lines introduced by Interpublic: Saatchi/Compton (Saatchi & Saatchi Worldwide) and Backer & Spielvogel/Bates Worldwide. In March 1988, Dorland was integrated into the first network. This flood of mergers left its traces: hundreds of employees were blown about by the winds of restructuring; several clients, fearing that the new proprietor would no longer give them exclusive deals on particular products, took their budgets to other agencies. For example, the sweets and chocolate company Rowntree-Mackintosh, one of Saatchis' oldest and most profitable clients, was put to flight by another chocolate manufacturer, Mars, a client of Ted Bates. Thus, in the six months following the announcement of the merger with Bates, the Saatchi group lost $450m in transferred budgets, a sum for which new clients scarcely compensated.

The lack of historical roots in advertising was not the only difference between the British group and Interpublic. The American group, in its policy of diversification, counted above all on the multiplication of its services and advertising products (marketing, packaging, design, promotion, company literature, etc.). On the other hand, the project on which Saatchis embarked in the early 1980s was to bite bits off from other sectors previously controlled by specialist firms. In extending their portfolio of skills, Saatchis proclaimed loud and clear their desire to transform the advertising agency into 'a global superstore of services' in which enterprises could use the ensemble of their know-how to manage their affairs better. 'The Saatchis' ideal conglomerate', a *Newsweek* analyst remarked, 'would combine the advertising skills of Saatchi & Saatchi, the consulting prowess of a McKinsey & Co., the accounting acumen of an Arthur Andersen and the financial clout of a Goldman Sachs.'[10] They aimed to transform the advertising agency, to become an operational think-tank capable of intervening in every segment of what Saatchis, in its annual reports, calls the 'business culture', and to compete openly on their own terrain with the leading consultants, market research companies and accountants.

In 1986, Saatchis enticed away an expert from Arthur Andersen, a leading American company in research, consultancy and accounting, to make him president of Saatchi & Saatchi Consulting. In 1988, the brothers were accused of using him to poach clients from his previous employer. The previous year, the British group had tried to put into practice their project to expand into finance: they launched a takeover bid against Midland Bank, fourth-largest bank in the UK. But this was a miserable failure.

MEDIA AUCTION

'Would you be more careful if it was you that got pregnant?'. A first media coup: a hoarding with this legend and the photo of a pregnant man for a campaign on contraception commissioned by the Health Education Council.

From its first babbles on, the world's future foremost advertising group took special care of its relations to the media world, beginning with the professional press (like the UK advertising industry journal *Campaign*), then the economic press, and lastly the mass media proper. When Saatchis put their name to Ted Bates, it made the front page. This public reverberation surprised even the Americans, who commented that 'the trade press in the UK is much more interested in new agencies than the US, so it's easier to become well known quickly.'[11]

A savvy dose of press-releases, rumours, denials, off-the-record comments of the 'Certainly, but don't quote me' type – here as elsewhere the mediatised echo has become a fundamental element in the apparatus of the takeover bid. Not the cult of personality (the Saatchis rarely give interviews) but the cult of the Saatchis' label. The creation of events through the acts and gestures of the agency itself.

With Saatchis, the advertising industry and high finance are mutually implicated. Quoted on the stock exchange, the agency issued shares to enable it to raise the funds it needed. If the firm's communications policy has had the not insignificant aim of enlarging its clientele, its primary objective has been to make its expansionist projects more credible to stockholders, large and small, and to the financial community as a whole. For the main success of the British group in this phase of its social and economic ascent has really been to persuade a reticent stock market of the speculative value of the advertising sector. This is a merit which its international rivals freely acknowledge. According to an executive of the Parisian agency Roux-Séguela in 1987, 'The example of Saatchi & Saatchi fascinates me totally for its financial results, and for the way the English stock exchange has sustained its growth, without the slightest faltering. The financial market has completely overvalued it and they have been able to buy their competitors cheap. But you have to acknowledge their genius.'[12]

Thus the Saatchi brothers are not the proprietors of their own enterprise. Pension funds own 39 per cent of the ordinary shares; 30 per cent are in the hands of unit trusts, insurance and investment companies; 18 per cent are held by individuals; the remaining 13 per cent is ascribed to 'others'.[13] The Saatchis' power – extremely fragile, since they themselves hold no more than between 2 per cent and 4 per cent – remains uncontested as long as, year by year, their shareholders collect the dividends of a growing company. Between 1977 (the year Saatchis were first quoted on the stock exchange) and 1986, profits climbed from £1.2m to £70.1m and dividends per share grew more than fifteenfold. On top of this first innovation, which consisted in triumphal entry onto the stock market, Saatchis have added another, by taking advantage of new financial techniques: the procedure known as 'earn-out'. The victim is paid off in two instalments: the first payment is made in cash, raised through fresh share issues; the second represents a stake in the performance of the firm acquired, since it depends on the profits over the next two or three years.

But this recourse to a new kind of financial pump does not explain everything. There is no way to understand the Saatchis' resounding success and high profile over the last few years outside the context of a politically conservative England. And there is no way to account for its sustained progress without reference to its direct participation in the three victorious electoral campaigns of Margaret Thatcher and the Tories. As one journalist wrote in the *Financial Times* in October 1987: 'What cannot be disputed is that the two have been good for each other. The agency has helped Mrs Thatcher win three elections in a row and in so doing is widely judged to have advanced the art of political advertising. Saatchi, meanwhile, has grown from a middle-sized domestic agency to a global communications conglomerate with annual pre-tax profits of over £100m.'[14]

These electoral campaigns were especially aggressive towards the Labour Party: witness the famous hoarding produced in 1978 to denigrate the Labour government of James Callaghan: an endless queue of people of all social sectors outside a job centre emblazoned with the slogan 'Labour isn't working'. As the indirect fallout of this close alliance between the Saatchis and the Conservative neo-liberal government, since the end of the 1970s the agency has handled substantial budgets on behalf of public enterprises like British Airways, in addition to numerous institutional campaigns.

The first sign of *malaise* in this long and unclouded cohabitation appeared in 1987, when the Conservative Party saw its leader's ratings in the opinion polls beginning to sag. Even so, the Iron Lady was re-elected hands down, but for the first time the Tories engaged additional agencies to carry the campaign through. In particular the firm of Tim Bell, defecting president of Saatchis and long-time friend of Mrs Thatcher, who at the time presided over the destinies of the agency Lowe Howard-Spink Marschalk & Bell.

Three months after the poll, an exchange of letters between the Prime Minister and Maurice Saatchi confirmed the separation, and for the agency the loss, of one of its most prestigious accounts. The official reason for this rupture: to avoid giving grounds for complaint in view of the agency's plans to take up an option for two channels on the Astra

11

television satellite. In his letter to Mrs Thatcher, Maurice Saatchi wrote:

> Saatchi has been moving into areas which are bringing us increasingly into contact with government and government regulatory authorities. We are conscious that this might open the company, public authorities and Ministers to misrepresentation. . . . We intend to play a significant commercial role in developing new broadcast initiatives such as DBS and you will be aware of our interest in the financial services sector.

Commercial links with the party, he added, could only complicate the task of all concerned. The Prime Minister could only acknowledge the decision and pay tribute to Saatchis: 'We have worked together successfully, with the government carrying through policies which are right for Britain and with Saatchi presenting our policies skilfully and effectively.'[15]

This planned retreat in the British Isles does not signify a chill in enthusiasm for electoral campaigns on the part of the world's foremost network. In April 1988, Saatchi & Saatchi was engaged by the Dutch Labour Party for the general elections of 1990!

A GIANT WITH FEET OF CLAY?

The rotation of mega-kings in the advertising world reflects the acceleration of the circulation of merchandise and financial capital on the world market. This is demonstrated by Saatchis' short history.

In 1988, the British press pointed out how vulnerable was the advertising sector – especially Saatchi & Saatchi – from a financial point of view. Called to account, the world's number one replied by publishing a two-page insert to prove the opposite. But a year later it had to admit that the 1989 results would be lower than previously, thus marking the group's first year without growth since it was founded. The response of the stock market was to bring its shares down by 16 per cent. It was not long before rumours of takeover bids spread like wildfire. The leader-writer in the American advertising trade journal could not refrain from rubbing salt into the wound by writing in April 1989:

> Now that the Brothers Saatchi have announced that pretax fiscal 1989 profits will fall below last year's disappointing level, a thunderclap that left their investors gasping, they would do well to reconsider their 'ability to attract, reward and retain' talent.
> Especially management talent.
> It's one thing to assign 'power of scale' benefits to whatever they termed 'improved global information systems, increased technological resources and increased access to a broad range of communica-

tions and consulting expertise.' It's another thing to *manage* this business mix effectively on a global scale.

After the earnings shocker, it's up to Maurice and Charles Saatchi to show the world what they're made of. They must attack their management problem with the same fervour they showed during their 16-year climb to the top.

If they can succeed in setting matters right, they'll have demonstrated they really are quite the business geniuses their press clippings have been making them out to be since the early 1970s.[16]

In June 1989, after seeing their profits cut to a third, the world advertising leader announced its intention to part with its consultancy activities and fall back on its primary métier, in order to check the fall in profits. 'We have realised', a spokesperson for the group explained, 'that we're not able to get on top of the consultancy business, though it still brings us in about a quarter of our gross revenue.' Among other things, the American market had not been as remunerative as predicted and, above all, the restructuring of the group had not produced the anticipated results. In scarcely six months, the profits from advertising had been halved.

Taking advantage of the precarious condition of the world's number one, new shareholders joined the company, including Silvio Berlusconi's Fininvest group. In October, with the announcement of the half-yearly financial results – profits had fallen by 50 per cent – takeover rumours got worse. The names of possible purchasers began to be mentioned: Silvio Berlusconi, with a 1 per cent shareholding; the Japanese agency Dentsu; and Southeastern Asset Management, an investment fund based in Tennessee, which at that time was Saatchis' largest single shareholder with 10.2 per cent. To try and re-establish the confidence of their investors, the Saatchi brothers gave up their jobs as joint chief executives and handed direction of the group over to a new chief executive, a Frenchman who was a senior executive of the North American firm Dun & Bradstreet. Finally, in 1990, the consultancy branch – the Hay group – was acquired by its management.

As an image of what is happening in the economy as a whole in the era of speculation, the appeal to reasons of 'industrial synergy' to legitimise a strategy of megamergers begins to lose credibility. Other important explanations emerge: to keep adding to the turnover; to grow in order to resist takeovers. But in wishing to expand, one thereby signals to competitors that one is vulnerable. The strategy of over-borrowing to finance expansion adopted by the new British megagroups of the 1980s has made them particularly sensitive to fluctuations and recession in advertising expenditure. This has affected the Saatchi brothers since 1988. It has also caught up with the other empire-builder, Martin Sorrell, and his WPP group, whose market value plummeted by 70 per cent in two days in November 1990 after it announced the collapse of its pre-tax profits. By the end of 1990, WPP's debt mountain was expected to reach £315m. The servicing costs for this debt amount to £40m in interest, £32m in the repayment of principal, and a further £10m in deferred payments for earlier acquisitions. Pre-tax profits were estimated at around £90m.

TRILATERAL PACT

Beyond the triumphalist successes and stinging failures, beyond the cleavage between fierce competitors and partisans of megamergers, the order of the day is, above all, the imperative towards the internationalisation of the networks.

In July 1987, the biggest American agency, the foremost French group and the number one Japanese agency came together to create a world-scale advertising agency, HDM: H for Havas (through the intermediary of Eurocom of which it controls 43 per cent); D for Dentsu; and M for Marsteller, subsidiary of Young & Rubicam. We observe in passing that Young & Rubicam is the premier international agency in the French market – where it occupies fourth or fifth place – and the one with the most French of profiles: its manager is *not* an American; 75–80 per cent of its revenue comes from local clients; its relations with Havas do not date solely from this agreement; the director of its subsidiary Marsteller is the ex-boss of Agence France Presse (AFP). Faced with the model embodied by Saatchi & Saatchi, and confronted by the difficulty of setting up subsidiaries in highly competitive markets, this so-called 'intercultural' marriage represents an alternative strategy. 'We have chosen a third path,' explained a Eurocom official, 'that of alliance between partners who are leaders in their own countries. A strategy which respects national cultures and know-how. When they penetrate the Japanese market, French industrialists need Japanese heads and not a French commando on foreign soil.'[17]

The French advertising industry shares at least two characteristics with the Japanese. On the one hand, historically they are among the few who have succeeded in keeping the American networks in check. In 1969, the Americans had a tenth of the French market, in 1979 they had 36 per cent; while in Japan, the Americans have never earned more than a bare living. A privileged situation for France and Japan, not only in comparison to England in the 1970s, but also in comparison to countries like Italy, Federal Germany and Spain, where American subsidiaries have almost always been the leading force. On the other hand, the Japanese agencies resented as much as the French the need to catch up for lost time on the international markets, the former because they hadn't followed their own exporting industrialists promptly enough and set themselves up abroad, the latter for lack of international enthusiasm for French industry.

14

In Japan – the world's second-largest advertising market – the advertising scene is under the thumb of two large agencies which account for 65 per cent of the turnover of the ten leading companies in the field. At the summit is Dentsu, first- or second-largest agency in the world depending on the year, which collects a quarter of the country's advertising bills, while its immediate competitor Hakuhodo gets 10 per cent. With its turnover and its tradition – it was founded at the end of last century – Dentsu has no reason to envy the big British or American agencies except for their degree of internationalisation. For over the years in which Sony, Toyota, Honda, Panasonic *et al.* overtook their competitors worldwide, it was Western intermediaries who had charge of their foreign advertising and promotion budgets. It was only in 1981 that Dentsu sealed its first alliance with Young & Rubicam after several years of bargaining. Its main competitor Hakuhodo had taken the same step in the 1960s by linking up with the Interpublic group via McCann-Erickson.

In the second half of the 1980s Dentsu stepped up its involvement in the world's three most affluent markets. In addition to the HDM alliance – a network operating through a total of ninety-five offices in twenty-four different countries – the Japanese company centralised supervision of its international operations with the establishment of the Overseas Operation Headquarters in Tokyo. It formed wholly owned subsidiaries in Germany and Spain, it acquired shares in the British network CDP (Collett Dickenson Pearce) in order to construct a European network of its own, and planned its entry into the Eastern Europe markets. It created a new holding company, Dentsu Australia Pty Limited, and looked for entry into Taiwan, Hong Kong, Singapore and Malaysia. Dentsu's new international plan was to boost its non-Japanese billings from 10 per cent to 20 per cent before 1992 and to set up its own network – to serve Japanese clients – by finding strong local partners. In a major move to globalise its public relations business, Dentsu concluded an agreement with top-ranking PR agency Burson-Marsteller to establish joint operations through new offices in Tokyo and New York.

In the early 1970s in France, only one agency, Publicis, seemed at all concerned to set up its own international grouping, by playing the European card. The point of departure for this expansionist strategy was the purchase in 1972 of the Amsterdam network Intermarco, followed by the Swiss firm of Farner a year later. We owe to Marcel Bleustein-Blanchet, president of the Publicis group and patriarch of the advertising community, one of the few pronouncements of the time in the quality Parisian press about the megamerger between McCann-Erickson and Lintas and its possible consequences:

For advertising men 1978 was a year of reinforced American presence in Europe. 1979 will be Europe's year. In concert with Europe,

French advertising must continue to make its voice heard. It is a vital necessity. . . . France will only win through with its own brand-names. . . . One thing is certain: for French advertising, the match will take place in Europe. One of the world's principal advertising agencies, Lintas, in which European interests hold the major part of the capital, has just been bought by Interpublic, the Madison Avenue giant. This acquisition was the major event of last year. It is no use crying over spilt milk. It is better to learn the lessons of the phenomenon of concentration which is now, after so many other sectors, taking hold of the advertising profession. . . . It is now up to us. Are we going to lower our guard or follow the American example? Before the war, the big European agencies were English. Where are they? In Germany, in Italy, the leading agencies are American. Only France holds up the torch. . . . We must persevere . . . our commercial spirit is at stake.'[18]

As for Publicis, its receipts in 1987 put it at number nineteen in the world table, with 40 per cent of its turnover outside France (its rival Eurocom-Havas had scarcely 30 per cent in foreign business) which came from a network comprising twenty-three agencies in twelve countries, plus fifteen associate agencies in the majority of European countries.

At the end of May 1988, the typically French Publicis linked its destiny with that of the American agency FCB (Foote, Cone & Belding Communications), created in New York in 1942 from the vestiges of an agency founded at the end of last century. By exchanging 26 per cent of its Publicis-Communications division for 20 per cent of the capital of FCB, Publicis became its principal shareholder. As a result of the operation, in the following year Publicis became the largest European network, occupying sixth place in the world market. FCB retains its own activities in the United States, Latin America, Asia and the Pacific, while the European activities of the American agency and the international activities of Publicis have been regrouped into a joint subsidiary, Publicis-FCB, with 51 per cent control by Publicis-Communications.

In October 1989 its eternal rival, Eurocom-Havas, reached the heights of the leading international groups through the acquisition of 60 per cent of the advertising branch of the British group WCRS. Through this operation, the leading French group has established – together with its mixed network HDM – another network with both a European and a world reach, baptised EWDB (Eurocom-WCRS-Della Femina-Ball – the last two being subsidiaries of the British agency).

THE BROKERS

Concentration produces more concentration. Fear of the competitor initiates a spiral of further *rapprochements*. This is what is revealed by the process of formation of specialised companies for the purchase of advertising space. The pioneers are the British and the French, who created this new function of intermediary wholesaler in the 1970s for their own national territory. These specialised media-buying companies play a strategic role in which their accumulated negotiating power determines the level of the discounts obtained from the media. Today this role of advertising broker has been internationalised. Some twenty years after their creation in France, the system has been adopted by the big transnational networks. With very rare exceptions like the pioneers McCann-Erickson, the American agencies have not felt the need to conduct this activity through subsidiaries, still less to internationalise it, and least of all, to create specialised companies.

In February 1989, two American groups, Omnicom and Ogilvy, joined a few months later (following Ogilvy's takeover by WPP) by J. Walter Thompson, set up an important international specialist media-buying firm, The Media Partnership. Primary market: Europe. The justification for the operation, according to a European official of Omnicom:

> Media-buying on behalf of our advertisers, which constituted the advertising agency's original activity, has received a battering with the emergence of specialist companies a few years ago. We need to fight back in the face of the formidable concentrations going on in the media. The only chance is to concentrate our own means. Following the example of industrialists who increasingly purchase their primary materials in common in order to get the best terms, we too have regrouped our forces for the purchase of this strategic primary material which today's advertising space has become.[19]

This initiative was partly a response both to concentration among multimedia groups, and to powerful megagroups in advertising like Zenith, created by the Saatchi brothers in 1988 to bring together all media-buying for themselves and their subsidiaries.

The redrawing of the advertising landscape has also accelerated. In the wake of large-scale distribution, the advertising apparatus is now organising itself more and more around large-scale media-buyers. The evidence can be seen in the changes recorded in France in the very formula *'centrale d'achat'* ('head purchasing office'). On stage are three large groups: Carat Espace, Publicis and Eurocom. These alone combine 60 per cent of media-buying in France, the remainder being divided between almost seventy other companies. In order to reach second place, Publicis linked up with the American group Interpublic. On the

ADVERTISING INTERNATIONAL

European front, in 1989 Carat Espace bought 49 per cent of the foremost
German media-buyer (Hiemstra Media Service) and acquired almost 30
per cent of the capital of TMD, the largest British media-buyer before the
arrival of Zenith-Saatchi. In September of the same year, Carat Espace
passed under majority control by the British group WCRS. The following month, the latter's media-buying branch acquired full control of
Carat Espace International, and then Eurocom became a minority
shareholder in the English company, which was renamed the Aegis
group. In this concentration of centralised buying, France leads the
dance. Some 83 per cent of all advertising spend is controlled by such
space brokerage groups, as against 16 per cent in Britain, 45 per cent in
Spain and 60 per cent in Belgium.[20] Although the construction of these
big central buying agencies mainly affects Europe, few countries can fend
them off (for example, Brazil, where the first buying group was
established in 1989). But the national agencies oppose such moves and
even attempt to argue that they are illegal.

The regrouping of the big agencies within these powerful transnational alliances does not happen without producing problems. These begin
with the question of client confidentiality, when the client begins to
worry about the cross-links with agencies that handle their competitors'
budgets, and with whom they are therefore liable to come into conflict.
The second big problem is that of the transparency of the tariffs. In a
milieu in which the operative principle is the discount and the power of
negotiation, nothing is less evident. The proof is found in the conclusions of a report by the French Council for Competition* of 1987
which describes in detail how the growing power of the specialist buyers
may put pressure on the media, threatening, if they refuse to accede to
their commercial demands, to deprive them of advertising. This report,
which at times takes on the appearance of a prosecutor's charge-sheet (in
contrast to the excessive prudence of its recommendations) explains in
particular how the opacity of negotiation could give rise to important
detours of money to finance political parties or electoral campaigns, or
simply for personal ends.

The function of these new transnational advertising brokers is clearly
not limited to the act of purchasing advertising space. In a context of
hyper-competitive supply, the buyers also have to counsel advertisers on
the appropriate purchases. From this function comes the strategic place
of research. 'The objective of our agreements', according to an official of
Publicis, 'is to constitute the most important force in the field of media
research in Europe.'[21] Indeed, the companies involved in market research,
opinion polls, audience ratings and counselling are highly esteemed

---

* Conseil de la concurrence, created at the end of 1986 to replace the Commission de la
concurrence and the Commission des ententes.

within the media world, with every segment of the communications and information industry wishing to take advantage of these reservoirs of grey matter. We shall come back to this.

COMMISSION

By the end of the 1970s, a major upset had begun to occur in the way the various actors in the advertising process functioned. The decade had begun with a real provocation when Saatchis, having scarcely entered the trade, threw a stone into corporate waters. In a landscape dominated at the time by J. Walter Thompson and other American heavyweights, they had dared to place an advertisement in *The Sunday Times* which announced the death-struggle of the 15 per cent commission, proclaiming it one of the small new agency's intentions to abandon the system.

The system of commission is one of the golden rules of the advertising industry: the agency which places a booking on behalf of an advertiser receives a commission of 15 per cent. The principle developed soon after the first modern advertising agency was set up in the United States around 1840, the only difference being that in those days the pioneers charged as much as 20 or 25 per cent. A golden rule because it defined the commercial relations between advertiser, agency and media.

If the principle is universally recognised, the methods of calculation are often different. Whereas the commission in most countries is paid by the media (this is the French case), in others it is paid by the advertiser (notably, in the United States). This has direct repercussions on the remuneration of the agency: in France, the amount which the agency pays for a spot is less than the sum it charges the client, and the advertiser pays the agency according to the official tariff; in the United States, the agency bills the client for the actual price it pays for the spot.

Before 1970, there had been only one serious attack on the commission system in the entire history of advertising: in 1929, at the time of the Great Depression, when advertisers reduced their budgets. To avoid any possible misunderstandings, advertisers and agencies jointly turned to a professor at the University of Chicago to write an independent report. His conclusion was that even though in theory it was not ideal, in practice there was no better method of remunerating the work of the agency. This creed had become so solid that at the time it celebrated its centenary in 1964, J. Walter Thompson affirmed that the conclusions of the report

are still and in one sense even more valid now than they were 30 years ago. The rate of commission is not only not excessive, but is steadily becoming less adequate as additional services are added to the variety performed by agencies. As agency services become increasingly broad

19

and complex, more competition is essential ... and therefore commissions will ultimately have to be supplemented by additional fees. But most attempts to substitute fees for commissions (rather than to supplement commissions with fees) are hopefully designed to reduce the agency's compensation – a condition which they consider unrealistic.[22]

The challenge which Saatchis launched against the leader of the industry consisted in just this: to substitute fees for commissions. To play the game of competitive prices to the last round.

With great risk to the agencies, this first upheaval in century-old habits took place in the late 1970s. No need to guess where: Great Britain. In November 1976 the Office of Fair Trading ruled that the traditional advertising agency commission system was an illegal monopoly under the Restrictive Trade Practices Act of 1976. (The Office of Fair Trading, set up in 1973 following the Fair Trading Act, had the responsibility, among other things, of overseeing advertising practices.) The results were not long in coming: the blossoming of a generation of small agencies which profitably employed the modified tariff system, and the rise of specialist media-buyers through which the newcomers were able to evade the need to provide the media proprietors with financial guarantees (in five years the number of these 'media independents' tripled, most of them set up by ex-directors of the media departments of the big agencies). The development of WCRS, Lowe-Howard-Spink and many others dates from this time; however, they didn't all share the same destiny. Faced with the gigantism of the Saatchi megamergers in the 1980s, some of them created federations between themselves, as their composite trade names often indicate. Nine years after its launch, WCRS had taken its place among the transnational groups.

The late 1970s were fertile in debates on the need to abandon commission. This question was the order of the day in Switzerland, Sweden, the Netherlands and elsewhere. France was not spared. In 1978, the advertisers left the agencies without a leg to stand on: the occasion was the removal of price controls by the government of Prime Minister Raymond Barre. The advertisers' trade association, the UDA (*L'Union des annonceurs*), demanded 'the right to buy space without [the intermediary of] an agency, and ... to negotiate the final agency bill without an imposed percentage'. The agencies' organisation, the AACP (*L'Association des agences-conseils en publicité*) retorted: 'The 15 per cent commission is accepted in every country of the world. If we suspend it here, we will be discriminating against French advertising.'[23]

If we are to believe the advertising people themselves, ten years later the problem is far from resolved. In many countries it is a burning issue, beginning with the United States, one of the last places to subject the question to review. As late as November 1987, at the end of an inquiry into advertisers, *Advertising Age* concluded that:

> Agency compensation looms as 1988's most significant and controversial issue for advertisers and agencies. A festering problem for several years, compensation now threatens to overshadow creativity as the chief determinant in new-business reviews. Some agencies have turned down new accounts because of disagreements on this subject. Whether straight commission, fee, commission-plus-fee or sliding scale arrangements, new action is being taken on payment structures. The changes have the potential to reshape the rules of the $100,000m-plus ad industry. . . . Also general economic conditions seem to be exacerbating the problem.[24]

Transnational advertisers are divided. Procter & Gamble continues to accept the commission, but its new holding Richardson-Vicks follows the system of commission-plus-fees. General Motors and other automobile manufacturers have negotiated a reduction in commission to 12 per cent and are hoping to reduce it further to 10 per cent.

The firm of Nestlé has asked the four networks that service it around the world (Lintas, McCann-Erickson, Publicis, J. Walter Thompson) to come up with concrete proposals aimed at harmonising the method of payment, and bringing about what in its jargon of global communications it calls 'a totally integrated centralised communications orchestration'. If expressions like these are offensive to musical sensibility, they at least point to the stakes involved in the reform of remuneration: the deployment by the companies of communications strategies on a global scale. It is not only a question of rationalising costs, but also of bringing to bear new modes of evaluation of the efficacy of advertising campaigns. 'With the removal of commissions', said Nestlé's director of visual communications, 'the fee system could be augmented with incentives geared to the success of the brand and based on set criteria such as sales volume or brand share.' Suspecting its partners' reticence, it is careful to specify that 'the proposed new approach is being masterminded by Nestlé's Swiss headquarters, but its success depends on acceptance by the national operating companies as well as Nestlé's agencies.' As the same executive put it, revealing a little more of the implications of the debate for the principle of commission, 'We're discussing with agencies ways of improving the relationship with the agency as a consultancy.'[25] One debate conceals another: the debate about the new synergy between the different partners in the process of communications management.

At the end of the 1980s, few countries escaped this deregulation of the commission system. In Brazil, in 1989, agency remuneration became a topical subject. The usual rate – supported partially by legislation – is 20 per cent on media and 15 per cent on other services. The trend is for more freedom in arrangements between an advertiser and its agency if they so wish. In Canada, the commission system is being re-examined in the light of developments in the United States where major transnational corporations have cut back on commission with an additional percentage offered as an incentive for performance. In New Zealand, since the removal of the non-rebate clause from media accreditation agreements in October 1988, many agencies are being forced to operate on lower margins.

But the deregulation of the methods of payment also gives rise to secret practices on the borders of legality: hidden discounts, super-commissions, a variety of gifts, automatic kick-backs within the agency, every form of so-called parallel remuneration which is able to profit from the opacity of the financial transactions. These practices are all the more prevalent in certain countries, for example as we have seen in France, where the agencies retain part or all of the discounts which they negotiate with the media. In December 1987 some of these practices were denounced by the report commissioned by the French Council for Competition. However, stifled by the profession, the report had little echo in the media. In one of the few articles about it in the press, a Parisian journalist described the most subtle technique, known as 'free replay', of which the authors of the report had taken note:

> The method is simple: imagine that the medium (magazine, radio or TV) responsible for putting out an advertisement, makes an error which impairs the advert (inaudible soundtrack, bad printing . . .). Quite properly, this deficiency gives the right to an equivalent free spot, in reparation for the damage. Thus far, there is nothing illegal. Things get serious when certain operators abuse this practice by overclaiming such deficiencies. The medium yields, for fear of not being paid. But the advertiser, unaware of the juggling act, pays for the space a second time! And since the medium is part of the plot, the payment is divided fifty-fifty. In certain media, the rate of replays reaches 20 per cent of advertising receipts. The money thus collected is often put to purely personal ends.[26]

The misdemeanour of the insider.

THE HARD CORE

As a result of the waltz of acquisitions and the alliances of the 1980s, three of the world's leading advertising groups have their general headquarters in London (Saatchi & Saatchi, WPP and WCRS) and two have them in Paris (FCB-Publicis and Eurocom-Havas); and the British have managed to reduce the American share in the turnover of the top twenty agencies in the domestic market to 30 per cent. Two more networks remain based in

New York: Interpublic and Omnicom. Only Interpublic and Eurocom already existed as groups at the end of the previous decade. Omnicom was only born in 1986, through a regrouping by three American networks: BBDO Worldwide, DDB Needham and Diversified Agency Services, founded in 1928, 1949 and 1925 respectively.

Following worldwide agency ranking, the club of the top twenty includes two Japanese, two French, six British, and one of mixed ownership (HDM), with the remainder belonging to the US. Ten years earlier, apart from the two Japanese, all were American.* What remains virtually unchanged is that ten years ago and more, the top places were shared by Dentsu of Japan and the American agency Young & Rubicam. On the other hand, the legal status of these big agencies has changed radically in the last ten years. Few of the networks have remained independent, that is to say, outside the domain of financial speculation. It is rare for an agency not to be quoted on the stock exchange. This, however, is the case with Young & Rubicam, which has been in private hands since 1923: about 1,000 of its 10,000 employees own shares in the company, with a maximum individual holding of 5 per cent. This leads its president to explain: 'This kind of private management lets us work more calmly. Our managers are not forever keeping an eye on the stock market. We can concentrate our attention on our clients' interests and invest millions of dollars in training, which benefits the clients.'[27] Of the twenty largest independent American agencies of previous years, only four do not now have their shares listed.

All these groups and agencies are trying to diversify their activities to the maximum. Even if the great majority have never been seduced by the Saatchis' project of diversification into the domain of management consultancy, they are increasingly extending their 'non-media activities': design, graphics, market research, sales promotion, direct marketing, audiovisual production, video communications groups, sponsorship and public relations. Spending by this so-called 'below-the-line' sector has steadily outpaced 'above-the-line' expenditures.* In the late 1980s, the ten leading world advertising groups increased their annual revenue from the conventional media by 18 per cent; the growth rate of non-media

---

* This follows the classification of *Advertising Age*. One should add that in many countries – France, for example – advertising people have never bothered to define the difference between 'group' and 'agency', nor have they agreed on common and public rules of accounting or systematic auditing of accounts: hence the divergences which occur in different sources.

* The terms 'above the line' and 'below the line' in advertising do not mean the same as in film and television production. 'Above the line' originally meant the five media which paid commission to advertising agencies, namely, the press, radio, television, outdoor advertising and cinema. 'Below the line' was used for direct mail, exhibitions, point-of-sale displays, etc. This terminology has now largely lost its significance, due to the interpenetration of these areas and the explosion of non-media activity. [Translator's note.]

activities was 102 per cent. 'Integrated communications' is the new buzzword. So as to offer clients as many facets as possible of the various marketing and communications services provided by units of the same group or agency, new concepts are emerging which reveal the search for the integration of services: 'Whole Egg' (Young & Rubicam), 'Orchestration' (Ogilvy), 'Cross Referrals' (WPP), or more simply 'Full Service Communications' (Dentsu, new definition announced in January 1987). Among the most diversified agencies or groups are: J. Walter Thompson (almost half of the revenue came from research, public relations, design, sales promotion, video communications, etc.); Ogilvy & Mather (worldwide leader in direct marketing and specialist in public relations and research, with 38 per cent of the revenue coming from these non-traditional domains); Dentsu (30 per cent of its gross billings derives from multi-dimensional activities such as sales promotion, public relations, 'urban development' or expertise in mounting exhibitions as a means of activating local economy, promotion of large-scale sporting and cultural events).

Two sectors in particular within the international advertising market have forged ahead: sales promotion and direct marketing. In 1989, companies in the fast-moving consumer goods sector in the United States, Canada and Europe devoted 55 per cent of their marketing budgets to sales promotions and 45 per cent to advertising. Twelve years earlier the proportions were 40 per cent and 60 per cent respectively.[28] The figures come from a study by the Ogilvy Center for Research and Development of 314 firms which devote at least 10 per cent of their sales turnover to marketing their products. The reason why point-of-sales promotion is so highly valued by the industrialists is that in the United States, according to reports, this is precisely where two-thirds of purchasing decisions are made. Another indicator is the growth in 'telemarketing' which in 1988 in the USA represented twice the amount these enterprises invested in advertising spots.[29]* This development is obviously sustained by the new logistics of information and communications technology, including the growth of databases and data banks which can be used to target consumers with increasing precision.

Another stimulating challenge: the rise of micro-marketing, with its more tailored or niche approach, which follows the shattering of the market and the growing heterogeneity of the public, as well as the relative decline of mass-marketing with its concept of homogeneity of customer and market. What is the extent of this non-traditional advertising sector within total advertising investment in different countries? Although it is difficult to answer with any precision, due to the incompatibility of most

* 'Telemarketing' refers to selling through the television screen with follow-up either by telephone or through teletext systems such as the French Minitel. [Translator's note.]

of the estimates, it appears that in 1989 this sector already represented 47 per cent of advertising costs in Italy, 38 per cent in France, 36 per cent in the US and 34 per cent in Japan.

Whether forefathers of advertising or newcomers, these groups and agencies make up the hard core in the globalisation of the networks. Each according to its own style – by means of subsidiaries, federation or cross-holdings – they can be found unfailingly in every latitude, regardless of the nature of the political regime or the level of economic development.

The battle rages everywhere. Before the big manoeuvres of the 1980s, there were only one or two agencies of European origin among the top ten linking the various markets of the Old World. In scarcely five years, the relation of forces has been inverted in favour of London and Paris. There are now few countries left where local agencies, which had managed to survive the preceding decades, have not been worried by the approach of the networks. There was Young & Rubicam setting foot in Portugal in 1988 and acquiring shares in Team, for a long time the leading independent agency in Lisbon. Two years earlier Ted Bates absorbed the Alas group in Spain. In the Netherlands and in Federal Germany, the ten top agencies all have majority holdings by the networks. In Italy, only one of the top five agencies is nationally owned. In Belgium, where all the heavyweights are American, British or French, the last local agency succumbed to Ogilvy in 1978. Its Belgian owner explained at the time:

> A key motivation for HHD in the merger is that our agency has remained a purely Belgian agency and has consequently suffered from the lack of international linkages that are increasingly necessary to compete for accounts assigned internationally. With O & M, we hope to become the leading agency in Belgium and intend to recapture some clients who had to leave us for international reasons.[30]

Ten years later HHD/Ogilvy & Mather were indeed among the leaders of the local market, and the hopes of its previous owner for globalisation were in train.

Although in Latin America, nationally owned agencies succeeded during the 1980s in dethroning the subsidiaries of the American agencies, as occurred for example in Brazil and Mexico, the 'transnational connection' increasingly passes to the foreign networks. In 1988, two significant events attracted the attention of the specialised press in Mexico and Brazil, countries where the alliance of nationals with transnational networks operates through the big American agencies, since other networks have little hope of competing with them in the subcontinent. Even Saatchis had minimal presence in this $3b advertising market. In that year, the British group launched an attack on the two largest markets in Latin America. It approached Brazil's second-largest agency with the proposal of an alliance, but the company preferred to turn to the American BBDO Worldwide, to whom it ceded a 19 per cent stake in ownership. Saatchis also engaged in negotiations with the top company in Mexico, with the object of finding a formula for association. The need to reinforce its network in Latin America was all the more urgent due to Procter & Gamble, the international detergent manufacturer which was one of its principal clients, laying hands on one of Brazil's leading companies in perfumes and toiletries, with the intention of using this glittering acquisition to launch a new marketing and distribution strategy on a continental scale.

In the so-called Era of the Pacific Rim, the networks have also redoubled their interest in Asiatic markets, especially South Korea and Taiwan – the two largest advertising markets in the region after Japan – plus Hong Kong, the Philippines, Thailand, Singapore, Malaysia and Indonesia. In Hong Kong, for many years, the advertising scene has been dominated by subsidiaries of Leo Burnett, Ogilvy, J. Walter Thompson and Ted Bates, with the addition of HDM and WCRS. Taiwan and South Korea, on the other hand, have long resisted the foreign networks, enabling them to build up their own local heavyweights. But the opening up of the advertising market has brought the arrival of the big networks or the reinforcement of their presence. In South Korea, in 1988, Ogilvy, Bates and Young & Rubicam sealed the first alliances with the big local groups, while in Taipei, JWT-WPP installed their own office and Saatchi & Saatchi took over its affiliate.

In the French-speaking parts of Africa, where several 100 per cent local agencies that appeared at the end of the 1970s became competitors, a market consisting of twenty countries is shared between two agencies: the French Roux-Séguela and Lintas-Paris. With a presence going back several years, the French network has progressively replaced its subsidiaries with less costly franchise or partnership agreements. Then in 1989, McCann-Erickson set up its first subsidiaries in the Cameroon and the Ivory Coast (the latter represents more than a third of the region's advertising market) – a highly symbolic move because it was following its principal client, Coca-Cola. This was some forty or fifty years after its first establishments in Latin America.

If the world of the networks corresponds to the North/South axis, it is also now beginning to involve an East/West dimension. In 1988 Y & R signed an agreement to set up the first mixed-ownership enterprise in the Soviet Union, with a 49 per cent holding in partnership with Vneshtorgreklama, the country's largest advertising and international communications organisation. The objective was to offer a full range of consultancy and communications services to the increasing number of Western enterprises doing business in the country. It is true this agreement was limited to an organisation attached to the Ministry of Foreign Commerce and did not extend to Soyustorgreklama, which comes under the Interior Commerce Ministry and constitutes the other pole of Soviet advertising. But in a country where the term 'advertising' is unknown and the function is designated by a russified French word (*reklama*) which is now, in French, archaic (the current French word is *publicité*), these developments indicated a small revolution. In 1980, the entire budget for promotion of Soviet products in the press and on the airwaves, in a market of some 300 million consumers, amounted to scarcely $750m,[31] or the same as the *increase* in advertising expenditure in Italy in the same year.

Another important development in media and communications in this region of the planet, also in 1988, was the exclusive three-year contract obtained by Publitalia (a company owned by Berlusconi) for advertising space on the three Soviet television channels for companies in Western Europe. Silvio Berlusconi has thus become the necessary intermediary for European enterprises wishing to reach the 180 million Soviet television viewers. It is stipulated in the agreement that content must be adapted to the local context: traditional spots run from thirty seconds to six minutes, but short publicity films of up to fifteen minutes can be used to portray different companies or types of products (with the exclusion of tobacco and alcohol).

A year later, in 1989, Ogilvy opened a Moscow subsidiary in association with a Hungarian agency and Soyustorgreklama, while Saatchis were named as advertising and marketing consultants to Gostelradio, the government committee in charge of TV and radio in the Soviet Union.

In 1990 McCann-Erickson/Novosti (owned 51 per cent by the American agency and 49 per cent by Soviet news agency Novosti) set up office in Moscow. In 1988, McCann made its first move into Eastern Europe by opening McCann-Interpress Hungary in Budapest to handle the accounts for Coca-Cola, Nestlé and Camel. As an editorial in *Advertising Age* commented in February 1990:

> Having played out the string on their takeovers, hostile and otherwise, at home, American business executives now must turn their attention overseas and provide our unique marketing know-how to the new entrepreneurs in nations made ready for a solid injection of capitalism. The Brand Name War is about to replace the Cold War. . . . Our advertising and marketing community is getting a new frontier.[32]

All the big agencies – and similarly the multimedia groups – are making their presence felt in Eastern Europe. In 1990, Berlusconi created Publi-Europe, a media-buying company to sell advertising time and space for

Eastern European media. The first agreements included the TV state channel in Poland and Czechoslovakia.

THE AGE OF THE STRATEGISTS

'In recent years', according to JWT's personnel manager in London in 1986, 'advertising has been competing more and more with management consultancies and merchant banks, and they have been paying huge starting salaries to attract the talent.' In a typical year, he explained, the leading twenty agencies in London which recruit graduates tend to have four or five vacancies. By contrast, the large accountancy firms have 300. In 1986, London-JWT sent 2,500 application forms to students expressing interest in joining the agency; 650 were returned, and 87 candidates were interviewed – roughly half from Oxbridge. Of the six offered jobs (as trainee account handlers), four were men, two women; three were from Oxford, three from Cambridge.[33]

If the advertising networks change, so do the men who run them. Even if finance still has the edge as a preferred career choice, advertising is in the process of becoming a professional activity valorised by higher education. Consider the opinion of the director of the French magazine *Communication & Business*:

> In future, account managers will suffer the pressure of the market. This is a new phenomenon. For the last fifteen years, the creative staff have been the ones who in large part had to respond to the demands – quite justified – of the clients. They were always in the firing line. Today, the creative element is 'trivialised', or rather normalised. . . . There are few obvious differences, fewer disparities between one agency and another. On the other hand, the demands of advertisers now mainly concern strategy. Strategies for brands and for enterprises. The advertisers need high-grade people to elaborate policies for commercialisation and communication. . . . As the close of the century approaches, the tendency will be accentuated. . . . Where to find this new talent? In the schools of commerce, marketing and management, and elite teaching centres like the *Centrale* or the *Sciences Politiques*?* . . . It will perhaps be necessary to seduce afresh the graduates of the *École des Hautes Études Commerciales* who for some time have felt themselves better equipped for the career of 'golden boy' in a financial establishment.[34]

To gauge the significance of this shift in the professional hierarchy, remember that the account manager is the person in charge of relations

---

* Equivalent of the London or Harvard Business Schools. [Translator's note.]

with the advertiser and is responsible for the 'copy strategy'. This is the basic document which defines the message to be communicated to the purchaser, and the profiles of the consumers who make up the target. The 'creative staff' – the art director and the copywriter – produce ideas for the campaign, including the slogans to be used, and co-ordinate its production. They work to the brief provided by the account manager and the third component in the scheme, the media department. Here the planners select the media to be used. Some agencies have separate personnel to carry out these negotiations, while others employ media staff as both planners and buyers, engaged both in planning the schedule to be used and then in buying the slots; the idea is that the planner knows the overall objectives of the campaign and so can buy more effectively.

The real portrait of the top advertising strategy-maker is far from the common news-mongering accounts of the life of the 'business generation'. Take this report from the Belgian capital, for example:

> Semi-worldly, semi-marginal, sporting a trendy wristwatch, he left McCann-Erickson after two years, and Young & Rubicam after three. He writes about advertising, appreciates luxury but detests every form of conformism. He also gets rapidly fed up with the agency grind. Advertising is dead, long live communication! So he stakes his claim to a little piece of territory with his accomplice. . . . Their aim is to transform the client's brand image, develop communication strategies. . . . In fact they hate the institution of advertising, the same as their elders in the 1960s. Aficionado of Walt Disney and Kundera . . . he has opened his own restaurant. Out-and-out individualist and elitist. At night he plays poker with his buddies, sometimes losing 500 Fr. He works in town from nine till eight, uselessly meddling in one thing or another; suddenly goes to visit friends from the days of student demonstrations or sits down to watch *Star Wars* or *Business, Business* on video. . . . What does he really like? New gadgets! 'I like surprises! Mitterrand once said *"Vive la modernité"*.' That's good![35]

The last element in the tableau: the strategist-entrepreneurs in the construction of the global communications business.

Who knows Marion Harper besides a few chroniclers of the history of the profession, and employees at the New York headquarters of McCann-Erickson who, every day at 485 Lexington Avenue, cast a distracted glance at the portraits of previous company presidents? Who knows the managing directors of the big networks and other American multimedia conglomerates? The Saatchi brothers, on the other hand, have in less than five years carved a legend for themselves as predators in high financial places and in magazines with worldwide circulations – and their disfavour in the media following their poor financial results is the measure of the cult which they formed around them in the preceding years. The same celebrity has gone to the new bosses of the transnational audiovisual industry. The names of Berlusconi and Maxwell have become their own trademark. Their entourage only strengthens the legend by mimicking their unspeakable halo of narcissism. There is no pity for the impertinent, with the audacity to reject hagiography.

Such self-glorification in the media has the effect upon Americans of evoking their nostalgia for the epoch of their own 'megamoguls', the big bosses of cinema and television. 'In a way', writes a journalist in *Variety* with admiration, 'the fact that so much development can be pinned on individuals rather than faceless corporations indicates European commercial television has some parallels to early TV ownership in the US. It wasn't just CBS, NBC and ABC, it was William S. Paley, David Sarnoff and Leonard Goldenson.'[36]

But the comparison, to have any validity, must stop there. The first age of television is in no way comparable to the context which gives rise to these new witch-doctors and their communications groups. If these men are captains of industry, they are also prudent political strategists. In a competitive environment spiked with the rules of the nation-state, where the question is how to overcome the barriers that belong to the old-style national institutions, strategies for industrial expansion are also strategies for cross-alliances. The high-visibility politics of the star players are only the perceptible part of a communications network where personal relations with politicians bring about decisions much more rapidly than the noisy broadcasting of opinions.

2

CULTURE SHOCK
The decline of the imperial model

BROKERS OF DEMOCRACY

The formative history of the international advertising networks is that of the first steps towards the media in all their modernity.

In effect, it is by means of these networks, through a flow of messages of transnational dimensions, that a permanent, daily and generalised connection is developed between particular societies and cultures, local, regional and national. Hence the primary confrontations between the public cultures belonging to the particular territories of the nation-state, and the cultures of the private sector and the market, with their universalising tendencies and ambitions. Also, the prime tensions between scattered popular cultures and the centralised mass culture which is produced industrially.

If this is so, it is because behind the concept of advertising in its instrumental sense – namely, 'the multiple and impersonal announcement of goods, services or commercial ideas by a named advertiser, who pays an agency and a transmitter (the medium, or advertising support) to deliver his message to the market' – behind this concept is hidden another, an idea deeply rooted in the history of the mode of communications: that of a new model of social organisation, a new means of creating consensus, of forging the general will.

This is advertising as the fundamental apparatus of the democratic marketplace, democracy of and for the market – for this is effectively the substance of the message. The fatherland of aggressive advertising – the place where it was inscribed directly into the logic of the marketplace – the country which first assumes this new vision of the world is the United States. As the president of the American Agency BBDO recalled in 1968:

Democracies with high living standards are at the top of the list of countries spending a high per cent of national income on advertising, whereas communist dictatorships with relatively low living standards are at the bottom of the list. . . . Freedom must have its advertising, or else it will surely run into danger . . . the American

31

marketing system has as its basis that sudden upsurge of the idea of human freedom.[1]

While the Old World, together indeed with some of the other new worlds, refuses to reduce 'popular culture' to 'mass culture', the US advertising industry has always regarded them as one and the same. In an article entitled 'The rhetoric of democracy', specially written for *Advertising Age* to celebrate the bicentenary of the War of Independence, the historian Daniel Boorstin claimed – with singular disregard for distinctions which have been made by innumerable anthropologists, sociologists and cultural historians:[2]

We are perhaps the first people in history to have a centrally organised mass-produced folk culture. Our kind of popular culture is here today and gone tomorrow – or the day after tomorrow. . . . When we turn to our popular culture, what do we find? We find that in our nation of consumption communities and emphasis on Gross National Product (GNP) and growth rates, advertising has become the heart of the folk culture and even its prototype. American advertising shows many characteristics of the folk culture of other societies: repetition, a plain style, hyperbole and tall talk, folk verse, and folk music. . . . How do the expressions of our peculiar folk culture come to us? They no longer sprout from the earth, from the village, from the farm, or even from the neighbourhood or the city. They come to us primarily from enormous centralized self-consciously 'creative' (an overused word, for the overuse of which advertising agencies are in no small part responsible) organizations. They come from advertising agencies, from networks of newspapers, radio and television.[3]

It is precisely by means of such a biased misconception that what at first appears no more than a 'technique for the modernisation of selling' turns into an American offensive after the Second World War, in the first great wave of internationalisation. The conviction that these international networks were not simply new promotional circuits for industrial and commercial products, but also networks of cultural and political influence, was flaunted in broad daylight. According to a writer in *Advertising Age International*:

It could be said that advertising and marketing can be a nation's unofficial diplomat overseas, representing a country's way of life more dramatically and realistically than official state department or foreign office ambassadors. The tremendous international impact of marketing and advertising in the United States, in fact has led to the coining of the word "adplomacy".[4]

'Advertising and marketing techniques are by far the most successful American export' – and national agencies which fall under the control of the American networks breathe fresh vigour into this image. 'It is the Americans who have taught us how to conduct advertising and marketing.'

After World War II a body of marketing knowledge existed in the US; in Germany the very word 'marketing' was unknown. If it hadn't been for the subsidiaries of US corporations which exploited their parents' marketing know-how, probably it would have taken until the late 1960s for anything similar to evolve in German companies and universities. To me this head start in knowledge of methods is among the main reasons for the spectacular success of American companies in Europe during the 1950s and 1960s.[5]

Summarising this educational mission, an analyst in the specialist press writes:

Certainly one of the greatest contributions made by American advertising agencies has been their role as training centres for the ad communities around the globe. A Danish advertising man commented to *Advertising Age* last year that in the 50s when marketing as a conscious skill was dawning in Europe, those who knew the basics 'were the real winners', and generally speaking, that meant Unilever-trained managers and middle-managers. They were the ones that scored the points and stood out from the rest. In Mexico, Colgate-Palmolive, Procter & Gamble, General Foods, Anderson Clayton, and Richardson-Merril have filled the role of educator. Virtually every agency had at least one marketing man who was skilled in one of the American multinationals. 'Colgate, particularly, is constantly feeding our industry with people,' says Augusto Elias, head of the Publicidad Augusto Elias agency. On the agency side, many of today's Mexican agency owners came out of the executive ranks of Chicago's now-defunct Grant Advertising agency.[6]

DECLINE OF THE IMPERIAL MODEL

V*eni, vidi, vici*: this pioneering phase of the internationalisation of the advertising networks, in which the leading player and the imperialist colours are both Yankee, came to an end at the start of the 1970s.

The world economic framework altered: the flow of direct international investment took on different colours. In the period 1961–7, the US share in the total foreign investment of the thirteen member nations of the OECD reached 60 per cent; between 1974 and 1978 it fell to 30 per cent. The German Federal Republic saw its own share increase from 7.2

to 16.7 per cent; that of France from 6.9 to 7.8 per cent; Japan went up from 2.4 to 13.2 per cent, while over the same period, Britain's share declined from 8.7 to 7.9 per cent.[7] It was only during the second half of the 1980s that this proportion increased.

Another shift that followed in the second half of the 1970s was the redirection of investment by the big European companies towards the United States, with the Japanese falling into step the following decade. During the 1960s, the US received around 10 per cent of the flow of world investment. By the end of the 1970s this figure had tripled. In the late 1980s, it fluctuated at around 50 per cent, and the United States had become the principal destination for foreign investment.[8]

In parallel, the manner in which investment in Europe by American firms was financed was modified. Beginning during the second half of the 1960s, this alteration took full effect after 1972. From this date on, subsidiaries of American enterprises appealed less to metropolitan capital than to local capital (through credits or profits obtained locally). This process thereby contributed to a real brake on investment, which some-times ended in the disappearance of European subsidiaries – especially in the case of enterprises which first crossed the Atlantic in the 1960s, when the United States, in order to resolve a classic crisis of overproduction, launched an assault on those economies which were still in sound condition. This is much less true for firms established abroad before the tidal wave – headed by the big spendthrift detergent companies and their advertising agencies – who have continued to develop. So too have others of whom little was said during the 1960s: companies which headed the 'American challenge', introducing the latest technologies (electronic and nuclear, for example), intensifying their activities throughout this per-iod. Firms like ITT, General Electric and Westinghouse, which generally tended to adopt a low profile that furthered other forms of relationship with national economies, like remote control through their ownership of patents.

As for the Third World, the image of a group of countries interchange-able with one other has given way to a splintered reality consisting in the petrodollar countries, with colossal balance-of-payments surpluses; 'newly industrialised' countries, like South Korea, Taiwan, Singapore, Hong Kong and Brazil; and a huge mass of nations whose economies are stagnant or in regression.

Reflecting these upsets, financial institutions have entered on the second stage of their internationalisation. The first stage had begun in the 1960s when the rapid growth of commercial exchange (plus the growth in exports by the industrialised countries), together with the increase in direct investment, forced American and European banks to follow their clients in becoming transnational. The second stage sees a powerful growth in the Euromarkets provoked in the first place by the appearance of an American deficit and then reinforced by the OPEC surplus.[9]

These years are characterised above all by the consolidation of national advertising markets. In 1953, advertising expenditure in the United States made up three-quarters of advertising industry receipts worldwide. Twenty years later this figure had dropped to 62 per cent. Local agencies, where they continued to operate, created difficulties for the American networks, who were usually always in front in international markets, and competing for the same clients. In short, this thrust by internal advertising markets (in some countries, the rise of a national industry) created new power relations which obliged the American networks to re-examine their mode of conduct on foreign territory.

Even if the particular form of relationship with the locals is worked out case by case, since it depends precisely on the negotiating capacities of each party, certain networks elevate the principle of the willing and agreed 'nationalisation' of their operation to an article of faith. According to the president of Kenyon & Eckhardt at the beginning of the 1970s, after a reconnaissance trip through Europe and Latin America:

> I think the local nationals have an absolute right to control their own destiny. The American affiliate can own up to, say, 49 per cent and put in its technical expertise. . . . The Common Market is going to make countries more nationalistic than ever. . . . Every place I've gone, I've talked to many people, including consul generals and even presidents, and all of them subscribe to this theory. K & E is interested in buying into or merging with agencies interested in moving ahead. We want to buy into a shop where there is good young talent and not where the management is 65 and ready to retire.[10]

The professional press in the United States saw which way the wind was blowing. In 1977, after fifty years in which it addressed the advertising business in the Old World in the same way as its American counterpart, *Advertising Age* decided to launch a European supplement. A short while earlier, the French had decided to set up a bi-monthly called *Stratégies*, modelled on the English fortnightly *Campaign*, itself a distant imitation of *Advertising Age*. The supplement's opening editorial, headed 'Why we are here' declared:

> There was a time when European admen eagerly looked to the US for the latest trends in advertising and marketing, and so it was sufficient to give our European readers the same fare as our US audience. That time has passed. Europeans today are creating the trends themselves, are setting their own creative style. And so the time has come for our newspaper to publish a European section for

European advertising and marketing people and reflecting the innovations originating from Europe.[11]

In the same edition, the director of a subsidiary of an American network based in Düsseldorf was already drawing conclusions and sketching out the strategies which American firms should apply if they wished to carry on prospering in this market: 'The United States is no longer the pacesetter for Europe, where creativity is the name of the game. . . . European countries have learned their lesson well over the last twenty years . . . and are now formidable competition.' Centralised headquarters made sense fifteen years ago, he continued, because New York had 'the clients, the flying teams and the know-how. This is no longer the case: the know-how is here [in Europe]; we can solve problems on the scene with local managers providing continuity.'[12]

Two years later, after this overture towards Europe, *Advertising Age* announced the formation of a Latin American council with the following comment: 'This advisory Council, headed by Richard B. Criswell of Leo Burnett in Chicago, will serve as a sounding board on major advertising and marketing issues affecting Latin America.'[13] The various countries of the subcontinent were represented by the directors of the big agencies, to whom were added the commercial directors of big multinational advertisers like Johnson & Johnson, Gerber and Nestlé.

Third-generation networks emerged in the 1980s, and corresponded to the growing movement of interconnection and integration between markets and economies. If the first generation could be confused with the so-called process of Americanisation, and if the second could be defined as the internationalisation and consolidation of national protagonists, then the present generation is deeply marked by the process of interpenetration of firms and markets. To follow the parallelism sketched out above, the 1980s also saw the start of the third phase in the internationalisation of financial institutions, also led by the growing integration in this case of the capital and exchange markets, which redefined the activity of the financier. To the semantics of 'international capital markets' is added the jargon of 'global markets'. The new conceptual map employed in the financial networks resembles that of the advertising and media networks: *deregulation, globalisation*. The accession of the advertising agency, and more generally of global communications enterprises, to the stock market and the world of speculation, completes these relations of kinship between the two pillars of the so-called 'service society' (and its synonyms: the information society, communications society, tertiary society).

The US market remains the largest. Investment in the advertising industry worldwide in 1989 (in TV, print, radio and outdoor advertising) had reached $177b (nearly $240b if you include below-the-line business).[14]

36

The North American market absorbs about half of this, Europe 28 per cent, Asia and the Pacific 19 per cent, Latin America 2 per cent, Africa and the Middle East less than 1 per cent. Advertising expenditure in US media as a percentage of Gross Domestic Product (at market prices) amounted in 1988 to 1.55 per cent (as against 1.32 in 1980). For the countries of the European Community it was 0.99 per cent (0.73 eight years earlier). But the range bracket was extremely wide: 0.74 per cent in France (0.48), 0.93 per cent in Federal Germany (0.88), 1.12 per cent in Switzerland (1.08), 1.54 per cent in Spain (0.63), around 1.44 per cent in Finland and Britain (which eight years earlier stood at 1.10).[15]

Britain thus spent twice as much on advertising as did France, while its GNP was less than a fifth of the size. At the same time, the average rate of advertising investment in the three biggest televisual markets in Latin America – Brazil, Mexico and Venezuela – outruns that of Switzerland which enjoys an income level several times larger than do these countries. At the bottom of the scale, and confirming the disparities of integration of Third World countries within the networks of the international market, are India and black Africa, where the rate varies between 0.3 per cent and 0.5 per cent.

Still the Madison Avenue advertising networks are everywhere. But they are no longer hegemonic. Their system of advertising and marketing has become institutionalised and shared by other nations. Americanisation has metabolised into what the French historian Jean Chesneaux refers to as 'world-modernity' (*modernité-monde*).

In the days of America's uncontested hegemony over the world economy, it used to be said maliciously that when New York catches cold, London and Paris cough. Today, in the age of trilateral world economy, one should add that when Tokyo falls ill, New York sneezes. In 1977, American manufacturers of television sets still controlled 48 per cent of their internal market. Ten years later, their share had fallen to 14.5 per cent and the world's foremost video market now imports three out of every four television sets and the entirety of its stock of recorders. If this witticism is ever more accurate in describing the relegation of numerous sectors of the American economy (mass electronics, automobiles, banks, trading companies), it would still be highly imprudent to eliminate American power from the hit parades of the big communications networks.

The weight of evidence and the fact of the matter is this: in the new global architecture of the telecommunications networks, the United States – and the processes which are taking shape there – remain determinant for the future of other national and regional realities; even if they each have their own form of access to the communications world in consequence of the historical weight of their domestic institutions. Every society, one could say, gets the kind of modernity it deserves. On the new

37

global stage, the prompter is still there, but there is no longer any *deus ex machina*.

APPROPRIATION

Like the indictment of Americanisation, the oaths of allegiance and the recognition of debt towards Madison Avenue have for long obscured the analysis of the encounter of particular societies with the know-how exported by the world's most advanced industry.

In the alchemy of relations between economic and cultural forces, the transplant of modernity by means of new sales techniques has often produced contradictory processes where adherence and connivance are mixed up with both rejection and mimetic behaviour, and the more or less critical appropriation of external contributions. More exhaustive work remains to be done to examine in detail this difficult gestation of both universalising modernity and territorial singularity, this permanent dance of unequal exchange. That is not our main intention here, which is more modest: merely to throw a little light on this process of interaction, using examples taken at random from articles, reports and testimonies collected in the trade journals of different periods.

The first representative example: France

If the founders and theoreticians of modern aggressive advertising are mainly American, the inventor of the advertising agency, albeit still in a primitive form, was none other than a Frenchman, Théophraste Renaudot (1586–1653), better known as promoter of the *Gazette de France*, the ancestor of the modern French newspaper. It was in 1630 that Renaudot set up an agency in the form of a bulletin board which at the end of the seventeenth century served in Britain as the model for the first advertising bureaux. As one historian has noted, the invention of the advertising agency:

> only acquires its full significance as part of an ensemble of public services set up with the encouragement and protection of power. This attempt at the secular rationalisation of what until then were religious charities, has only, it seems, a distant relationship with modern advertising; it seems to belong rather to the modern history of the welfare state, since its avowed objective consisted in the regulation of the poor. This *ancien régime* of publicity had a social end; the recourse to advertising, by aiding the development of exchange, aimed more profoundly than material prosperity at the amelioration of human commerce. In this sense, all publicity is commercial; but entering into the bosom of political economy, it

turns the means into an end and the incitement to consume becomes the instrument of sales promotion. Public assistance gives way to private enrichment, and publicity becomes a 'source of riches'.[16]

In adopting the root-word 'public', the concept of '*publicité* ' reveals the genesis of these institutions within the territory which it invents. On the other hand, the English language adopts the old French Renaissance term *advertissement*, which becomes 'advertisement, advertising', and confines 'publicity' strictly to public relations. And while the French advertising apparatus was created following the Renaissance through the prolongation of the institutions of public benefaction, the American apparatus was born directly in the spirit of competition. The historian's commentary on the French advertising institutions clearly indicates how the irresistible rise in aggressive advertising best enables one to grasp the slow transformation of the idea of a public service, and shows how it clears a path through the resistance offered by a certain cultural heritage and historical tradition.

France, not having discovered the techniques of aggressive advertising itself, went to the United States to learn them. Consider the confessions of the founder of modern French advertising, Marcel Bleustein-Blanchet:

At age 18, without knowing a word of English, I left for America, the one place I knew I would learn what advertising really was. I was like a Muslim going to Mecca. What I learned was very simple: You can't have good advertising for a bad product. My admiration for the United States comes from two things: democracy in communication and respect for public opinion. I returned with one desire, to make advertising a respected, responsible profession, something more than shrill claims and slogans. My father was horrified when I told him. 'Advertising?' he said, 'That's like trying to sell the wind.'[17]

This idyllic liaison between Madison Avenue and the young tiro of advertising in the years before the war turned out far from normal when the American agencies, at the end of the 1940s, resumed their interrupted activities in Paris by establishing their first subsidiaries: 'Advertising seemed to be viewed, especially by the Resistance fighters after the war, as the new occupation force', admits the international editor of *Advertising Age*. To the reproach addressed to the American networks that they stole local budgets away from the French, he adds that of 'failing to understand French psychology'.[18]

Between 1961 and 1973, when they arrived in force, many of the New York or Chicago networks had already drawn the lessons of their predecessors and proposed, before this practice had become general elsewhere, forms of association with minority participation. By the end of the 1970s, in the specialised press in the United States, one loses count of the articles and interviews bearing the seal of 'cultural difference'. The president of Young & Rubicam in Paris,

> sees the [French] educational process as being detrimental to the overall image advertising has in this country. At Y & R, Mr Boulet claims he has Americanised his employees to a Procter & Gamble-like efficiency level. But he still contends that people coming out of schools in France aren't ready for Americanised advertising. 'Eighty per cent of the teachers in the French school system are socialists,' he says. 'You can't get the type of spirit necessary for competitive advertising from that type of education.'

For his part, another advertising executive remarks that:

> Advertising in France, because it's younger and less jaded, has fewer restrictions than in the U.S., with a greater flexibility of approach. The Americans are too pragmatic. They see one solution to a problem. The French see 36 solutions and have a little trouble making up their minds. But they usually come to the right decision. I think it's a compliment to be accused of being too aesthetic – it's like being called too innovative.[19]

More than ten years later, if the first comment has been shot down by the rise in the legitimacy of advertising and the media and the new regime of truth thus installed, the second remains valid. As the actor Peter Ustinov explained in April 1988, the great difference with the United States is that French advertising respects the personality more: it seems to have been created by a single brain for a group of individuals. American advertising, on the other hand, appears to be the result of research, analysis and consensus; there is so much money invested that creation is hugely filtered before reaching the public.[20] The tribute to be paid for this originality: 'French advertising is very fine advertising. But it's not exportable. That's the big problem. And nor are French advertising people. That's another story.'[21] The same problem suffered by French television production in foreign markets.

Second example: Italy

Here US advertising transnationals have the lion's share. Jean-Luc Godard once said that 'the best Italian cinema is undoubtedly *Carosello* '.[22] *Carosello* (Carousel) is the style of advertising which began at the end of the 1950s under the aegis of Italian public service television (RAI). Two-thirds spectacle and one-third commercial message, a real story followed by a spot, *Carosello* lasted almost fifteen years. It disappeared from the small screen during the 1970s, the decade of audiovisual deregulation. The story is told by an Italian advertising producer:

> Going back to the 1960s the production of Italian advertising films was largely in the hands of the producers who, in turn, ran the creative team. The agencies made suggestions and focused on the target . . . *Carosello* was the product of Italian advertising culture, it expressed an identity which others perhaps could not understand. It was the natural result of the *commedia dell'arte* which is all ours and only ours. . . . We must not feel ashamed of being what we are. We had minstrels, the troubadours and the *cantatori* [singer-composers]. This language of the artisan class has come down to the industrial era thanks to many enterprises. With the development of the American agencies in our country, the problem of creativity has been displaced from the production houses to the agencies. This is also because, bit by bit, marketing was becoming a science and the creative staff were coming under the rule of marketing . . . . When I refer to *Carosello* I do not mean that the same language would still be valid today because the language has to evolve. . . . Today the language is that of *Flash Dance*, produced moreover by an erstwhile employee of J. Walter Thompson. . . . In the past decade, Italian advertising has hardly distinguished itself in advertising festivals, largely because we have lost our identity. This may seem incredible because the whole world considers us the best artistic creators. Italian design is our highest expression. Like fashion, and the car designers who put their names to the automobiles of the Japanese, the French, the Germans. . . . The reproach that can be made against certain Italian advertising people is that they have given more importance to other people's discoveries than our own.[23]

Third example: Brazil

Among the ten largest markets in the world, Brazil on the other hand, since the start of the 1980s, has indeed received many prizes in these same festivals. Since 1981, and the 18th Advertising Film Festival at Cannes, Brazil has taken sixteen awards, including two golden lions, two silver and one bronze, thus for the first time overtaking the United States and Japan. At the Ibero–American advertising festival (FIAP) held at Punta del Este (Uruguay) in 1987, Brazil had more than 300 entries. It shared with Spain, another place full of creativity, some 70 per cent of the prizes, with Argentina placed third, while not a single prize went to Mexico.

Brazilian historians of advertising locate the first encounter with American know-how in 1926, through the advertising department of General Motors. 'It was this firm', says one of them, 'which brought us the whole experience of the competitive market of American advertising. It carried in its baggage a whole new school of thought about advertising which used strange expressions like *layout, copywriter, media, slogan, market research, headline, caption* and many more.'[24] A short while later, J.W. Thompson and N.W. Ayer arrived, and rapidly became, according to the same historian, 'veritable training-ships' of advertising. In the face of growing demand, obliged to set up 'locals', JWT transformed its agency into a site of practical training. It instituted a system of trainees: each trainee had the chance to go through every stage of advertising production in a short space of time. All the big agencies, Grant, Lintas, McCann-Erickson, who set up bases in Brazil in the following years, adopted this formula. It was not until 1951 that a national institution took over this role, with the creation of the first teaching establishment under distinguished patronage: the School of Propaganda of the Museum of Art of São Paulo. Despite its authoritarian connotations, the term *propaganda* was preferred to *publicidade*. (It had long been the same in many other countries.)

When television transmissions were inaugurated in São Paulo and Rio de Janeiro in 1950–1, J. Walter Thompson called on an American producer, Harry Herrman, who with a young Brazilian assistant proceeded to create the first commercials for Brazilian television on behalf of Ford. Some thirty years later, the television giant Globo, fourth-largest network in the world, has its own production enterprise for advertising programmes which employs 200 people full time, utilises ultra-modern equipment, and is capable of producing in English at half the cost of the United States.

Since the end of the 1970s, the big Brazilian agencies have overtaken those who taught them the rudiments of the modern techniques of advertising and publicity. In 1981, the founder of one of the most important Brazilian agencies, Mauro Salles/Interamericana de Publicidade (and an ex-Minister), became the first Latin American advertising agent to be elected president of the International Advertising Association (IAA) by an assembly of 1,100 delegates from fifty countries.

At the end of the 1980s, four agencies with national majority ownership were the leaders of the Brazilian market. McCann-Erickson, who in 1970 had the lion's share, amounting to almost double its nearest competitor – a Brazilian agency – had fallen back to sixth place, with a turnover one-and-a-half times below that of the national number one.

Just as in the case of its television industry, Brazil has thus succeeded in establishing a national base of advertising agencies without recourse to measures of protection (at least direct ones, for as in many other countries, state budgets, for example, are given by priority to local agencies). This strategy contrasts with the nationalist policies of the Brazilian state which, to support the progressive construction of local industry in the fields of informatics, aerospace and especially cinema, has passed a number of very strict regulations to protect national initiatives and products. But beyond the differences in scale, informatics and aerospace as much as television and advertising are built on the appropriation of the know-how of the big industrial countries. In the domain of industries involved in visual production, however, this stage has long ago been left behind, and Brazil has succeeded in producing a style and genres quite its own.

EXPROPRIATION

Other countries in the Third World have tried to resolve the problem of their advertising industry in a very different fashion from that of the South American giant. India, for example, has limited the participation of foreign networks in agency ownership. Thus, in 1987, Hindustan Thompson Associates, which led the field, was affiliated to the JWT network; the second, Lintas India, held only 40 per cent of its subsidiary, the same as the third, Ogilvy and Mather; while the Saatchi & Saatchi/ Compton network had minority interests in the fourth, Everest Advertising. Indication of a timid opening, in 1988 Lintas became the majority proprietor of its subsidiary.

'Go home, or become a minority partner.' This policy towards foreign advertising networks forms part of a global strategy of 'indigenisation' of the economy. Its origin is found in a law passed in 1973, the Foreign Exchange Regulation Act, which reduced the participation of foreign enterprises in their Indian subsidiaries to 40 per cent. But not all foreign companies have responded with the same docility as their counterparts in advertising. In March 1978, Coca-Cola abandoned India where it had established itself twenty-eight years earlier when the British departed. The reason for the divorce was its refusal to yield to the provisions of the exchange market, and above all its refusal to comply with the 40 per cent law. It made much of the fear that the secret of its famous fizzy drink would be out. The same year, IBM in turn shut its doors, abandoning the country where it had first arrived in 1951.

During the 1970s, many countries of the South adopted the same principles. Some, like Venezuela, which led the discussion in the international debating chambers on 'the new world order of information and communication' and 'national communications policies', were also the first to propose a series of measures intended to regulate the activities of foreign firms. In those years, the most diverse political regimes adopted similar legislation. Beyond restrictions on property, they forbad, for example, the importation of advertising material conceived abroad, obliging foreign firms to translate their adverts into the national language and sometimes local dialects, as well as controlling the transfer of royalties and profits. To the demands of national identity was added the desire of local bureaux to preserve the market for their employment: to give work to their producers, their artists, their agencies and their products, and above all to assure the creation of a national base for their post-production industries.

As early as 1975, the *Wall Street Journal* showed disquiet at the rise of these new brakes on advertising activity.

Several years ago, Latin America's growing consumer markets looked like a fertile territory for U.S. advertising agencies. Half a dozen moved in to grab the lion's share of the promising Latin business. But now, with nationalistic sentiment running strong throughout the region, the U.S. ad agencies are encountering a variety of difficulties. Some Latin lands, for instance, recently agreed that a foreigner can't own more than 19% of a local ad agency. They tend to view advertising as part of their national communications facilities, and therefore, an area to be kept from foreign domination. Among these countries are the so-called Andean group of Venezuela, Colombia, Ecuador, Peru, Bolivia and Chile. As a result, in two years McCann-Erickson, Young & Rubicam, and J. Walter Thompson must sell 81% of their operations in these lands to local interests. This is particularly painful in Venezuela, where each of the U.S. agencies has an operation. Venezuela, with mounting oil revenues, had seemed an especially promising market for advertising.[25]

At the end of a study carried out in 1978, the IAA evaluated the rise of policies which members of the association judged to be a 'blow to the liberty of commercial expression'. This diagnosis also established that the patriotic reflex was not necessarily a monopoly of developing countries.

Such restrictions in Western countries are principally motivated by economic considerations. Foreign-made materials take away potential jobs from local producers of print and particularly audiovisual materials. Graphic and broadcasting unions as a result have gotten protection from foreign encroachment in the form of labor-management contracts in Mexico, the U.K. and U.S. In non-Western countries, motivating factors are nationalistic and cultural in orientation – whether to remove the stigma of colonialism, to forge a new common national or regional identity, or merely to resist the anglicization of the local language. For example, Peruvian regulations stress the protection and enhancement of the national culture and of the 'Peruvian man', and therefore try to ban foreign-inspired models and materials. The Philippine government urges the use of the Tagalog language to express that country's 'independence from foreigners'. Nationalism, too, is not just a non-Western phenomenon. French law forbids the use of foreign words and expressions when French equivalents can be found in the official dictionary (while this law is rigorously applied to tv commercials it is not followed to the letter in the print medium).[26]

The French law to which this international report refers is the Auriol Law, passed by the government of Raymond Barre in 1977. Conceived in the spirit of 'the quality of the language contributes to the quality of life', the law forbids foreign firms employing Anglo-American terminology in their advertising and promotion, as well as instructions for use of their products. It was particularly badly received by the manufacturers of computers, spare parts, and electronic and aeronautic components, who considered themselves the most affected by these linguistic barriers. The arguments they advanced to try and mitigate the application of the law demonstrate where, in their opinion, national frontiers end and the reign of universal standards begins: 'The language of most high-technology fields is English', they point out, 'and specialists, wherever they are, are taught from standard American texts and manuals', adding that 'translation would be prohibitively costly and time-consuming'.[27]

In numerous countries, laws and decrees passed in the 1970s have scarcely gone beyond a declaration of principles. In those which devised the most extreme measures, such as Peru, 'the most restrictive of the most restrictive' according to the IAA report, today McCann-Erickson and J. Walter Thompson occupy the top places and retain 100 per cent ownership of their subsidiaries in Lima. In Venezuela, McCann-Erickson, the third-largest agency in the country, bought up the entire shareholding of its local partner in 1986. J. Walter Thompson has retained full ownership of its subsidiary. Only the second – fruit of a union between Ogilvy & Mather and a national company, Corpa – still rigorously observed the 19 per cent law.

The welfare state voluntarism of the previous decade, with its wish to counterbalance the excessive commercialisation of the ensemble of audiovisual systems, has given way to the quiescence of neo-liberal governments which prefer to rely on market mechanisms. The Manichaean confrontation prophesied by the US delegation to UNESCO (between, on the one hand, increasingly authoritarian states, progressively imposing their regulations in the domain of culture, information and communication, and on the other a private sector, defending its idea of the freedom of commercial expression) has not taken place, and public power has been forfeit to the opposite camp.

AGGRESSIVE ADVERTISING

Ironically, the only state, up to 1988, completely to have locked up its advertising system was South Korea, one of the historical allies of the American superpower. And this was for reasons of national security quite as much as for political economy.

All foreign investment in the sector was forbidden. Further, the law stipulates that all advertising, before transmission by any audiovisual media, must be approved by KOBACO (Korean Broadcast Advertising Corporation), which is controlled by the government. Set up in 1980, KOBACO collects a 20 per cent commission on all advertisements which it approves for radio and television. In turn, it pays a commission of 7 per cent for television and 8 per cent for radio exclusively to those agencies which it recognises. The only problem is that more than four years after it was set up, this recognition had only been extended to four out of sixty advertising agencies. Out of these four, three were members of large local conglomerates, such as the Samsung group, and the fourth was an independent agency founded by an American resident who owned one-third of its shares. As a Korean resident owning shares in a Korean company, this individual investment was not subject to government approval. Nevertheless, repatriation of profits from the investment was not allowed. However, it should be added that it was only thanks to direct pressure from the American Chamber of Commerce in Korea and the US Ambassador that the agency was recognised by KOBACO.

But the snags which had to be undone in order to overcome the legal barriers to entry into the audiovisual advertising market did not end there. The three agencies owned by the conglomerates received preferential treatment. With the security provided by the groups they belonged to, they enjoyed unconditional sixty-day credit, while the independent agency had to obtain a guarantee from a Korean insurance company for its payments to KOBACO.[28]

In 1988, as a result of heavy lobbying by the US government and transnational firms, the South Korean government opened up the advertising market. Foreign agencies won the right to take a minority share of local agencies during the ensuing two years, to hold majority equity as of 1 January 1990, and to set up wholly owned branches as of January 1991. All in all, the situation provided a fine opportunity for South Korean advertising agencies to plead the relationship between freedom in general and freedom to advertise, but history teaches that this equation is far from simple.

In fact the history of relations between advertising agencies, democracy and freedom is full of compromise. For every agency like the French company of Robert Delpire, who on the day of the coup against the popular government of the constitutional President, Salvador Allende, publicly renounced the budget of the Chilean airline Lan-Chile, how many multinational networks have not lent assistance to dictatorships? In Chile, McCann-Erickson had provided back-up for the street demonstrations by a seditious opposition between 1970 and 1973 and its clamour for the intervention of the *putschists*, while J. Walter Thompson dressed up the public relations of the Greek colonels in 1967 and the Ministry of the Interior of General Pinochet's government in Chile in 1974. Similarly, in 1978, Burson-Marsteller prepared an international strategy to improve the image of the military junta in Buenos Aires. The classic example, however, is that of the aggressive employment in 1954 of the firm of Edwards L. Bernays, nephew of Sigmund Freud and father of the public relations industry, in the campaign for the mobilisation of American public opinion in anticipation of the overthrow of the constitutional President of Guatemala, Jacobo Arbenz, who had dared to launch an agrarian reform in the banana republic where United Fruit ruled the roost.[29]

The American advertising networks were certainly better advised when in 1987 they refused approaches by supporters of the Contras and the protagonists of Irangate. In May 1987, *Advertising Age* revealed how the firm of Bozell Jacobs Kenyon & Eckhardt had just avoided getting involved in this scandal. At the moment they were about to sign a contract which had been presented to them as an 'educational programme' on the account of the National Endowment for the Preservation of Liberty, the agency realised that it was actually a psychological operation against the Sandinista government in Nicaragua. The more prudent agencies Burson-Marsteller and Ogilvy & Mather had already turned it down. The foundation was forced back on a small firm dealing in political publicity, Goodman & Associates, of Towson, Md.[30]

Does this mean that grand schemes of imperial intervention, where the private multinational acts directly in the service of the geopolitics of the state, have been returned to the props store, and they now constitute unfortunate exceptions? At all events, one thing is certain: the redistribution of roles, on stages both national and international, between state and private sector, is upsetting established geostrategy.

3

THE LIMITS OF THE GLOBAL SCENARIO

Imagining the Other

THE DOCTRINE

We live in an era of global communications. Scientists and technologists have achieved what militarists and statesmen down the ages have attempted to establish but without success – the global empire. There is no doubt that the world is becoming one market-place. Capital markets, products and services, management and manufacturing techniques have all become global in nature. As a result, companies increasingly find that they must compete all over the world – in the global marketplace. This new development is emerging at the same time as advanced technology is transforming information and communication.

(Saatchi & Saatchi Annual Report 1986)

The first remodelling of the international networks which came about under the guidance of Interpublic occurred without authoritative statements about the justice of the cause. The style and content of the American group's annual reports employed the laconic language of economic war communiqués rather than that of overarching or seductive movements. When it came to megamergers, the language which the advertising industry applied to itself shed its skin, extolling a discourse of legitimation with theoretical pretensions. What then does this global perspective consist in, which inspires predators and serves as a rallying cry for advertising and marketing professionals?

Long since part of the practice of several transnational firms like Coca-Cola or Lévi-Strauss, this approach to the market became doctrine at the beginning of the 1980s. It began with an article by Theodore Levitt entitled 'The globalization of markets', published in June 1983 in the *Harvard Business Review*, which Levitt, professor of business administration at the Harvard Business School, himself edited.

According to his central thesis, there is increasing intervention in foreign markets; more and more industries and services are arriving at

48

'worldwide competition'; the accruing internationalisation translates into integration of markets on a global scale; world markets emerge for 'globally standardised products'; the increase in competition on a global level demands a global strategic vision of market planning; a powerful force leads the world towards what Levitt calls 'a converging commonality', namely technology.

The key to success in the exploitation of international markets is found in the global launch of products and brands, that is to say, in worldwide marketing of standardised products. The doctrine holds that 'universal standardisation' depends on three hypotheses: the homogenisation of world needs; a universal preference for low-priced products with an acceptable level of quality; and the need for economies of scale in production and marketing. The American professor does not deny the existence of segmented markets – he knows that markets are composed of different social, economic and demographic groups. But he postulates that these segments respond more to a global than to a national logic. Similar groups of people living in different countries can have the same needs and the same demands for the same products.

Levitt is a management theorist, and undoubtedly he and Peter Drucker are the two leading representatives of the breed in the United States. One of his decisive contributions is the concept of the global corporation, which alone, according to him, is capable of 'decimating its competitors' in a hyper-competitive worldwide market.[1] Products, services, distribution and communication must be conceived in global terms. 'The global corporation operates as if the entire world (or major regions of it) were a single entity; it sells the same things in the same way everywhere.' This quotation is prominently displayed in Saatchis' 1986 Report.

On the question of advertising, Levitt is hardly verbose. Even less so about the new media environment. But from the start of the 1980s his hypotheses about the main trends in the world market provided a theoretical foundation for intuitions and analyses employed in the British company's annual reports. The 1981 report refers to the need for pan-European policies, while the following year it goes further and preaches the idea of 'world markets'. In the intervening twelve months, Saatchis acquired a world dimension when it took over the American company Compton International, its first large transnational network. A global firm needs global targets. Assumptions about the globalisation of markets and advertising campaigns necessarily lead to the axiomatic notion of the 'global company', in other words, itself.

The scheme is simple: there are three major tendencies, the first two comprising four aspects, the third comprising three:

1 **Four key influences** on the media landscape: consumer convergence;

49

technology; the need to become a low-cost producer; the growth in advertising expenditure.

2 **Four major trends:** the globalisation of the media and the big communications groups; the increasing size of media-owning companies; the segmentation of the media; new media and new kinds of opportunity.

3 **Three types of effect:** the increasing pace of globalisation; pressure on governments to liberalise broadcast media; increase of attention to the function of the media.[2]

With conjugations and permutations depending on who is being addressed, this same thread of argument runs through all the documents, reports and interviews issued by the company. There is no better way to illustrate these notions than to review the annual reports of 1985 and 1986. What do we find?

A definition of the merits of the process of merger and concentration: economy of scale and the power of scale

Movements which affect the field of advertising are in symbiosis with those which affect industry overall: 'The top three advertisers in the world, each with a combined advertising spend exceeding $1 billion in 1984 in the US alone, have all been created by "megamergers": Procter & Gamble and Richardson-Vicks; Philip Morris and General Foods; R.J. Reynolds and Nabisco Brands.'[3] (In fact, in the United States, of the 100 leading national advertisers in 1980, a third had ceased to exist as independent companies ten years later.) To reinforce the hypotheses, a comparison of the parallel balance of concentration in the advertising industry: in the course of the last decade, a small group of multinational agencies has grown by 311 per cent, compared to 130 per cent for domestic agencies. This small group today controls 20 per cent of worldwide advertising investment as against 12 per cent ten years earlier. In five years, the number of large groups in multinational advertising has decreased from twelve to eight. This, then, when speaking of the doctrine of globalisation, is the basic statistic: a handful of transnational companies consuming one-fifth of the world advertising cake, which nourishes eight networks. Indeed it is difficult to understand the discourse of 'universal standardisation' adopted by global networks except in terms of a core at the heart of a two-speed world economy.

The prognosis for the evolution of global megagroups in control of advertising on the planet between now and the year 2000 always adopts the nuances of certain specialists in global marketing. For example, a professor at the University of Southern California in Los Angeles, Jagdish Sheth, says:

In general, with globalization I see that eventually we will see maybe

three or four super global agencies that are truly worldwide. . . .
Saatchi, Dentsu and Young & Rubicam are the most likely major
agencies in this group to emerge by the turn of the century at the
latest. . . . Then, you will see second-tier players who will begin to
specialize by industry, and they would like to go global . . . but in a
niche market. In these cases, agencies would have a few large clients
on a worldwide basis or several smaller ones in industries such as
banking and telecommunications. A third tier of shops will
specialize in a single medium such as print advertising, TV or direct
mail.[4]

However, the financial fragility of a number of megagroups – beginning
with Saatchis – plunges the impartial observer into perplexity whenever
there is speculation about the emergence of 'an elite group of truly global
agencies chasing panregional accounts'!

It is not enough to argue in terms of economies of scale, that is to say,
how to produce more cheaply. It is also about the power of scale, that is,
how to do it better. This is exactly the advantage which is offered by the
agency with global dimensions.

Power of scale in advertising means increased flexibility of resources,
the ability to attract, reward and retain the very best talent, superior
media-buying clout and better media-buying systems. It means
increased resistance to adversity, a greater willingness to accept risks
and greater ability to invest in research and development. And it
means improved global information systems, increased technological resources and increased access to a broad range of communications and consulting experience. . . . The company is a family of
business experts.

(Saatchi & Saatchi Annual Report 1986)

A definition of the so-called holistic approach

The notion of globalism is geometrical in nature. Horizontal when it
designates the networks' geostrategy, vertical when it concerns their
strategies of diversification. The quest for a global target is inseparable
from that of the global communications enterprise – to enlarge to the
maximum the fronts on which the profession intervenes. But above and
beyond this search for cross-fertilisation, there is, above all, a conception
of the way the organisation and management of the large enterprise –
whatever branch of activity it belongs to – ploughs its furrow.

The movement towards global business management affects each
member of the organisation and not only the function of marketing and
advertising. Because 'in essence, the workings of a company are not
dissimilar to the workings of one's body. There is no point in trying to

51

get fit just by dieting, because regular exercise is needed as well, coupled with the right diet, and the right psychological conditions.'[5]

For the enterprise to think in terms of global marketing is to recognise the need to change its organisational structure, its information system, its system of research and development, its production system, its system of premiums, etc. Within this totalising perspective, it is necessary that every party to the enterprise pushes in the same direction. It needs a clear strategy, a simple structure of organisation, people who are highly motivated working with better information, properly focused marketing, good internal communication within the team and with consumers.

> To achieve the optimum business system for its industry, every aspect of a company's activity has to be seen holistically – or the organisation is shackled by the weakest link in the chain, or worse, by elements that actually work against each other. A brilliant new strategy is of little use if the people in the company do not understand it, or are not motivated by it. And highly motivated people are not much use either of they are acting on the wrong information, or are not communicating clearly with their customers.[6]

And again in the words of Theodore Levitt:

> The business firm has to be systematically self-conscious about every commercial message it sends out – whether it concerns its ads, its product design, its packages, its letterhead, how its salesmen dress and what they say, its point-of-sale materials, its trucks, or the condition under which its products are displayed and sold. This requires a carefully planned and fully co-ordinated programme . . . an integrated organic whole.[7]

Here in a few words, using a model taken straight from systems theory and vulgarised by persons of lesser talent, is Saatchis' justification for the diversification of the global network into management consultancy and the aim of providing a 'services supermarket' for every enterprise. The financial setback which this project suffered in 1989 clearly doesn't mean the disappearance of this logic of global integration, which is used to vindicate the reorganisation of social relations within big companies and the restructuring applied to the sphere of professional communications practice through amalgamation.

A definition of 'consumer convergence' ('the global approach')

[Today's] sophisticated marketers are recognising that there are probably more social differences between midtown Manhattan and the Bronx, two sectors of the same city, than between Midtown

Manhattan and the 7th Arrondissement of Paris. This means that when a manufacturer contemplates expansion of his business, consumer similarities in demography and habits rather than geographic proximity will increasingly affect his decisions. . . . All this underlines the economic logic of the global approach.

(Saatchi & Saatchi Annual Report 1985)

The globalisation of the media stimulates the global campaigns which now address themselves to segmented audiences, identifiable by their particular interests, their lifestyles or their occupation.

But parallel to this segmentation of audiences, the time has come for transnational advertisers to *'capitalise on universally recognised cultural symbols and references. . . .* Without TV and motion picture education about the virile, rugged character of the American West, the worldwide proliferation of the Marlboro brand would not have been possible.' The global convergence of consumers consists in just this: 'This cultural convergence is manifest too in the worldwide popularity of films like *Rambo* or *Ghostbusters*, pop music idols like Madonna, and books, both fiction (for example Jackie Collins' *Hollywood Wives*) and non-fiction (for example Victoria Principal's *Body Beautiful*).'

(Saatchi & Saatchi Annual Report 1985)

Observe, incidentally, that if the doctrine of globalisation (the way it is defined and employed by the foremost group in the world) is constructed on the ruins of the doctrines of Americanisation, it reveals no less a fascination for the products of the US culture industries, those 'natural supports of universality', as a member of the agency puts it.

A definition of the 'new consumer age' – that of the 'advertising literate consumer'

This is a rupture at the same time theoretical and practical.

In the early days of commercial TV advertising, many theories about the ways in which advertising achieved its effects were based on the simple model of a passive, uncritical viewer to whom the advertiser transmitted a message. As long as the advertiser kept his message simple, demonstrated his product's attributes straightforwardly, and repeated the message often enough, sales would follow. Modern theories recognise that different advertisements achieve their effects in a variety of ways, and the consumer is not just a passive receiver of advertising 'transmissions', but someone who is used to seeing advertisements, who knows what they are trying to do, and who responds actively and often critically to them. Modern television audiences across the world are no longer just consumers of products, they are *consumers of TV advertising* too, and they have become sophisticated evaluators of that advertising product. . . . The

53

'advertising literate' consumer of the 1980s is quick to identify, and to disparage, the unimaginative, the second-rate, the 'cheap' production and the commercial cliché – and is liable to extend those judgements to the advertiser's brand.

(Saatchi & Saatchi Annual Report 1974)

In strong contrast to earlier years, the Saatchis' Annual Report for 1989, the year of the fall, is unusually subdued. Instead of a document full of photos, graphics, quotations from eminent economists or businessmen and theoretical observations, the presentation is bland and consists largely of the company accounts.

THE THEORETICAL CONTROVERSY

Can there be global product policies? If there is a definite temptation for companies to exploit their brands in different countries using the same form of marketing, the answer to this question is less settled than Theodore Levitt and the Saatchis' experts would lead us to believe.

The clearest criticisms are found in the arguments of other academics in the same departments who are opposed to the marketing theorists. One of the most fundamental is that of Yoram Wind and Susan Douglas, professors in the Wharton School of the University of Pennsylvania and at New York University respectively. Their work, entitled *The Myth of Globalization* takes exactly the opposite position to Levitt's article on the globalisation of markets.[8] Their thesis is this. The latest developments in information and communication technologies and networks, as well as the growing integration of markets, certainly needs a global perspective in the planning of strategy, but such a perspective does not necessarily imply that it must be based on the commercialisation of standardised products and brands throughout the world.

The two authors therefore throw out the three hypotheses which underlie the doctrine of 'universal standardisation' and propose their own scheme for the real logic and mode of development of globalisation. In particular, they show that there is no proof the world is becoming homogeneous, and it is consequently difficult to claim that forms of response in the markets constituted by different countries are increasingly similar. Even if there are certain products and markets for which similar reactions can be identified across the globe, one also finds other sectors within these markets which differ considerably from country to country. They illustrate the point with numerous examples. For instance, while leading perfumes are marketed in a global fashion, the use of eau de toilette and eau de Cologne varies considerably from one country to another, in the same way as preferences for the smell of spices or flowers.

For the two American experts, moreover, forsaking preferred products in favour of others which are new but standardised and competitively priced cannot be verified either. At present, certain global products, like still photograph cameras, sell very well at high prices. Furthermore, the argument frequently invoked in favour of globalisation, that of economy of scale, becomes at least partially questionable because of new technologies of production, which allow a product to be modified and personalised without great effect on costs. Standardisation is therefore no more than one solution among the different possible strategies. Between the two extremes, that of a product which is identical worldwide and that of thorough differentiation according to a strategy specific to each country, in most cases the necessary strategy is semi-international. Thus, two apparently antithetical developments are occurring simultaneously: a proliferation of micro-markets for individualised ('designer') products and the internationalisation of major markets for mass consumer products.

If they recognise the relevance of investigating the similarities, the majority of critics of out-and-out globalisation – and they are numerous – stick to taking the differences apart and insisting upon the consequent need for adaptation. The majority of international flops, they observe, are the clear result of a lack of cultural sensibility, a lack of recognition of values and attitudes that make a successful strategy in one country inauspicious in another.

A point of contact between adversaries and partisans of the doctrine is found in the global campaigns of transnational giants like Coca-Cola, Pepsi, Marlboro, Levi Strauss or Esso-Exxon. Their performance in the synchronisation of their advertising operations worldwide has even become a theme of self-promotion and a slogan: 'Here is the new image of Marlboro Lights. The new episode of the fantastic Marlboro ride. It has been conceived in France. It could have been conceived anywhere in the world. Here is an image which speaks, in all countries, in every language. Here is an international campaign.' The recipe?

> We have a single brand that permeates 155 countries around the world. Essentially, in every one of those countries, our target consumer is the same target consumer. We have divisions around the world, all of whom are responsible for their business. Strategically, we set our strategies together. We have what has become sort of a cliché in our company: one sight, one sound, one sell. We have been able to develop an effective advertising and marketing approach, and at the same time give ourselves and our brand some control over what is said, how it is said, how it looks and where it is.[9]

Yet even with these transnational vectors at play, it is best to add nuances. On the one hand, for example, Coca-Cola also trades in regional and local brands; regional brands like Fanta in Europe, Latin America and

55

the Middle East, and local ones like Georgia and Aquarius in Japan. On the other hand, if their slogan 'It's the Real Thing' resounds on television and cinema screens across the world from Sydney to La Paz, it is also true that this standardised line of promotion coexists with local variants. Think of the relatively low profile which Coca-Cola maintained in France during the 1970s compared to neighbouring countries. In 1976, the advertising spend in French media by the Atlanta company was six times smaller than in the German Federal Republic and three times smaller than in Britain. This disparity was still there in the 1980s, when West Germany served the US transnational as a laboratory for a pan-European marketing strategy. French consumption stood at five litres of Coke per inhabitant per year, as against twenty litres in West Germany and forty-four in the United States. And this in spite of a tenfold increase in advertising expenditure in France since 1980.

Objections to the doctrine of globalisation of a less technical nature than those of the marketing theorists are made by a new and motley generation of advertising people who are allergic to macroscopic visions. To Saatchis' slogan 'The Bigger the Better', the new entrepreneurs oppose the virtues of small-scale, horizontal relationships, micro-processes and micro-analysis. Their disagreement with the macroscopic vision is evident in their proposal and legitimisation of another type of communications firm, comprising small and flexible teams capable of 'thinking the unthinkable, thinking what the big organisation cannot think of'. According to the British research and marketing company Taylor Nelson Group:

Contemporary values have ceased to be homogeneous and stable. It is not only possible, but desirable, to aim different messages at different groups. . . . Given the new socio-cultural values, the best placed firms will be those which are flexible, adaptable and non-bureaucratic and which develop fast and varied systems of information. It also appears that they will be those who reject global marketing. The concept of global marketing, given this new scenario, is overly simple and takes no account of the complexity of social change. . . . In the past, marketing communications were organised around the strategies of order and authority. But these are ceasing to be effective. . . . Big corporations in the future may have to invent alternatives to the themes of power and dominance, accommodating themselves to contradictions, generating as much communication *towards* the centre as from it.[10]

This strategy is necessary, they conclude, in order to offer the services of their flexible teams to big and small alike.

Micro or macro, even then the alternative is left behind in terms of the organisational model of the enterprise. For what the crisis has taught and set in motion is that small is complementary to big and vice versa. A double line of evolution is being drawn: on the one hand, the rise of global firms; on the other, that of small autonomous units, eventually inside the big structures. In short, the well-balanced coupling of centralisation and decentralisation which has been put into practice in the French firm of Havas and the Japanese Dentsu. In 1978 Eurocom-Havas offered its new services to associations, local administrations and public and semi-public institutions through the creation of the first agency specialising in 'social communication'. They called this small and flexible unit Eleuthera. In 1984, Dentsu launched an agency for women directed by women. Its ensign was Dentsu Eye (E for Egeria, Y for Youth and E for Early Bird).* Its staff consisted of twenty-seven women, and four men who made up the administrative personnel.

The same articulation between 'micro' and 'macro' is also found in the strategies of 'regionalisation' or the establishment of local roots by the macro-networks – especially as demonstrated by Young & Rubicam's policy of territorial deployment in the countries of the European Community, or that of Eurocom, which has reorganised its network in the French provinces through joint ventures with local independent agencies or by restructuring its own bureaux. The hypothesis which guides this preparation for the single market is that the role of the 'region' as a significant marketing space can only grow to the same degree that national identities are eroded. 'Region' in this sense should not be confused with the political-administrative 'regions' but may ignore or extend beyond the frontiers of the nation state. Thus, alongside the notion of the region as an entity fomented by the European project, there also emerges that of new intra-regional relations.

REDEPLOYMENT

It is no longer possible for a country to exist independently from the rest of the world. Whether we like or not, the next logical step in the evolution of mass communications is global communications. It is a form of communication that transcends national boundaries and language and reaches to the hearts and minds of people. Global communications must speak personally to every individual; at the same time its message must be universal. Each country has its own culture and industrial system. Understanding and respecting diverse ways of life is important, and trying to strip the diversities and

---

* *Egeria*: in Roman mythology, the nymph who was transformed by King Numa into an inexhaustible fountain. *Early Bird*: the first Intelsat television satellite, launched in 1965. [Translator's note.]

consolidate different cultures into one convenient mass culture is a terrible mistake.

This was the message delivered by the president of Dentsu in a speech at the 31st IAA (International Advertising Association) World Advertising Congress held in Sydney, Australia, in May, 1988.[11]

With or without this nuance, there can be no doubt that the logic of globalisation is both a mental reality and a real presence in the marketplace. The networks increasingly respond to its pressure by reorganising their local branches in order to offer their clients centralised services co-ordinated internationally. They also favour the interchange of ideas and the transfer of experience from one market to another, from one subsidiary to another. The systematic meetings which are held between members of the same network in each major region have become routine. Here they not only discuss the problems created by the co-ordination of this or that account, but also the political and economic context in which subsidiaries in this or that region are called upon to operate. Owing to commercial secrecy, the participants are generally very reserved. But the chatterboxes sometimes surprise you with their confidences.

In February 1988 there was a meeting in Caracas between delegates of thirteen Latin American bureaux belonging to Ogilvy & Mather, one of the most important regional networks in the subcontinent, under the presidency of the group's world director (a North American) and the regional manager (a Brazilian). These meetings had been held regularly for five years. At this one in the Venezuelan capital there were twenty-three delegates, from Honduras, Guatemala, Costa Rica, El Salvador, Mexico, Ecuador, Colombia, Brazil, Paraguay, Uruguay, Chile, Argentina and the host country. They discussed the management of common accounts, how to purloin the regional account of Ford from a competitor, and a good deal more.

Questioned about these general aspects of the agenda, the Brazilian representative elaborated his vision of the region:

I emphasised at the recent meeting that 1987 had been a very difficult year for Latin America. The economy was very depressed, with alarming hyper-inflation and constant monetary devaluations. I also referred to political instability, the rebirth of a very old trend of nationalism in some countries and xenophobia in others. Nor can one leave aside the drama of the external debt and fabulous fiscal deficits, mixed with excessive state intervention in the private economy. The latter is repeated in almost all the countries of the area: the brutal presence of the state, which reduces the freedom of the private economy and impedes the development of business creativity. Perhaps Chile is the exception. It is the only country in Latin America which has reduced the presence of the state in the economy. In economic terms I would call it the country with the greatest freedom of enterprise; there are not even any price controls, something which I regard as a regional syndrome. However, in political terms there is still much to be done and as yet there is little space for criticism and discussion. The ideal would be to combine political freedom with economic freedom. In the long term, neither can survive alone.

As for the reflections his network had made on the social function of advertising, the Brazilian expert added:

> At Ogilvy we have a duty to involve ourselves in these questions every day. We have a duty, because we are free citizens and our business only survives in freedom. I consider myself a professional in freedom, because there is no advertising in the Soviet Union and all those communist countries where the economy is totally dominated by the state. As an advertising man, I believe we should speak of the need to impose more freedom and less state, less government, more private initiative and the definitive elimination of hyper-bureaucracy.[12]

Another index of international, if not global pressure is the networks' redeployment of the supervisors and co-ordinators responsible for transnational clients, an affair which obviously didn't start yesterday. The European co-ordination centre for J. Walter Thompson, located in London, employs a team of some thirty of these supervisors, and the British capital serves to co-ordinate Europe-wide and sometimes worldwide accounts for Bacardi (since 1977), Burger King (1977), De Beers (1978), Ford (1970), Kellogg (1977), Kodak (1977), Kraft (1982), Nestlé (1974), Rolex (1946) and Warner Lambert (1985). It is worth recalling that it was also London where McCann-Erickson set up their pan-European and world media-buying office in 1986. Ogilvy & Mather, who at the end of the same year opened a European centre in Brussels for the same purpose, employed some ten supervisors covering Europe who operated in different capitals, including Amsterdam for Philips and London for Unilever. Regional supervisors in the British capital are in charge of the Polaroid accounts in Europe and the Middle East, while that of Mattel, the American games giant, is run from Paris. Young & Rubicam, who have worked with local firms in different European countries for some time, have stayed with them in the course of their expansion into external markets. In this agency the general rule has been to direct the transborder account from wherever the client has its headquarters: Adidas in Germany, Pernod-Ricard in France, Barilla in Italy. Their best trick is a well-established experiment in developing indicators of homogeneity in the market, fed by a research programme into lifestyles and the values known as the four C's (Cross-Cultural Consumers' Characteristics).[13]

DDB Needham Worldwide has moved its international headquarters from New York to Paris, adding a new executive vice-president in New York to run global accounts. BBDO Worldwide and Lintas Worldwide set up a European board of directors and an 'executive group'. They have also named executives or new agency units working 'cross-culturally' and 'multilinguistically' and with exclusive management of multinational accounts.

On the horizon of the international networks' restructuring of European operations is the coming of the single market in 1992. The arrival of the first transborder technologies has raised the ante. With the satellites of Sky Television, Super Channel, etc., the search for a unique advertising platform has accelerated. The two eternal transnational rivals, Coca-Cola and Pepsi Cola, provide the first indication of the pan-European transnational television battles to come. 'The reason we have centralised the account is because the pan-European media are coming of age', declares the director of Pepsi Cola. A British advertising executive comments:

> The move confirms the belief of many advertisers that existing approaches to multi-country media will change radically as marketers review the cost-effectiveness of their buying in the new electronic age. . . . Pepsi Cola's use of satellite television for a European offensive against arch-rival Coca-Cola is dramatic evidence of the way big advertisers are reacting to the new electronic media.[14]

A LABORATORY

At times there is disillusion. Cross-border satellite projects are far from achieving financial balance. There is not an overabundance of products that could be described as international, consequently the manna of advertising is still very much a national prerogative. The projections made by the London branch of J. Walter Thompson are modest: 'The fuss made about satellite television can seem out of all proportion to the opportunities it offers', according to the executive in charge of 'new media'. 'Sums on the back of an envelope suggest potential pan-European advertising spend on television to be more than 5 per cent of the total potential in Europe during the next ten years.'[15]

Many of the objections to globalism find their *raison d'être* in this European laboratory. The mosaic of languages and regulations and a long tradition of marketing conceived from and for a national base are not about to disappear. Domestic advertising spaces exist: there are differences in legislation and industrial structures; there is a different balance in each national media system; and above all, a diversity of cultural dispositions. How could it be otherwise when it emerges that in 1985, advertising was still prohibited on Sundays on German and Dutch television, on radio in Ireland, and similar rules applied to Good Friday and other religious festivals in Greece and Italy!

Products are not necessarily employed in the same way, nor do they respond to identical needs. The motivation for making purchases varies. The Danish and the Germans apparently buy fluoride toothpaste to prevent their teeth falling out; the French and the Italians for cosmetic reasons. While BMW and its network, which covers more than thirty countries, tries to maintain the same international image everywhere, Volvo puts the accent in France on status and leisure; in Sweden on economy, durability and security; in Germany on performance; and in Switzerland on safety.

As for brand-name policies, things are far from homogeneous. The same product may be sold in a different packaging in response to local requirements. In Europe, for example, Kellogg has evolved different promotional themes, distribution strategies and packaging for each country, while in Latin America (as well as the Far East), it has standardised promotion throughout the region. The same may even be sold as a different brand from that of a neighbouring country. This is the case with various detergents – Cif can become Viss, Jif or Vif – all made by detergent manufacturers who, none the less, have a long history of internationalisation. This may also happen with bulkier products. In Italy, Volkswagen has been obliged to 'nationalise' the name of its Jetta model because of a negative connotation, since the prospective purchaser is not very inclined to purchase a car which might bring bad luck.

These disparities translate into an incompatibility in statistical data: the nomenclature and tools of measurement established within national frontiers do not measure up to an international future. According to the research director of Britain's Advertising Association, the challenge of harmonising advertising data in Europe is considerable. 'Investment, location, acquisition and many other decisions require the comparison of the relative importance of advertising expenditure across countries, industries and markets, yet the information currently available is extremely difficult to interpret.'[16]

There are essentially four problem areas. First, some countries produce statistics based on surveys of the volume of advertising purchased (e.g. pages or TV spots) multiplied by the rate card cost of buying it. This type of calculation fails to take account of any market discounts (which in the deregulated Italy can reach 70 per cent). Second, the data may be of varying degrees of accuracy. For example, some data may be collected by a sample survey of expenditure and some by a census. Third, some countries include the production costs of advertising expenditure and/or the advertising agency commission payable, others do not. Fourth, some countries measure expenditure in direct mail or sales promotion ('below-the-line' or non-media advertising), but most concentrate on the 'classical' media (print, radio and TV, cinema and outdoor advertising). Once all these problems are sorted out, there remains another: conversion into a single currency. Massive variations in the value of the dollar relative to other currencies require some other method, through the calculation of 'purchasing power parities': the units of each currency required to purchase the same basket of goods or services in each of these countries.[17]

As if this were not enough, there is another general difficulty, which consists in the information which is held back by various participants in the advertising process on the grounds of 'commercial secrecy'. Then there is also the incompatibility of data arising from trivial problems like the different classification of the same products: some countries include chocolate-coated biscuits under 'confectionery' and others under 'sweet biscuits'; some give health and beauty products according to weight, others according to units sold. This also affects the selection of variables chosen to measure this or that political behaviour, not to mention, more prosaically, the domain of eating habits. The only people who manage to escape this patchwork jigsaw puzzle of definitions, distribution systems, motivations and brands are the firms which have already conceived their products in global terms. Though not yet operating on a planetary scale, the Italian company Ferrero distributes its Nutella throughout Europe according to the same commercial policies, while Gillette, in anticipation of the single European market, has launched a new natural deodorant (Natrel Plus) in Britain, Spain, the Netherlands and Scandinavia.

If most of the polemics about globalisation are stimulated by the multimillion promise of the single European market, somewhat similar debates have arisen almost everywhere, wherever big unified markets are created or relaunched. In the first place, the new global regional space promised by the Canada–USA Free Trade Agreement, and the project to open it to Mexico, thus creating a single market embracing some 350 million of real or potential consumers from the Arctic Circle to Yucatán; also the Asia-Pacific macro-market with Japan and the 'new industrialized countries' of this new geo-economical area as the engine. But the globalisation stakes also have repercussions on the Southern Cone of Latin America (with the future regional common market linking Brazil, Argentina and Chile); the Economic Plan for Central America (PAECA); the Caribbean Common Market (CARICOM); and the consolidation of the Australia–New Zealand Free Trade Agreement (NAFTA). Some reservation is needed: if experiments in regional integration in Latin America – some of which go back more than twenty years – show that the obstacles to the harmonisation of technologies and government economic policies are immense, they also reveal how a common consumer and advertising culture has been created through commercial television. This releases 'mega-marketers' in many of these countries from the need to postulate questions concerning the varied heritage of television in the nation states of the Old World.

One thing is certain, however (and how could it be otherwise?), the doctrine of globalisation – in the form expressed in professional discourse – is caught up in the idea of a world economy based on 'triad power'. This concept, elaborated in 1984 by Kenichi Ohmae, a Japanese employee of the American research company McKinsey, is dedicated to the idea of a tripolar world reality: Europe/North America/Japan and the four dragons. This is where 80 per cent of individual expenditure by the entire population of the planet is concentrated.[18]

Access to the problems of globalisation is only conceivable – in the judgement of the mega-marketers – in terms of operations which correspond to this trilateral form of life. According to one of them:

Increasing similarities between peoples, and increasing opportunities for global brands, are not confined to Europe and America. The Saudi Arabian wife, in strict purdah, spends liberally on French perfumes and cosmetics; successful Hong Kong Chinese have the highest per capita consumption in the world of the top French XO Cognacs and – despite awful traffic congestion – have more than their fair share of Rolls Royces, Porsches and Ferraris; and the Japanese, for so long eschewing foreign goods in favour of Japanese products, are embracing a new sub-group individualism (or, viewed globally, convergence) and responding increasingly to the allure of foreign brands, from Burberry raincoats to Aston Martin Lagonda motor cars. But convergence in global demand has not developed only among the wealthy or only for the most expensive brands. In Russia, Western travellers will be quietly propositioned for American or British cigarettes and Levi jeans; in Burma, the newly-arriving tourist will be offered considerable financial inducements to part with his bottle of Scotch whisky (stated brand preference being Johnny Walker Red Label) or carton of American/European cigarettes; and Coca-Cola, Pepsi Cola, McDonald's and the Sony Walkman are available, or desired, almost everywhere.[19]

The reality is different. The accelerated construction of regional global spaces leaves new inequalities not only between North and South, but also within these regions. The most striking example in the South is black Africa being left increasingly alone in its misery – especially since foreign investors have started to redirect their investments towards Europe, especially Eastern Europe, and Western geopoliticians have lost their fear that Africa will fall to the 'communist bloc'. In the North, the new single market widens the gap between different countries and regions. The 'golden triangle' of the European market, which comprises central and northern Italy, eastern France, most of Germany, and southern England, is evidently becoming separated from the European periphery – Europe's 'Third World', comprising Greece, Ireland, Southern Spain, Southern Italy and Portugal, with its higher rate of unemployment (20 per cent) and lower gross industrial product (approximately half the EC average). Economic globalism remains silent about this disparity, marked by a different potential, which is bound to adapt to the new conditions of competition, and to profit from the benefits of integration.

IMAGINING THE OTHER

'One of the constant features of all mythology', wrote Roland Barthes in the mid-1950s, 'is the inability to imagine the Other. . . . Confronted with the foreign, the established order knows only two responses, both of them mutilating: either to see it as a caricature or else to neutralise it as mere reflection of the Occident. Whichever, the main thing is to dehistoricise it. The myth, through the most powerful appropriation, *alienates* identity.' [20]

Long before the phenomenon of globalisation arose in advertising circles, much had already been written and said about the global pretension of the new culture of merchandise. The pretension which Jean Baudrillard demonstrated with great brio in one of his early essays entitled 'The moral of objects', when he spoke about international standards of living – the projection of a certain social class, a certain nucleus, throughout the world.[21]

The 'new age of the advertising-literate consumer' implies that we have forgotten these analyses and flashes of intuition which, at the time, changed the way we thought about 'here' and 'there'. And yet, proof has not failed to accumulate during the past decades concerning the negative repercussions of this model of development and growth, which ignores not only cultural differences but also the social and economic segmentation of the planet.

In August 1978 one could read in *Business International* the following advice to agro-food companies:

Strike their eyes and flatter their sense of color; make the product recognised and without using words, make them want to adopt the brand. In regions where illiteracy is widespread, a drawing or symbol characteristic of the brand can be a big help; create your own means of advertising when the country doesn't have any – for example, films or sound tracks; orient advertising towards women, who are the main consumers; choose the media most suitable for penetrating the countryside – in largely illiterate rural areas, the radio is sometimes the most efficient means of communication; try to give your products a Westernised appearance to give them social standing in regions undergoing rapid development wherein idea of modernization and Westernization are linked.[22]

These are the very practices which numerous anthropologists, doctors and organisations have been protesting about for the last two decades.

The best-known accusations are undoubtedly those which shook the firm of Nestlé over the years 1974–6. The charges, brought by a string of non-government organisations, concerned the bludgeoning advertising strategy employed by the company from Vevey in order to sell its powdered milk as a replacement for mother's milk, especially in Africa. Advertising messages transmitted an aggressive concept of modernity:

> Nestlé wants the baby's well-being/Bottle-feeding is modern, scientific, hygienic/It is Western, therefore prestigious/Rich people use the feeding-bottle, which makes it desirable/Advanced women use feeding-bottles/A feeding-bottle makes a baby strong, healthy, fat, happy and intelligent/A mother who loves her child buys Lactogène.[23]

They were reproached with failing to consider the environment in which their products were offered for consumption: a cultural tradition of prolonged lactation, closely linked to the natural spacing of births, defective hygienic conditions, lack of drinking water. They were also accused of using medical and paramedical bodies as guarantors of their powdered milk, which virtually turned the commercial product of an agro-food company into a prescribed medicine.[24] The repercussions of the affair gave the companies involved a real shaking, and certainly made them modify their attitudes to the markets concerned.

Few of these issues have escaped the vigilant attention of the networks involved in Third World action and investigation. Throughout the world there have been initiatives by the most varied groups aimed at evaluating the strategies employed in advertising policy, especially by agro-food and pharmaceuticals companies, for the purpose of applying remedies.[25]

Since long ago, even before the modern industry of aggressive advertising took off, producers of adverts and medicine were in complicity. It is not an accident that for a long time the excesses of both have earned them in popular imagination the sobriquet of 'charlatan'; nor that the first measures concerning advertising taken by the public authorities in the major industrial countries were frequently directed at pharmaceutical products, as well as foodstuffs and beauty products. This was particularly the case with federal legislation in the US.

In 1972 the International Organisation of Consumers' Unions (IOCU) undertook a series of comparative studies in more than twenty Third World countries dealing with the distribution of various medicines produced by the major pharmaceutical companies. (The IOCU was founded in 1960 by five consumer groups from the United Kingdom, the Netherlands, Belgium, United States and Australia; some twenty-five years later, it had 170 member groups in over fifty countries from Argentina and China to Uruguay and Zimbabwe.) These studies found negligence in the provision of information to the consumer; the application of double standards (strict observation of existing regulations in the mother country, laxity in the Third World); and the promotion of different uses for the same medicines, depending on where it was distributed. These practices were reinforced by the liberalism of local authorities, and the inadequacy of national legislation for consumer protection. In Mexico, for example, more than two-thirds of pharmaceutical consumption was self-prescribed. The studies also showed the profusion of brands in the marketplace: 11,300 pharmaceuticals in Brazil, 15,000 in Colombia, 16,320 in Mexico, 18,000 in Thailand, compared to 6,500 in France, 2,500 in the Netherlands, 1,600 in Sweden and Denmark. A profusion which, as indicated by debates on the future of social security systems, is not the exclusive inheritance of disadvantaged countries, since Italy markets 15,600, West Germany between 12,000 and 15,000, and Britain around 10,000.[26] To stem the tide, a number of Third World countries (notably Brazil and India) have adopted policies intended to reduce the list of indispensable medicines, which according to the norms established by the World Health Organisation (WHO) does not exceed 300. One of the smouldering issues facing the Brazilian government in 1988 was the opposition of the major pharmaceutical firms.

As for the impact of advertising on the models of food consumption, Mexico is probably one of the best-studied countries. It is also the country which has tried hardest – without success – to find a solution by establishing a 'minimum food basket' to slow down the galloping process of undernourishment. Numerous studies have sieved through the development of diet in the different social classes. One of them, carried out between 1976 and 1979, sums up:

The evolution of the food industry, and the forty subsectors which it comprises, leads to the conclusion that there is a tendency to produce sumptuary foods. We speak of sumptuary consumption not only because these products are consumed preferentially by the rich but also because they form a market alongside the middle and low sectors and are unnecessary for a good diet. On the contrary, their acquisition indicates that the lower classes are sacrificing consumption of the necessary basic foodstuffs.[27]

The authors establish a direct correlation between the spread of an increasingly deficient diet and the progress of the added-value foods industry which produces items like desserts, crisps and cornflakes. In Mexico this industry is dominated by four firms, Kellogg among them, who at the same time are the country's four biggest advertisers.

Thanks to millionaire advertising campaigns accompanied by excellent distribution networks, similar to the distribution of drinks, these firms have achieved unprecedented expansion for foodstuffs with low nutritive value. . . . Those who suffer most are the poorest classes, whose diet is composed of maize, beans, fats and oils. The consumption of fizzy drinks and desserts has increased the intake of pure sugar with detrimental effect. In other words, these calories become ever-more expensive. As for the middle and upper classes, animal protein predominates – meat, milk and derivatives – and wheat-based products are preferred to corn.[28]

This model of consumption is also a model of production. The cradle of the civilisation of maize has been converted into an importer, at ever-increasing prices, of what it previously exported. In the fields, sorghum has taken the place of the manna of the gods. In religious ceremonies, the indigenous people of the sierra have replaced maize alcohol with Coca-Cola. Meanwhile, the new chiefs have established their power with the aid of distribution networks for the products of the soda fountains in the north.

It is an aberration that Brazil, for example, should be at the same time the major world exporter of orange juice, the smallest consumer of orange juice, and one of the major consumers of Fanta Orange, which contains not the slightest trace of this fruit – and all this while vast sectors of the population suffer a high deficiency of vitamin C! Brazil has become the showcase for the champion of fizzy drinks, Coca-Cola. It has been established there for more than forty-five years and its turnover, in excess of $1,000m, makes it the company's second-largest concessionary, just behind the United States. It was Brazil where, in 1948, Coca-Cola entrusted its advertising to a subsidiary of McCann-Erickson. Strengthened by this first and successful experiment, the Atlanta company tore up the contract which since the beginning of the century had linked it to another agency, Arcy, and instead offered its entire world advertising account to McCann-Erickson – an account for which the network still has the exclusive business.

4

MEDIA WORLDS
Cosmopolitan flexibility

THE FIRST STEPS

The question of the globalisation of advertising campaigns and markets only makes sense in relation to the supporting media. On this point, analysis by the partisans of megamergers stops short. After launching the idea of the need to capitalise on the universally acknowledged symbols and cultural references of super-productions and best-sellers, and taking their hats off to their counterparts in the new multinational multimedia groups, the doctrine remains silent at just the point where the real problems begin. They also had to confront the various sectors of the cultural industry that began to set up subsidiaries in the international market years, even decades ago. Their record shows how difficult it is, and continues to be, to reconcile global objectives with concrete cultures and realities. It also indicates how far 'international', as an operative concept, has imperceptibly evolved towards 'global', as much in the case of the press as in audiovisual media. And it also shows how this history is that of the relation of forces.

Because of its age and the diversity of its genres, the domain of magazines and periodicals is one of the most instructive. Its international trajectory has long been tied in with the very models of the North American press, not to mention the 'American way of life'. Around fifty years have passed since the first North American publication began to circulate internationally, while the French women's magazine *Elle* achieved sales of one million in the US market.

The monthly which was first on the scene remains today the most famous: *Reader's Digest*. Its director is wont to say: 'When you think of global products, you say Coca-Cola, or Xerox, or IBM. You really should also say *Reader's Digest*.'[1] Twenty-eight million copies, 39 editions in 17 languages, printed in 24 different locations, 34 per cent of sales in international markets – the most significant index of its transnational influence is the price of a full-page advertisement. In 1988, the cost of a page in black-and-white stood at $240,370 – the highest tariff among the global press (to use the terminology of *Advertising Age*, which adopted it some time ago to refer to publications as diverse as *Time, The Financial Times, USA Today, Wall Street Journal, Business Week, International Herald Tribune* and *Newsweek*). The tariff for a comparable title, *National Geographic*, another monthly classified as 'global', with a print-run of ten and a half million, is $127,720: virtually the same as for the weekly *Time*. To merit inclusion by *Advertising Age* in their 'Global Media Lineup', the following criteria must be fulfilled: substantial mass circulation in at least three continents; world circulation of at least 50,000, and a circulation for international editions of at least 10 per cent of domestic circulation; editorial content of global scope and primarily in English; advertising in all editions purchased through a central office.

It was 1940 when *Reader's Digest*, founded in 1922, launched its first foreign language edition: in Spanish, for Latin America. The principal motive was to participate in the war effort and help counter the forces of the Axis in the region, where numerous armies maintained private links with Fascist Italy and Nazi Germany. The French edition came out seven years later.

How does *Reader's Digest* put together this global product? According to a representative of the world co-ordination centre, with its offices a few miles outside New York, 'There is constant communication between the staff and the individual editors. They work together. If an AIDS article was to run in the US, the editors of the French or African divisions, for example, would have the option of running the article as is or changing it to adapt to local interests and culture.'[2] But if it becomes imperative for 'the widest-read magazine in the world' to bend to local habits, so too with the development of universal themes. This explains the commendation of David Ogilvy: 'The editors have discovered that subjects which are important to people in Iowa, California and New York are equally important to people in France, Tokyo and Rio.'[3] Launching its conquest of foreign markets at the dawn of North American hegemony, the *Digest* has had its ups and downs, and learned to modify its discourse. As the deputy managing director of the company confessed in 1979, 'Multinational has unfortunately become an ugly word. . . . Unlike *Time*, which calls itself international, though published in only one language, we prefer to describe ourselves as a national magazine in a large number of countries.'[4] 'Our share of the market', he continued, 'is established. The circulation of our local editions has remained stable over the last ten years. This is what has enabled us to become an integral part of the market in each country.'

On the other hand, the public relations manager in the London office – a supporter of the European market – adds: 'But each edition carries a considerable amount of locally-generated material, and a team of staff writers based in Paris write European stories which are also available to

69

local editions. We like to say that the menu is basically the same, though the ingredients differ from country to country.'[5] Some three years earlier, the Canadian government put pressure on the *Digest* to ensure that 80 per cent of the editorial content differed from the original edition, and demanded the transfer of ownership of the local edition to national hands. The same with *Time*. At the end of the 1960s, these two publications had between them monopolised more than half the advertising accounts invested in Canadian magazines.

Pioneers in the conquest of the international market, *Reader's Digest*, *Time* and *Newsweek* have long maintained their lead. Indeed it was a quarter of a century before other publications took the same route. On the whole, the timing follows closely on developments in the advertising networks: after the North American advance in the second half of the 1960s, there was also consolidation among national magazines, and the internationalisation of the most important of them ten years later.

The internationalisation of the magazine business was accomplished through the franchise system. This formula is the outcome of strategic reflection on the conflicting relation between 'national' and 'international'. The title's proprietor cedes the right to utilise the name to a national publisher, under specific conditions and in exchange for the payment of royalties (generally 10 per cent of the income of the new magazine). The franchise allows the local publisher to launch the new title without excessive outlay and with less risk of failure. The concessionary benefits from a brand-name, a reputation, a format, know-how, the fruit of many years of experience. He connects with a transnational network. He acquires, from the start, an address book of advertisers: advertisers already accustomed to purchasing space in the parent magazine will be well disposed to its offshoot. Sometimes he gets the opportunity to participate in brainstorming sessions with editors of other local editions. Examples of successful North American franchise operations include *Cosmopolitan*, *Scientific American*, *Family Circle*, *Playboy*, *Glamour*, and *Good Housekeeping*.

COSMOPOLITAN FLEXIBILITY

What lessons can be learned from the progress of these magazines, all of which adopted the vernacular in order to blend in better with the national landscape?[6]

Variations of geometry and geography

There is no unique formula. Every publication finds specific modes of association with the parent publisher. The balance of 'local content' is resolved case by case and is susceptible to evolution. For example: the

French publication of the North American popularising journal *Scientific American* (*Pour la Science*) started out in 1977 with seven articles translated from the North American edition of two months earlier, and an eighth piece of French origin. The same formula was adopted by most of the other foreign editions, especially those of Italy, Japan and Spain. At the time, this unequal treatment provoked serious reservations. Michel Debré, one-time Prime Minister under General de Gaulle and an ardent defender of national independence, sent a written question about it to the Secretary of State for Scientific Research. He asked him 'to intervene to put an end to such projects and to maintain a policy of encouragement for a scientific publication by French publishers'. Around the same time, Doin, a pillar of French medical publication since 1874, was acquired by the North American group CBS and its Saunders division.

Out of step

A magazine is not internationalised everywhere at the same time. There is a vanguard as well as a rearguard. Thus the women's magazines of the Hearst group (*Good Housekeeping, Cosmopolitan*) set up Latin American subsidiaries in 1966, while their first European venture took place eight years later, in France. Between the first foreign editions of *National Geographic* – one for Latin America and another for Spain – and the French and Italian editions, there was a delay of nearly five years.

Geographically restricted globalism

A magazine is not necessarily adaptable to every country. Many have foreign versions – which even so differ considerably from the parent publication – in only a limited number of markets. This is the case, for example, with *Family Circle*, which is issued in Great Britain, Australia and West Germany. The general norm, according to a British editor, is that:

> Magazines for young people – by which I had better mean single people – since marriage and parenthood have an instantly aging effect – are likely to be transplantable so long as they are not parochial or ultra-topical. However, home-interest magazines are not yet exportable except in the broadest and most general terms. They are unable to bridge the cultural and social chasms between countries. *Good Housekeeping* and *Family Circle* have very little in common with the original *Good Housekeeping* and *Family Circle* in the USA. *Cosmopolitan* and, more recently, *Playboy* will easily transplant because they 'travel light' with little domestic baggage.[7]

71

Social globalism

The target envisaged by local versions of international publications is mainly the upper reaches of the 'middle class'. 'Middle class' is defined by its purchasing power. Here are some examples, gleaned from the promotional literature for the titles mentioned. *National Geographic*: 'About 82 per cent of the 275,000 readers are in the upper-middle class or higher, according to a survey conducted by the Mexican affiliate of Gallup International Research; 47 per cent are company owners, presidents, administrators or managers; while 20 per cent are doctors, lawyers, engineers, etc. Another 64 per cent own their own houses.' 'The readers of *Reader's Digest* have a high level of education, are "far from poor", enjoy domestic living.' The formula of *Buen Hogar*, the Latin American version of *Good Housekeeping*: 'Our magazine is directed at young modern married Latin Americans, with good education and housing. Their interests are no different from their North American equivalents.'

Breaking away from the typical class of modernity, which is necessarily connected to high standards of living, comes the internationalisation of 'down-market' products aimed at the 'general public'. Their origin is not the big US publishing groups but Italian and Spanish companies, the original publishers of *fotonovelas**, plus a publishing group of Cuban origin based in Florida and set up by anti-Castro émigré Cubans.

New transnational protagonists

European groups, especially French and German, have internationalised themselves extensively. The weekly *Elle* was granted a licence for a Japanese edition in 1969, and five years later for an Arab language edition. The German *Burda* launched a British edition in 1973. In 1979, the Bertelsmann group which has produced *Géo* in Germany since 1976, set a new pattern by competing with the North Americans on their own terrain when they launched both a French and a North American edition.

The year 1983 was a pivotal date for French groups in search of international markets: *Marie-Claire* went abroad and within five years brought out five international editions; Elle now has fourteen foreign editions, including one in the US. *Elle*'s latest versions are in Brazil, West Germany, Popular China and Greece. The formula for this furious internationalisation consists in a licence or link with a local publisher, preferably a mixed enterprise, and due regard for the ideology and design of the model and the magazine's development. The head office of *Marie-Claire* explains that

---

* Fiction in the format of comics but using photographs instead of drawings. Equivalent of the *telenovela*, which we know in English as the soap opera. [Translator's note.]

the editors of local editions may additionally buy, adapt, or find inspiration in articles published in the French *Marie-Claire* or other editions. In fact, while all the magazines with multiple editions draw from a bank of common articles, only exclusives, or journalistic scoops, appear on the front pages in several countries at the same time. An exclusive with Arthur Miller about Marilyn Monroe, or an interview with Robert Redford, sells like hot cakes. A piece of original reportage on women prison officers can only hope for adaptation.[8]

The target is the stereotypical 'young Western urban woman': 'active woman of 18–30, who travels abroad' – except for the countries of the Gulf, where modesty is required.

In 1987, *Burda* made a sensational appearance in the Soviet media landscape by inaugurating the first magazine to carry advertising.

The end of sectoral dependence

The creation and diversification of a production base for national publications which developed in many countries during the 1970s reduced the lack of competition in national markets for many genres. What is more, when local and foreign products begin to compete, the former generally wins by several lengths.

From the comic to the *fotonovela* by way of the news magazine, many countries which were previously supplied from abroad are now self-sufficient. According to one testimony from Mexico, comics are now 80 per cent national. The remaining 20 per cent come from Walt Disney or Marvel Comics. 'Production is essentially national. Even if it's inspired by foreign models, they have been assimilated, 'redirected', with the addition of the typical situations and deplorable conditions of daily life in Mexico.'[9]

An endless process

Transplants via franchise seem never to end. New fronts are ceaselessly opened up, often profiting from the absence of a local alternative within the sector. Thus, in February 1988, came the appearance of French editions of *Glamour* and *Fortune*. Two very different publications: the first is a women's monthly for 18 to 30-year-olds published by Condé-Nast, French subsidiary of the Newhouse group which already publishes *Vogue*, and *Vogue-Hommes*. The second is a version of the financial magazine *Fortune*, belonging to the Time-Life group, and published in France by Hachette.

The French publishers, who harboured doubts about the title, thought of changing the Hollywood-like name of *Glamour* to *Miss Vogue* or *Vanity*. As for *Fortune*, it came gift-wrapped in the old discourse of US magazine publishers on universality, already brought up to date:

Adapting successful American publications to markets overseas has a big future. Advertisers are looking for these types of publication. In February, New York-based Time Inc. and French publishing giant Hachette-Filipacchi will begin publishing a monthly French-language edition of *Fortune*. Time Inc. also publishes a Japanese-language edition of *Money* and a *Fortune*-style magazine, called *President*, in Japan. Globally, American-based magazines in the English language are huge and will remain huge.[10]

In less than two years this triumphalist approach was bitterly discredited, demonstrating the contradictory character of alliances between national content and global formula. In July 1990, *Fortune-France* ceased to appear. The reason for this collapse: a disagreement over concept and content. According to a press statement by Hachette, 'The magazine needed more sparkle, to appeal to a wider public and not just to managers. But the concept was far from this.' The American proprietors responded: 'This is a magazine which circulates throughout the world, including Europe. Local editions must observe certain criteria. We shouldn't lose our image, or deceive the readers.'

THE GLOBAL NEWSPAPER

The appearance of certain franchises is far from innocent, and it does not necessarily broaden the range of choice simply to add another title.

It is no accident if the appearance of a French *Fortune* coincided with a general crisis in the French economic press. In 1987, Dow Jones, publisher of the *Wall Street Journal*, had taken a 14 per cent holding in the Expansion group, while the Italian De Benedetti, at that time owner of, among other things, the publishing group Mondadori, acquired a controlling interest in Dafsa (Banque de données économiques et financières, or Bank of Economic and Financial Data). In 1988, it was the turn of the foremost French economic newspaper *Les Échos* to fall into the hands of the British group Pearson, owners not only of the *Financial Times*, but also a publishing empire which includes Longmans, Penguin Books, the New American Library, Viking, Hamish Hamilton and Michael Joseph.

It is precisely the field of the economic press where strategies for the creation of 'global newspapers' are most apparent. While in other sectors of the press the concept of globalisation often repeats basically the same strategies of internationalisation, the redeployment of the economic press on a world scale suggests the operation of a new logic, secreted by the most advanced stage of interconnection between markets, capitals and the globalisation of financial networks. Two giant institutions are in evidence: the *Financial Times* and the *Wall Street Journal*, founded respectively in 1888 and 1889.

The *Wall Street Journal* kicked off the internationalisation of the economic press on 2 September 1976. The project was in preparation for six years. The chosen terrain for this première was Asia. By launching the *Asian Wall Street Journal*, the American daily hoped to adapt itself to the slippages of the world economy. Its diagnosis was most lucid:

> The U.S. is Asia's biggest customer, and trade between nine East Asian nations and the U.S. is now greater than trade between the U.S. and the nine members of the European Economic Community. . . . the GNP of the nine East Asian countries has grown at a rate that is nearly triple that of the industrialized nations of the world.[11]

Over the preceding years, the American daily had acquired 49 per cent of the economic weekly *Far Eastern Economic Review*, published in Hong Kong; 10 per cent of its partner on the review, the newspaper *South China Morning*, belonging to the same city; and, together with the Japanese daily *Nihon Keizai Shimbun*, had founded a media-buying office of world reach. Above all, it had succeeded in convincing these two partners from Hong Kong and Japan, plus the *Straits Times* of Singapore and the *New Straits Times* of Malaysia, to embark on the adventure of the *Asian Wall Street Journal* together. From the very first number, to prove that it was indeed a common enterprise, the editors included no more than half the editorial content of the New York edition.

A pioneer in the transmission of pages by satellite, which it began in 1975, it was also the first to decentralise the printing of its national and international editions, which now roll off the presses in Hong Kong, Singapore, Tokyo, the Netherlands, Switzerland and seventeen different locations in the United States. (In this respect, only the experience of the *International Herald Tribune*, the first multinational newspaper of a general character, printed in ten cities around the world, is at all comparable.) It was also – as shown by its alliance with a big Japanese daily in the 1970s – a pioneer in the sale of advertising space on a global scale. A simple telephone call allows an advertisement to be placed in the main newspapers in the UK, Italy, Japan, Australia, Hong Kong and Malaysia. In 1987, to complete its incursion into Asia, the *Wall Street Journal* purchased the entire shareholding of the *Far Eastern Economic Review*, the 'Asian managers' weekly'.

The *Financial Times*, those pink pages whose heyday was under the British Empire, waited till January 1979 to take its first step into Europe. Since then, even if it remains an English consumer product – 70 per cent of its advertising revenue comes from local advertisers – the financial community has awarded it the title of 'Europe's business paper'. With a circulation of 312,000, the British daily sells 258,000 in Europe, 20 per cent of this on the Continent. It is printed in Europe in three locations: London, Frankfurt, and, since July 1988, Roubaix. In 1987, it opened a fax centre in Philadelphia to try and penetrate the American market, with the objective of reaching a circulation of 25,000. At the same time it was studying the possibility of printing an Asiatic edition with the Japanese group Asahi Shimbun.

In January 1983, the *Wall Street Journal* took up the European challenge when it set up office in Brussels. The publisher reckoned on a circulation of 12,000. Seven years later sales had climbed to 46,000. Above all, the paper had been 'Europeanised': 60 per cent American information to 40 per cent European information, with around half the advertisers European.

The *Wall Street Journal* drew its strength from its American base of operations. Its circulation is almost seven times that of its British competitor: more than 2 million. By way of comparison, *Les Échos* sells no more than 70,000. At $109,300 for a page of advertising in black and white, the *Wall Street Journal* is nearly four times more expensive than its rival. A mass newspaper in America, where its circulation is double that of the *New York Times*, in Europe it becomes an organ of the elite. The average annual income of a European reader: $116,000. Doubtless this explains why the American daily looks after its circulation by having copies delivered by messenger service to high places in European finance and commerce.

By acquiring shares in the French group Expansion, the *Wall Street Journal* paraded its ambition not to internationalise exclusively under the banner of the Anglo-American language. Business realism, certainly, but of a certain shade. Outside Great Britain, French is still the language most used by business in Europe. According to a pan-European survey among business people in 1986, 37 per cent used the language of Descartes, 34 per cent used German, and 31 per cent English. But this source also reveals that around two-thirds of them have frequent recourse to English, as opposed to a half eight years earlier, while 40 per cent read it, as against 30 per cent in 1978. Thus, as a British marketing advisor puts it: 'There appears to be a clear link between the growth in top executives with the ability to read English and the growth of international business magazines in continental Europe.'[12]

The question of language seems to be less problematic for the business community in East Asia.

English was selected as the only possible language for the Monday-through-Friday daily because, while Asians speak many different languages, a considerable number of business leaders there read English. . . . We would be happy to have 12,000 to 14,000 to start. We are not addressing ourselves to anyone but the decision makers.[13]

This was what an official of the Asiatic branch of the *Wall Street Journal* hopefully declared the month it was launched. Eleven years later, the Asiatic edition of the American mainstay of economic analysis was printing 33,500 copies, nearly ten times the circulation of the *Financial Times* throughout the Asian Pacific.

What is missing from the schemes drawn up by the financial press is any reference to the debt-ridden countries of Latin America – the target countries for the big offensive launched by the emblematic magazines of consumerism in the 1960s.

INTERNATIONAL CINEMA

It was neither the advertising industry nor the press which christened the concept of globalism. It was the film industry during the course of the 1970s. In proposing 'global films', the producers announced that they had finally discovered the main factor in optimising audiences.

The so-called 'global-oriented' film has several noticeable traits. Its cast is chock-a-block with big-name stars, usually of several nationalities. But the Lorens and Burtons and Caines who find themselves so prominently billed in films of this genre are rarely called upon for a tour de force of acting; three-dimensional characters depend on good dialogue, the nuances of which are lost in translation. And translation is what these films must excel at, so witty repartee, even by the likes of Neil Simon, is definitely out. Instead, the stars tend to serve as foils for action; they exist to shoot and get shot. For global films are also engineered to play heavily on the elemental magic of the medium; grand actions against exotic backgrounds. Mayhem and carnage need no subtitles.[14]

Confident in its hegemony over foreign markets, Hollywood has contributed greatly to imposing certain terms of comparison between American and international product. A conviction voiced in January 1988 – less aggressively than during the heated years of big anti-imperialist movements – by Jack Valenti, president of the MPEAA (Motion Picture Export Association of America), when he spoke of the 'global reach' of the American film.

In nearly every country where American films are exhibited, they are supreme, enticing people of every nationality, religion, color or turn of mind. Because what we create in this country captures so full a portion of the audience's affections, U.S. films, programs and home

77

video material return to this country, annually, more than $1-billion in *surplus* balance of trade. In order to grasp this singular fact, consider this: The U.S. film industry is one of the few American enterprises to have a trade surplus with Japan![15]

It is worth writing home about. The myth of American cinema is not dead. While a country like France, which had managed to build up a national film industry, was approaching the shores of crisis, cinema in the US was still sailing the high seas. In 1987, a billion admissions brought in a record $4.3b. The negative effects of competition from electronic media seemed like a bad memory. If the French abandoned the big screen, some 40 per cent of American households equipped with video recorders rediscovered it. 'After two years, viewers had exhausted the video stores and were no longer satisfied with watching films [on TV] with interruptions for adverts', noted the research director of the MPAA (Motion Picture Association of America).[16] The same thing has happened in Britain: here, although the video market continues to expand (with rentals up from £421m in 1987 to £566m in 1989, while sales increased from £96m to £300m over the same period[17] cinema admissions have nearly doubled over five years, from 53 million in 1984 to 90 million in 1989.[18]

The recipe for the recovery of cinema in both the US and the UK was to remodel the theatres and convert them to multiple screens (multiplex); to extend the high season; and create a new public, younger and more urban, with adolescents comprising half the audience. Even if films like *Platoon* and *Wall Street* – $180m each in earnings – have managed to enlarge this sociological base, the creation of this new audience has entailed sacrifice in the variety of genres and subjects. An inflationary spiral operates: average costs of production are $15m, with record expenditure of $80m for *Rambo III* (which included a fee of $20m for Sylvester Stallone). But if business is booming for giants like Disney, Paramount, MGM, Warner, Universal, Columbia or Twentieth Century Fox, for independents the situation is frankly worse.

Average advertising budgets are $10m. The speed of capital turnover dominates the process: to recover the costs of production in the minimum time. 'It is a vicious circle', explains a professor in the Faculty of Cinema at the University of California. 'A film must be consumed hot because of the investment incurred. But in order for it to be delivered to the audience boiling, the distributors burn up millions of dollars.'[19]

Hegemony of US cinema. Hegemony of the ensemble of image industries. Extreme polarisation of the world market: 79 per cent of exports come from North America, while half the purchases are made by Western Europe (which equals less than 25 per cent of its programming needs). In total, more than 40 per cent of world commerce in images (cinema-TV-video) comprises the European purchase of American products. Within this flow of audiovisual goods, cinema, in 1986, represented 40.5 per cent, television 41.5 per cent, and the rest was video.[20]

The audiovisual trade balance between Europe and the United States in 1988, according to the calculations of IDATE (Institut pour le développement de l'audiovisuel et des télécommunications en Europe): North American income in Europe had reached $693m in the cinema, $575m in television programmes, and $700m in videos. Contrariwise, Europe's sales of films to the United States amounted to no more than $43m, television programmes stood at $100m, and video rights were worth $60m.

Back home, the Americans remain protectionist. Foreign films distributed in the US together represent no more than 3 per cent of cinema attendance. And throughout the world, producers and directors ask themselves if they have to make their films in the English language. In March 1988, *Variety* reported that:

> The more enterprising Hispanics and Latins . . . are trying to shoot their films in English, often using Yank thesps. The idea has been kicked around for decades, but was again a major trend at the recently held American Film Market, where Europeans, Asians and Latins were plugging English versions of their product.[21]

Among items to be shot in English were films by two Brazilians, Bruno Barreto and Paulo Thiago. A producer added, 'English has become the Latin of the twentieth century, the *lingua franca* of the film industry. With production costs spiralling in Brazil, it is becoming 'increasingly difficult to produce just for the local market.'[22]

The language question also worries writers and directors in audiovisual production in Europe. In September 1988 on the eve of the Delphes Colloquium, the film-maker Jean-Charles Tacchella, president of the International Association of Authors, declared himself in favour of a European writers' charter:

> I am opposed to the stick of the market for a first run film; after that, it merits reflection. In any case, it is the author – alone – who should decide whether to shoot in English, which sometimes becomes obligatory. Discussion around this question has been forceful, with divergent points of view, and we have to agree about it for Delphes. The Dutch and the Danish sometimes prefer to shoot in English, and they need assistance. But the choice of language must remain with the director. After all, Alain Resnais shot *Providence* in English. One hopes it is not obligatory. Especially since the commercial result is never obvious. The English don't sell their films any better on the American market than us.[23]

The erstwhile head of Columbia – property at the time of Coca-Cola – has explained very well how the logic of globalisation on the part of the major film companies also functions as a logic of exclusion. David Puttnam, the English producer who won an Oscar for *Chariots of Fire*, had been as successful as anyone in penetrating the American market, but lasted hardly more than a year in Hollywood. He explained at the time to a French magazine that 'the moment of simultaneous global release, on a world scale, is rapidly approaching.' That is why Columbia had restructured its marketing department into a single world organisation, because in his view, the main opportunity lay abroad,

> But to reach an international audience you have to shoot in English. That's the reality. A few years ago, someone like Bertrand Tavernier stood out against this phenomenon in the name of autonomy, independence and cultural identity. Now he shoots in English. I've asked Agnieska Holland, Doris Dorrie, Istvan Szabo, Lino Brocka, Eumir Kusturica, to make films for us. In English. It's not their language, and their previous experiences are not always convincing. They'll learn, they'll sharpen their ears, there will always be someone behind them to help. I know that directors, particularly in Europe, are looked on as next to god. But they have to realise that we are not spoilsports.[24]

This globalisation is sustained by dumping and reinforced by advertising budgets which often exceed production costs. It is a form of superproduction in which preplanning covers the world. When Coca-Cola acquired Columbia in 1982 – practically the last American major to fall into the hands of a conglomerate – one of its directors envisioned the synergy between Columbia and the mother company: 'Purchase by Coke will undoubtedly mean additional funds, so that Columbia will be able to increase its production schedule significantly. Columbia is already respected for its distribution and marketing operations which would benefit from Coke's marketing expertise.'[25] It didn't work out. The form of marketing used to sell Coca-Cola did not produce the same result with films. In September 1989, Columbia was bought up by the Japanese for $4.3b – in fact by Sony. The acquisition links the software of Columbia's film library with Sony's hardware, in preparation for the launch of HDTV (High Definition Television).

This doesn't stop all the majors developing strategies for globalisation. In 1987, in order to prepare for single-market operation, United Pictures International (the international marketing wing of Paramount, Universal and MGM/UA) bade farewell to the agencies it had worked with in individual markets, and concentrated the entire promotion of its films in Europe in the hands of the Young & Rubicam network.

When one looks at the growing pressure to shoot in English, submitting 'other cinemas' to the profusion of global campaigns, without questioning thematic development or the genres which result, one may justifiably ask if the siren's song of the conglomerates doesn't make the kind of internationalisation many film-makers once dreamt about ever more remote.

Imagine a Swiss born in Iran and living in France, who shoots a film about the Middle East in Spain, produced by Luxembourg and in English, photographed by a Cuban cinematographer, with an American actress and a German actor: namely, the remarkable *More* by Barbet Schroeder. Imagine an American film shot in India with English actors by an Irish producer and a French director: one of Jean Renoir's best films, *The River*. These were the two examples mentioned by the French film-maker Luc Moullet at an international conference at Saint-Étienne in February 1983, where the theme was cultural identity and the identity of the cinema.

TELEVISION WITHOUT FRONTIERS

'French actor plays American: seeks employment! This is what we are reduced to': the ironic joke of an actor at an assembly of performing artists. Whatever its stature, no TV chain can escape the plain fact that often fiction must now be shot in English; though in France it is still financed – at least in part – by the official state body responsible for supporting audiovisual production! According to the explanation of the Minister of Culture: 'Dramas shot in English give French production a further opportunity for development by providing the means for distribution in non-Francophone territories, and thus to tap capital to reinvest in production.'[26]

You don't need a weatherman to analyse the wind of coproduction blowing through the European image industry. A new word has been coined which is already becoming common currency: 'Filmglish' – a term used by one of the production chiefs of the group Beta-Taurus, central plank of the German television industry and partner of Maxwell and Berlusconi in a pan-European consortium. 'It's becoming more and more important for actors to speak English. . . . As a practical consideration, a European project should not carry the stipulation that it must be shot in the national language.'[27]

A veritable godsend for American producers advancing through the breach, and henceforth free of all trace of cultural imperialism: 'But what kind of product will that multinational consumer want? And how can companies prepare to supply it?' asks the producer of *Dallas*:

To answer the second question first, producers will have to take a more global outlook in their planning. Financial and creative horizons will have to be expanded to encompass not just a domestic but a worldwide audience . . . coproductions, in addition to joint financial participation among international groups of investors, will become increasingly common. These coproductions will be more cosmopolitan in theme to attract the international viewer and will likely be made in English to appeal to the financially lucrative American, Canadian, British and Australian markets . . . . Coproduction, in fact, may help resolve a concern that has plagued the international market – the fear that the influx of our high-quality television programs will crowd out local productions and lead to the 'Americanisation' of other cultures. . . . Then, as international audiences develop, Americans will be exposed to the more international, European-flavor of coproductions. The eventual 2-way street in entertainment flow should reduce tensions about American 'cultural imperialism'.[28]

To produce in English and, for some, in American: this is the order of the day not only for European producers but also those in Latin America. Because in both places there are many who gaze longingly towards the United States. Thus the Miami company Coral Pictures, belonging to one of the two main commercial television chains in Venezuela, Radio Caracas TV, recently embarked on production of a soap opera in English, *Dawn of Promises*, 'directed, scripted and thesped by Yanks', as *Variety* put it.[29] Thirteen episodes of two hours, subdivisible into fifty-two half-hour episodes, plus a feature-length movie starring American actors like George Kennedy, Stuart Whitman, Troy Donahue, Edie Adams; in 35mm, with a shooting schedule of two or three weeks and post-production provided partly in Venezuela and partly in the United States. This English-speaking soap opera would then be dubbed into Spanish for sale throughout Latin America. The calculation they were making is clear, and confirms the old divide of dependency: viewers in the South already know about dubbing, those in the North never will. 'Neither experiment worked,' *Variety* concluded, 'largely, it is believed, because even when dubbed the series remained too patently foreign for domestic tastes.'[30] Nevertheless the Puerto Rican chain Telemundo, hoping to kill two birds with one stone, gambled on an identical project: a soap opera of 140 episodes which aimed to add the Anglophone audience to its Hispanic clientele.

But this Latin American resort to the English language remains limited. For if the Mexican and Brazilian multimedia conglomerates, Televisa and Globo, have augmented the dubbing of their soaps and series for the American market, neither has crossed the Rubicon, as opposed to certain film producers in these same countries. The president of Televisa is fiercely opposed to the idea of coproduction. As he reiterated in March 1988:

> Televisa's policy is to produce as much as possible in Spanish: musical programmes, humour, drama and especially *telenovelas*. Coproduction doesn't work. In our case, we prefer to run all the risks. We don't believe that everyone involved in a production – actors, directors, etc. – necessarily has to be Mexican. Our accent, for example, is not very acceptable in other Hispanic countries. But with the experience we have accumulated in our dubbing studios, we have seen that a salad of accents (Puerto Rican, Spanish, Mexican, Argentinian, Venezuelan) is accepted throughout America and even in Spain. We found the same thing when we began to dub the first American series: everywhere the language is spoken they were accepted. The same formula goes for soap operas: the actress could be Argentinian, the leading actor Spanish or Mexican, the director Chilean, etc. But the producer always works for the enterprise and the product is always Televisa's.[31]

The obsession with the conquest – always hypothetical – of English-language markets, conceals a load of lessons relating to the latest experience of television without frontiers. According to representatives of two pan-European satellite channels, Sky and Superchannel, which reach about 10 million homes each:

> They're . . . trying to make their pan-European services more 'European' and less 'pan'. [They] have realized the idea of a single superstation beaming exclusively English-language programming from the U.K. into Europe is a losing proposition. Sky now coproduces much of its own programming, particularly with Dutch broadcasters and the German Music Box service, and is experimenting with subtitling; Super is now buying-in some programming in other major Euro-languages.

And these same representatives conclude, after five years of activity:

> If cheap American programming is likely at first to fuel fledgling and/or financially strapped satellite services, good indigenous, originally produced material is probably the only way to guarantee a sizeable faithful audience in the long term. . . . It must be remembered that it is still national off-air webs which attract the majority of audiences across Europe, with substantial in-house production and the cream of the latest U.S. imports . . . they're not going to entice Euro-viewers to switch off their favorite local soap or their own national newscast.'[32]

Indeed, most of the projects envisaged for the new pan-European channels have been abandoned or reduced to a national scale. Rupert Murdoch, pioneer of supra-national television with his Sky Television, has already changed his mind and decided to concentrate his bouquet of new channels on the British market. Only Eurosport is still aimed at the big European marketplace.

News remains national. This is clearly revealed in small countries like Belgium after several years of thorough penetration by their neighbours' stations. Local series too often have higher ratings than *Dallas* and *Dynasty*. The same thing is demonstrated by audience behaviour in societies as varied as Australia, Brazil and Britain, although compared to television news, fiction is definitely more internationalisable. At least, as long as the viewers', intelligence is not underrated. For this is precisely the attitude of many of the global *nouveaux riches* who entertain little concern for the particular cultures and histories where their productions touch ground.

FIFTH COLUMN

There is a blemish in the protectionist network of the United States cultural industries: the growing Hispanic presence on their own territory. The phenomenon was brought out into the open in 1987, with the film *La Bamba* by Luis Valdes tracing the short life of the teen rocker Ritchie Valens. Why the sudden fascination? According to Edward James Olmos, star of *Miami Vice* and the film *Stand and Deliver*, itself inspired by the Hispanic theme, the success of *La Bamba* showed people there were good stories which hadn't been used because they weren't considered commercially viable. 'Today a lot of energy is being invested in Hispanic themes, but it's a strictly economic matter.'[33]

The advertising agencies were the first to survey the potential of this new ethnic vein. As early as 1974 – when Hispanics represented 4 per cent of the total US population – Young & Rubicam created a Spanish-speaking Latin department with a 29-year-old native of Puerto Rico as its first manager.[34] Some fifteen years later, the United States has 19 million Hispanics, or 7 per cent of the total population (or 25 million if one includes illegal immigrants). In the year 2000, this proportion will have doubled. What is more, these cultural minorities enjoy – in addition to numerous radio stations – three television networks of their own: Univision, founded in 1962 by Mexico's Televisa and sold to Hallmark Cards in 1987, which covers mainly the West and South-West (more than 50 per cent of the city of Los Angeles was Hispanic in 1990); Galavision, owned by Televisa; and Telemundo, the Puerto Rican chain, based on the East Coast (around 14 per cent of the Chicago population was Spanish-speaking in 1990, 21 per cent in New York, and nearly 60 per cent in Miami).

The breakthrough of these minorities is even more spectacular in the music industry: Hispanic disco – a mixture of four of the most influential currents in contemporary dance music (house, electro, rap and eurobeat) – is triumphant. In 1987, a third of national Top Thirty hits were Latin, either by overtly Hispanic groups like Miami Sound Machine, Exposé or the Jets, or by artists who systematically include Latin remakes in their albums, like Debbie Gibson or Jody Watley. In *Billboard*'s list of composers with the most hits over the year in the United States, Lewis A. Martinee comes first, thanks to four consecutive Top Tens written for Exposé. Michael Jackson came third and Madonna fifteenth.

The explanation of Jellybean Benitez, one of the creators of this musical wave:

I began to realize that certain records were immediately grabbing the Puerto Ricans, then getting picked up by the Italians and the Blacks. It was as if Latin records found themselves right in the middle, between the two communities. To capture the Puerto Ricans was therefore often to capture the others. . . . You know, there's an enormous Hispanic population here, culturally completely neglected. Two years ago, people thought the only Hispanic singers were Iglesias and Menudo. But now there's Gloria Estefan, Los Lobos, Exposé, the Cover Girls, and these people sell lots of records. And then you have Madonna and Barry White, who also sing in Spanish.[35]

5

THE VANGUARD OF DEREGULATION
Neo-liberal enterprise culture

LIBERTY BEFORE EQUALITY

Internationalisation isn't what it used to be. Yesterday it was confined to the sphere of exchange and balance of payments in cultural products; now it attacks the structure of the communication systems of national states. Increasingly attuned to the norms of world networking, a new phase is unfolding in the construction of the media world. To enter this new legal, economic and political regime, one word sums it up: *deregulation.*

The ambiguity of the concept comes from the place and manner of its birth: the America of neo-liberal economists and politicians in a context favourable to 'less government'. Contrary to what is supposed, it is not the fruit of spontaneous development, but the result of political will. Nor is it defined by absence of regulation, but by a quest for different regulations to introduce instead.

The process of deregulation shakes up the ensemble of networks, be they advertising, audiovisual or telecommunications. It affects the public as much as the private sector. While it sometimes corresponds to the process of denationalization (or 'privatisation') of public enterprises and networks, it should not be confused with it. One can deregulate the private the same as the public. Moreover, if privatisation is a sufficient condition for entering deregulation (for many enter it like a religion), it is not in fact a necessary one. The introduction of these conceptual hypotheses locates the process in the wider context of new modes of communications systems management, and beyond that, in new modes of organising society. For by pushing society's centre of gravity towards the market, the radical mutation of the organisational principles and structure of both enterprises and networks redistributes the hierarchy and the scale of priorities of the economic, social and political protagonists involved.

The project of deregulation is in fact a proposal to rearrange public space. For this very reason, it implies a redefinition of the notion of free

86

speech: the free speech of the citizen enters into direct competition with 'commercial free speech'. The implementation of this social project is traversed by a constant tension between the empirical law of the marketplace and legal norms, between the idea of the absolute sovereignty of the consumer – as both the subject of rivalry and guarantor of free enterprise and commerce – and the idea of the sovereign will of the citizenry, guaranteed by their elected assemblies.

Seen in this light, the process of privatisation can no longer be regarded only as a way of discarding activities and functions which the state was given to exercise over the private sector, in order to recover a sense of the global social process. What it amounts to, no more no less, is the extension of the law of value to zones of individual and collective life which had previously remained relatively marginal to the logic of commercial valorisation. The decline of freedom, both literally and figuratively. Or to employ metaphorically the buzzword in the deregulation of telecommunications networks: an end to equal tariffs. The need to approximate to 'real costs' overtakes the principle of compensation for inequalities and distances between major users and marginal sectors, both urban and rural, inhabitants of North and South, the 'solvent layers' with their teleports, technopolies, and financial telecommunications, and the mass of the abandoned.[1] A tension between freedom and solidarity. Invocations to individual freedom forestall talk of social equality. As a *Time* journalist explains very well about deregulation in the United States:

> From the beginning, American sentiment has been in tension, between the values of freedom and equality. Under Franklin Roosevelt, and for several generations afterward, the official American inclination has been toward equality. In Reagan's America, the value of freedom has reasserted itself, sometimes at the expense of the gentler instincts. . . . The freedom to win . . . a Darwinian theater.[2]

NEO-LIBERAL HOMELAND

The United States is where it all started, especially in such proportions. After 107 years of good and loyal service, the US telephone network, Bell Systems, belonging to AT & T (American Telegraph and Telephones), was dismembered. On 1 January 1984, after a long government anti-trust suit, the quasi-monopoly was broken; not just beginning a new era but definitively closing the old one, in which a private monopoly could acquire 80 per cent of the telephone lines and come to function, in effect, as a parapublic service.[3]

If the telecommunications sector unleashes passions, this is not where the era of deregulation was inaugurated. Before 1984, the process affected the banking system (where deregulation began in 1970, accelerating in 1975 when the Securities and Exchange Commission ordered an end to the practice of fixed brokerage fees for stock-market transactions); then the airlines (in 1978 the Civil Aeronautics Board (CAB) granted airlines greater freedom in pricing and easier access to routes not previously served); road and rail transport (in 1980 the Stagers Rail Act gave the railways new pricing freedom); and lastly urban trunk routes (1982). In fact, therefore, the process has been uninterrupted, and each year brings its own acts of deregulation. In telecommunications, for example, it has been going on for a quarter of a century, and in banking it has unfolded over more than twenty years. Every year also brings its bevy of objections to the cogency of the deregulations of the preceding years.

The first signs of *malaise* were apparent at the end of the 1950s, and first took the form of a theoretical investigation into the legitimacy of state intervention. The particular field of inquiry was transport, and especially the regulation of airlines.[4] Moderated by economists and political scholars, the contesting argument never changes key: the law prevents the law of the market from functioning; this leads to inefficiency and a break on technological innovation, and favours interest and pressure groups to the detriment of the consumer.

With the deflation of the welfare state, this academic hypothesis will become mediatised. Strengthened by the growing influence of the neo-liberal schools of thought of Vienna (von Hayek) and Chicago (Milton Friedman), these model arguments have been taken up, amplified and given generous publicity by a private research organisation, the American Enterprise Institute for Public Policy Research, an organisation not unlike the Adam Smith Institute in the UK.[5] The regulation of inno-vation in the pharmaceutical industry, the regulation of safety standards in food products, of the environment, of working conditions, of the audiovisual industry, all these areas where regulations are a 'nuisance', are sifted by economists who have turned into activists on behalf of deregulation. Their troubleshooting aims at the costs exacted from the consumer by the untimely intervention of public authorities. The reins of the anti-regulatory movement, with its strong whiff of neo-populism, were taken over by the neo-liberals of the Reagan administration, and the criticism generalised. At least in certain fields, for the process of deregulation – which was already fashionable under President Ford and strongly pursued by President Carter – is also deflected, sometimes squarely halted, in those areas which the most neo-liberal American presidents consider strategic. In 1982, whilst his predecessors had fulmi-nated against private monopolies in telecommunications, Ronald Reagan rejected a complaint by computer manufacturers against IBM for monopolistic practices.

What are the results of deregulation from the point of view of the system? Here is what the analysts of *Business Week* say:

> Deregulation was supposed to usher in an era of higher productivity and lower prices. And it did. Under the pressure of the free market's invisible hand, air fares and telephone rates have fallen. But a small group of companies increasingly dominate deregulated markets. If this concentration continues, deregulation may stifle the very competition that it was designed to promote.[6]

The domino strategy. The process of deregulation of telecommunications is largely internationalised, as one says about a conflict. The government of the United States had no trepidation in challenging the international communications satellite network Intelsat, which originally had a monopoly in this form of transmission. Intelsat is a network which they themselves set up in the 1960s, when it had exclusive possession of the technology, and managed to unite most of the market economy countries around an initiative directed against the Soviet system Intersputnik. In November 1984, President Reagan announced his intention to authorise private satellite companies to compete with the institution which represented the international telecommunications community. In July 1985, the decision to privatise space became law. The reasons given were first, that Intelsat tariffs were too high and the big transnationals saw their costs of communication, especially between computers, continually rising; second, to prevent further competition from European satellites which could already be felt.

The satellites run by Intelsat are used for international communications by 109 member countries, including 27 for their internal communications as well. The organisation provides for two-thirds of international telephone traffic and practically all intercontinental television transmissions. When it was set up, tariffs were fixed in such a way that industrialised countries, the system's main clients, contributed indirectly to subsidising links with Third World countries. The principle of equal tariffs is clearly placed in question by the decision to allow competition by private systems.

But it serves no purpose to launch a satellite if the installations are lacking on earth to capture its emissions. This makes it vital to obtain 'landing rights' in those countries liable to provide clients. And this implies conquering hesitation on the part of national administrations of posts and telecommunications. The first private international satellite above the Atlantic, PanAmSat, was directed to the government of Britain, which had already privatised British Telecom in 1984. Mrs Thatcher's response was not long coming: in 1988, an invitation to tender was issued for private operators of such specialised international satellite links.

ENTERPRISE FIRST, FOLLOWED BY CHILDREN

American audiovisual deregulation is particularly revealing of the political philosophy which animates the process that embraces the whole of economic life, and changes the rules of the social game. The paradox is that its most fervent promoter is the Federal Communications Commission (FCC), whose mission, since 1934, has been to regulate media and telecommunications. On the pretext of 'less government', the FCC became one of the most important administrative offices in Washington, the one with by far the highest profile. The increasing activities of this federal commission contrast strongly with the mode adopted for deregulation in other sectors. The Civil Aeronautics Board, for example, has honestly deregulated itself by adopting the simple method of melting away.

Audiovisual first front: attack on the 'Fairness Doctrine'

Dating from more than half a century earlier, and based on the idea of adjustment to 'community needs', the Fairness Doctrine required of radio and television stations a balanced treatment of matters of public interest or subjects of general controversy, and obliged them to take different points of view and opposing positions into account. A real right to reply for minority or dissident groups, the doctrine could equally apply to information and advertising. In 1970, for example, anti-smoking campaigners were granted free spots to present their case alongside the cigarette commercials. The FCC objected: the ruling contradicted the First Amendment to the Constitution guaranteeing freedom of expression, which protects the press from any intervention likely to limit this right. Against the will of Congress, the FCC sanctified this latter interpretation in August 1987.

To understand the forms of deregulation peculiar to audiovisual production and advertising in the US, it is useful to know that from the beginnings of the American advertising industry, federal regulation was always very touchy about the veracity of advertisers' claims, and therefore made a stand on questions of unfair competition and dishonest advertising. Nevertheless, for forty-two years, from 1872 to 1914, the only laws regulating this area of activity were the province of post office legislation, with its sanctions against fraudulent use of the post. It was not until the eve of the First World War that Congress approved the Federal Trade Commission Act, which widened the field of intervention by federal authorities in respect to advertising. This law prohibits actions which are unfair and misleading in general trade, and carries a number of articles that refer to advertising. It was preceded by a law specific to certain products, the Food, Drug and Cosmetics Act of 1906, which tried to halt fraudulent claims in advertising for food, medicines and beauty products. From its creation in 1934, the FCC in turn became responsible for advertising standards through its grant of licences for radio and, later, television stations.

The Federal Trade Commission (FTC), composed of five members nominated by the President and confirmed by the Senate, comprises two main bureaux: the office of consumer protection and the office of competition. The staff of the first, which deals with advertising, consisted at the beginning of the 1970s of 250 lawyers and 135 'consumer experts'. In 1972, the American consumers' movement managed to attract FTC support. Calling on the 'Fairness Doctrine', it claimed general broadcasting access in the name of necessary 'counter-advertising'. An FTC petition to the FCC contended that specific amounts of time ought to be set aside for public interest groups and others wishing to comment on the implications of commercials which, while not misleading in the legal sense or unfair under the FCC's doctrine, are 'incomplete'. The FTC initiative was as poorly received by the FCC as by the broadcasters. The practice was thus discontinued. This didn't stop the FTC trying again in 1973, with the publication of a report entitled 'Advertising and the Public Interest'.

In the special issue which *Advertising Age* dedicated to the bicentenary of the American Revolution (1776–1976), one of the magazine's editors openly attacked the excessive weight of regulation:

> Government regulation is *always* more costly than self-regulation. Government regulations will stifle advertising precisely as the Interstate Commerce Commission stifled the railroads (helped along by railroad executives who were just as short-sighted as some advertising people are today). Excessively regulated advertising cannot be adequately productive and that also means higher costs.[7]

The advertising industry thus took the lead in the emergent movement for deregulation.

Second front: children's programmes

In 1983 the FCC cancelled the special rules which governed advertising time within this programme category. It likewise abolished the requirement for clear separation between the programme and the commercials.[8] And this was in spite of virulent protests by parents' groups. The result is that the characters are no longer the product of the creator's imagination, but derive directly from the marketing strategies of the toy manufacturers. In fact, the main characters in new cartoons now tend increasingly to be toys already on the market or about to be launched. A toy is no longer a classic derivative product of a television series or an animated cartoon, of the type imagined by the Disney industry, but a synchronic fusion of television programme and the market.

According to comments by the president of the Senate Telecommunications Sub-Committee, appointed in January 1988 to restrain the tidal wave of deregulation, many children's programmes were already extended advertising spots.

> Further, this fall, several programs featuring interactive toys, toys that respond to a video or audio signal emitted from television, were introduced. These programs represent a quantum leap in the ever-increasing commercialization of children's programming. As we are witnessing a steady increase in the number of program-length commercials geared towards children, we are also witnessing a steady decline in the number of educational children's programs available on commercial broadcast television.[9]

It was predictable. With the new optical electronic devices which allow remote decoding of coded information within television programmes, a further bridge was built between the toy industry and the small screen.

However, reservations have arisen, and in the face of these new interactive programmes the US networks, ever-attentive to protests by family associations, have opted for prudence. This reticence is not always found when the coupling of programme and toy crosses the Atlantic. In France, private television stations show less consideration. *La Cinq* (the channel owned by the trio Hersant-Berlusconi-Seydoux) is ready to transmit a magazine programme which incites children equipped with a Mattel toy to aim and shoot at targets on their television screen. The station sees dividends in the sales of these mini-robots, and soon the first channel follows suit with the purchase of *Sab Rider*. British television, on the other hand, is more resistant, considering the idea unprofitable. Those who live under the most neo-liberal regimes are not always the most neo-liberal. One supposes that this interactive technique will not remain at this level, because never has the introduction of a technical innovation been so closely tied to a change in the law.

But it is not because the technology is there that children go for it. Fascination rapidly gives way to saturation. In 1985, as many as fifty merchandise-driven programmes were on the air in the United States. Five years later, the toy-driven shows beat a retreat. The kids did not come to the rescue of Captain Power and its sponsor Mattel! The battle for advertising within children's programmes is far from over. In 1989, the House Energy and Commerce Committee returned to the issue and proposed that Congress should approve legislation to impose restrictions on children's television. The bill ordered the FCC to limit advertising commercials on children's television to twelve minutes an hour on weekdays and ten minutes at weekends. An identical bill was killed in 1988 by President Reagan.

Third front: the changing regime of concentration

In order to avoid speculation in the media industry, the established laws forbad every new broadcast licence-holder from selling off his radio or television station for the first three years. This anti-trafficking rule was abolished by the FCC in 1982. Another repeal increased the limits of ownership by an individual proprietor from seven to twelve radio or television stations, as long as together they amounted to no more than 25 per cent of the national audience.

The tangible result of this relaxation of the laws, closely connected to the necessary fluidity of the transactions, was a veritable avalanche of takeover bids by multimedia or electronics enterprises, including Murdoch, Westinghouse, *The Washington Post*, Columbia, Paramount, *Times-Mirror*, Viacom and many more. By 1988, eleven of the top twenty broadcasting companies had merged or changed owners. In the field of film distribution, after forty years of restrictions which impeded cross-ownership between production, distribution and exhibition, Paramount, Metro Goldwyn Mayer and Universal have bought up in three years 2,700 of the 8,000 exhibition sites in American territory. These acquisitions can only be understood in terms of the strategy of reconquest of the public mentioned earlier.

Fourth front: cable television

Regulated by the Cable Policy Act of 1984, plus the tariff deregulation by the FCC in 1987, when the level of rents chargeable by local authorities and the obligatory number of channels were both reduced, and subscription charges freed. No restriction was put on horizontal concentration in cable networks, as if there were no obligation to observe anti-trust legislation. Cross-ownership between media is allowed in certain instances (for example, cable television and the press) but not in others (cable and telecommunications). The duty of local operators to carry local stations, both public and commercial (the 'must carry' rules), a crucial element in the development of low-power transmitters, has been modified. In 1985, this duty was declared anti-constitutional and not in conformity with the First Amendment. A few months later, a compromise was adopted which would again be questioned in the courts.

WHEN FINANCE CHIPS IN

With the removal of prohibitions, Wall Street has moved closer to the audiovisual industry. New actors have entered the scene: financial establishments and their investment advisors. According to a French investigator from the Ministry of Telecommunications, Bernard Guillou, on a study trip of the American media industry in early 1986:

> The growing importance of financial administration in management (cost control, debt re-finance, dividend policy) underlines the emergence of new type of manager who adopts a certain distance from the symbolic – and emotive – content of media enterprises. John Kluge of Metromedia, or Tom Murphy of Capital Cities (ABC) represent this tendency today, which is doubtless less colourful but in the eyes of the fresh graduates from Yale or Harvard who increasingly staff these enterprises, more effective than the style of the radio and television pioneers.

The direct consequence of all this is a slippage in the hierarchy of functions within the enterprise. Guillou continues: 'In audiovisual enterprises as much as telecommunications, management controllers (especially cost controllers) and sellers (of space and services . . .) stand at the apex, to the detriment of technicians and content specialists [viz., screenwriters and directors].'[10]

It is this same relegation of 'content' which motivates the main complaint of the advertising networks faced with 'merger mania', who refuse to go in for the stock exchange game. According to the president of Leo Burnett, an unquoted agency created in 1935 and owner of a world network:

> the only objective of Leo Burnett is to produce 'superior advertising', and not to grow for the sake of growing. That's our thesis. What's more, we don't need to grow, because we're a private company with only 200 shareholders who are all employees. We're not interested in people who have no understanding of the business, and we're not looking for people outside the company. The only relations we have are between us and the clients, and we turn away anyone who only listens to Wall Street. The other agencies are public, quoted on the stock exchange, their aim is to grow and improve their profits, and their shareholders are not interested in the quality of the advertising, because they know nothing about it.[11]

Perhaps neo-liberal America has gone too far in the destabilisation of its networks and media enterprises? Very probably. At least this is what many people think. And some already predict a new era of regulation, without always saying exactly what form it would take.

94

With America's First Amendment principles (free press, free speech) always at issue as far as the media are concerned, the courts emerge today as the leading force in media regulation. The constant involvement of the courts creates a turbulence in the business environment, because decisions come in bursts and invariably are modified in the tortuous appeals process. When regulatory decisions are made by the courts rather than the Federal Communications Commission, there is no coherent policy, and this creates an atmosphere of uncertainty. One thing is sure: court decisions are less likely to be related to market forces (and perhaps common sense) than the policies of the Reagan-appointed FCC.[12]

Burned into the collective financial memory is the shock inflicted by the Black Monday of October 1987. The careless enthusiasm of the early days of deregulation has not survived the market boom of unregulated capital, for the volatility of the financial and economic environment is also the volatility of investment in the media industry. The unanimous trust extended to Wall Street experts and investment advisers has been rudely shattered, and our financial journalist concludes:

Whatever the direct impact on companies of Black Monday, the residue of the stock and bond market crashes on the industry generally has been an attitude of pessimism. Planning and growth will require more nerve in the future. No entrepreneur will be able to plan in advance an 'exit' strategy based on a trip to the financial markets. And few will be able to tap the financial markets for funds as confidently as many had done before the crash.[13]

Deregulation has thrown finance into the arms of communication – and communication into those of finance: the convergence of two highly internationalised sectors, at the apex of network techniques, the vanguard in the process of globalising the market.

The search for consanguinity by these two parts of the deregulation process is like the merging of two fluids in circulation. Indeed, the contemporary literature of financial analysts has so many points of contact with that of the analysts of the communication and information industry that they are interchangeable. And what do the financial analysts tell us?

At present we are witnessing the growing autonomy of the financial function at an international level, that is to say, a disconnection between the sphere of reality and the sphere of finance. The result is a striking contrast between, on the one hand, the uninterrupted rhythms of financial innovation and rapid increase in transactions, and on the other, the stagnation of production, especially in the area of industrial investment. Hence there are many indicators pointing to a growth of speculative but unproductive financial space.[14]

On this globe, where the effects of the image prevail over the real, financial space and communication space are suspended, each in their own way, above the productive base, not to mention the concrete daily lives of the great majority of the people. Each contributes to intensified speculation and the growing risks of volatile conditions.

CONNECTIONS AND DISCONNECTIONS

Volatility for some is a lead weight for others. On one October day, Wall Street lost enough dollars to have cancelled most of the burden of the huge international debts of countries like Brazil, Mexico or Venezuela.

In these environments of savage capitalism, the principle of deregulation is nothing new. These countries tried it out ahead of time, for it has always been at the heart of their mode of access to modernity. One can mention the aggressive ecology of advertising on the small screen in Venezuela, which already in the 1970s had an advertising ratio 61 per cent higher than the norm on the North American networks. Then add the piracy rate in audio and video cassettes, which in the case of films sometimes reaches 80 per cent of the market; the proliferation of receiving dishes, which allows the well-off to watch North American television channels; and the permissiveness of a state complicit in hidden advertising and sponsorship; plus the laxity of professional codes of practice in these domains. Here is a situation close to the literal meaning of the concept of 'de-regulation': a space that is void of controls, lacking any kind of effective rules, even rules to promote deregulation. This environment of a media apparatus left entirely to itself and the laws of the market, contrasts with another reality equally characteristic of the communications landscape: the radio, video and telematic networks of a popular movement which during the course of the 1980s shook off old fears of technology and appropriated it instead. A contrast which perfectly captures Brazil after the dictatorship.

At the very moment of public debate about the new Constitution, and therefore about opening up the space of communication, behind the scenes the government of President Sarney was distributing radio and television concessions to its own supporters. More than 600 concessions were distributed in less than three years, the highest rate at any time in the country's broadcasting history. At this rate, the National Congress of Journalists in June 1988 estimated that there would be practically no frequencies left for anyone outside the private sector at the end of the five-year presidential mandate; this threatened to undercut any attempt to alter the logic of an audiovisual system where the Globo group controlled around two-thirds of the communications market.

This state of original and permanent deregulation does not therefore prevent 'more market and less state' also being the order of the day in this Latin America, which shelters the top three television powers in the Third World, its five leading advertising markets. A reality all the more complex because here the concept of the state retains the imprint of a politically authoritarian and censorious power, and the absence of a state of law, and haunted by the long tradition of nepotism and corruption.

In addition to the pressure from all those national business circles who favour more economic liberalisation, more airwaves and more cables, there is the dynamic of external influences. Shock treatment by the World Bank (a halt in social protection and income redistribution policies) in which social severity is coupled with *laissez-faire* in the marketplace. A grey market in debt, in which credits on foreign banks change hands below their value. The debt is converted into investment in national enterprises. An example is Mexico, which in 1987, after signing a highly devious agreement for debt remission with the United States, offered all sorts of finance facilities, in order to solve the crisis in the state film industry. For example, for the purchase from the Mexican government of debt conversion certificates to the value of $10m, known as 'movie-swaps', the foreign audiovisual producer would pay only half ($5m) but be able to utilise up to $10m in studio services in the capital, or the employment of local artists and technicians.[15]

In countries with a strong commercial tradition like Venezuela, the era of the government's whim to regulate the channels is well over. Added to the one public and two commercial channels in 1988 were another commercial station and a pay channel. The stake was the construction of a local industry to compete with Mexico and Brazil. For the first time in the history of Latin American television, the dubbing of series from the United States and Brazil was no longer the exclusive fiefdom of Mexico's Televisa. Caracas has its own trade.

In the rare societies where important public channels subsist, private transmitter and cable operators are authorised by the most diverse political regimes. For example, democratic Argentina privatised one of its channels in December 1987, while the Chile of General Pinochet, which had a public channel and four university channels, invited offers for concessions on eight private stations. For this purpose, the advertising ceiling of six minutes per hour was removed. All the same, the privatisation scheme failed, owing to opposition from both the existing channels and the public, as well as differences within the regime itself. The most savage case of deregulation has been Bolivia. In 1985 the public monopoly was literally overwhelmed by the irruption of private stations. More than forty transmitters started up within a few months. As a film-maker from La Paz puts it, the sudden appearance of so much television

in the middle of the worst economic conditions experienced by the country in its whole history, seems at first paradoxical. It is less so when you see how the channels function. Limited to a precarious technical infrastructure, they are mostly quite happy to fill their programming with feature movies pirated from foreign stations, usually the North American Spanish-language channels, or simply acquired on the illicit market in Panama and Miami.[16]

Deregulation goes after deregulation like money goes after money. The development of television in these countries, in terms of diffusion if not production, has reached its highest point. The viewer of the world's fourth-largest network can switch each evening between three soap operas produced by Globo which makes almost 80 per cent of its own afternoon and evening programming. The same viewer can admire the postmodern aesthetics of its in-house commercials.* But (lawful madness) three-quarters of the population are disconnected from the circuits of minimum vital consumption to such a degree that, as an economic journalist from Rio de Janeiro notes, the television-dominated advertising market is 'stunted and concentrated, containing scarcely one in three Brazilians within its profile of consumption of the goods and services which advertising acclaims.'[17]

The evidence of a growing distance between individual buying power and what is offered by advertising has become common currency. As *Variety* reported from Buenos Aires in March 1988: 'While TV audiences climbed to an all-time high in the Argentine capital during 1987, advertising sales remained at best steady . . . . Why this anomaly?' With an external debt of $55b (it is still paying for the arsenal lost in the Malvinas):

> Argentina must borrow more billions each year to pay for the interest on its external debt and no hard currency remains to invest in modernization and development. The economy stagnates and while a few make fortunes in the financial markets, most of the population has no other choice than belt-tightening to cope with the recession. More and more people are obliged to stay at home due to lack of purchasing power. They watch TV but are unable to buy the things tub-thumped by the commercials.[18]

(This is *Variety* reporting, the media-world's leading trade journal, whose purpose is not to foment subversion.)

The distance which has grown up between the ordinary people of the

---

* The Spanish original uses the word *clips* [Translators note].

broad majority and the models of life advanced by the media and advertising is such that Mexico's multimedia conglomerate Televisa has undertaken to 'moralise' its programming. In this country with its simultaneously centralised and paternalist traditions, the group's directors decided to reduce scenes of sex and violence (hence it refused to purchase *Miami Vice* which the public channel didn't hesitate to transmit instead), and to drop 'educational messages' into its soaps – but very short ones, so as not to become didactic. Integrated into the action, the characters and the decor, these subliminal snippets were meant to arouse social conscience over a wide range of themes (family planning, hygiene, pollution, vandalism, etc.).[19] During the 1970s, Televisa had gone further, producing soap operas, with the aid of psychologists and sociologists, aimed at promoting birth control. The formula was so successful that India imported the model.

In the group's presentation folder one can read the following pious vow: to renounce the A-B-C-D classification of social classes 'which implies observing the public from a single perspective, as consumer, and instead to adopt the concept of an audience divided not by purchasing power but by the 'code of communication', the 'language to which it is attuned', including speech, education, habits and costumes, cosmogony, ethics; and therefore to investigate 'the widest possible "codes of communication", in order to improve communication and feedback, and employ the established circuits to transmit a message which is richer and more socially conscious than mere selling.'[20]

But in July 1988 the boomerang of reality struck a blow: in the country with the highest degree of concentration in the television industry anywhere in the world, which figures among the top twenty investors in advertising but occupies sixty-ninth place in expenditure per capita in education, the government party – the PRI, or Institutional Revolutionary Party – which since 1929 has always won 99 per cent of the vote, was severely shaken by the very people whose votes it had tried to buy. A Mexican journalist commented:

> Useless and pathetic – and the Public Treasury paying for it! – all the expenses in advertising, in transport, in tourism . . . a pure and simple waste of time, the buying of television time, the candidate's telephone conversations with the public, the gross manipulation of journalists, the perks they were given . . . all for what? For nothing. Because the thousands who received these perks avenged the outrage to their dignity and voted against the PRI.[21]

6

THE NEW FRONTIER OF THE OLD CONTINENT
Fragmentation and planetary conscience

A FRAGMENTED MODEL

Britain is the first country – and so far practically the only one – to back the possibility of peaceful coexistence between a strong public broadcasting service and a private sector subject to the same obligations of public service. Having done so, it has created not only a model television system, but also a system of regulation of advertising practice.

American advertisers have never hidden their admiration for this regulatory system, and on occasion, in their contacts with the federal authorities, have referred to it as an exemplary achievement. In 1977, a professor of marketing at Massachusetts University School of Business Administration published a comparative study which was widely reported by the professional press. He said that the differences, 'stem from stricter British advertising codes, prescreening of TV and radio commercials by a public board, with the assistance of the private broadcasting companies, and a recently stepped-up self-regulation program for the industry which covers print and other media advertising.' He continued:

> The different control processes in the two countries result from different laws and from greater government and industry cooperation in the U.K., compared to the U.S. British government officials believe that industry control with public participation is more effective than direct government control . . . the British have no anti-trust laws to prevent industry and the media from working together to prevent publication of socially unacceptable advertising. And they have no counterpart to the U.S. Federal Trade Commission, which issues complaints against questionable advertisements after they have been run, but not prior to public use.
>
> In the U.S. . . . an adversary relationship exists between the advertising industry and the government, whereas in Britain, government, industry and the public are attempting to resolve together complicated advertising issues relating to subjects such as health, safety, offensiveness and advertising to children.[1]

In fact, the British system for the regulation of advertising is a hybrid, like its broadcasting. On the one hand, a system for media other than radio and television (print media, direct mailing, poster advertising, cinema), following the British Code of Advertising Practices adopted in 1961 by the Advertising Association (the representative body of the advertising profession), and applied by the Advertising Standards Authority (ASA), which was set up subsequently. On the other hand, a system for radio and television, instituted by Act of Parliament (the Independent Broadcasting Authority Act of 1973) and applied by the IBA. The IBA, now with responsibility for commercial radio, replaced the Independent Television Authority (ITA), set up by the Television Act of 1954 to supervise commercial television. It was this Act which made Britain the first country in Europe to create a mixed television system, consisting of the BBC plus the independent companies who made up ITV (Independent Television). Commercial radio was added later, but only local stations were permitted, which left the BBC as the only national radio broadcaster. However, this set-up changed in 1990 when the new Broadcasting Act became law, which for the first time legislated for national commercial radio stations.

The Act of 1973 controls the content, volume, distribution and forms of advertising. For example, a pair of visual indicators separates the advertisements from the programmes. The former are grouped together in commercial breaks. It is prohibited to employ situations or representations which might lead the audience to confuse programme and advertising material. Furthermore, nothing must be stated, implied or allowed to suggest that any part of a programme has been provided or inspired by an advertiser. Until 1989, when the IBA relaxed the rules, nothing resembling the American model of sponsorship was allowed. According to a new 'User's Guide' to television sponsorship published by the IBA in March 1990, in future all programmes except news and current affairs will be open to sponsorship.[2] Above all, the IBA is responsible for exercising prior control of advertisements and censoring those which contravene its Code of Advertising Standards and Practices. (The Code is periodically revised by the Advertising Advisory Committee, a consultative committee composed of representatives of the advertising industry and consumer interests, plus a group of medical experts for pharmaceutical products and surgical appliances.) The print media, with its system of self-regulation, is not subject to this obligation. Control is a posteriori.[3]

This is the famous British model of public service broadcasting which came under fire with the publication of a White Paper in November 1988, in which, with 1992 on the horizon, Margaret Thatcher's government proposed the radical overhaul of the laws of the television game. The IBA, now considered incompatible with the need to open up the commercial television system, is to make way for a flexible new organisation with much more limited functions: the Independent Television Commission (ITC). The ITC will grant concessions to private groups but will not exercise everyday control on the content, variety and quality of the programming. In 1992, the regional ITV franchises will be auctioned off. Channel Four – the channel which demonstrated an alternative type of commercial television to the kind dominant throughout the Continent – is retained but will now become self-financing. Until now, advertising on Channel Four has been sold by the ITV companies, who in return provide the channel's budget; now it will have to sell its own advertising. Originally it was proposed that the licence fee by which the BBC is financed (the BBC carries no advertising) should disappear, to be replaced by a subscription system; and that one of the BBC's two television channels should lose a slice of its night-time schedule to commercial broadcasting, but these proposals have been stymied. A fifth national channel is to be introduced.

With this voluntaristic project for dismantling the present system, the neo-liberal government of Margaret Thatcher was hoping to increase Britain's share of the media landscape in the new Europe-without-frontiers. But they bit off more than they could chew. Focusing on the proposal to sell off the ITV franchises to the highest bidder, without reference to established standards for programme quality, almost the entire television industry rose up in protest, with officials of the IBA and executives of the 'Big Five' ITV companies (Thames, LWT, Central, Granada and Yorkshire) joining trade bodies, trades unions and consumer groups in a defence of public service broadcasting. The critics pointed out that newcomers, eager to cash in on the promised boom, would overprice their bids and then be left with insufficient cash to make their programmes. What aroused the ire of the established ITV companies was the government's eagerness to ride roughshod over them. Among media analysts, mumbles were heard about unsustainable expectations of growth in the advertising market to finance the operation. One advertisement which the industry placed in the quality newspapers showed a full-page, full-figure photograph of Rupert Murdoch, proprietor of Sky (which was struggling to take off), and the legend 'If even he's not in favour of it, who is?'. Result? When the new Broadcasting Act was brought before Parliament, opponents began to wring concessions from a government which in other areas of policy, too, had begun to falter.

OVERCROWDING

'Italy and Silvio Berlusconi invented commercial television on the European continent', reported *Variety* in April 1986, in salute of the network's tenth anniversary. To which the director of Publitalia, the advertising branch of the group Fininvest, added: 'Berlusconi understood the advertising needs of the consumer industry and what commercial broadcasting could do to satisfy them. He also understood the conservative nature of the advertising agencies, operating for years between limited space on RAI and the equally conservative print media.' [4]

Italy holds the record for growth in advertising investment: between 1980 and 1987, television revenue went up 307 per cent in real terms, increasing its share of total advertising from 26 to 51 per cent. The European average over the same period went up from 19 to 24 per cent. [5] The Italian peninsula approaches the indices of countries like Brazil and Mexico, and in Europe comes at the top of the table with Portugal (53.6 per cent) and Greece (48.9 per cent).

The group's story can be read in its healthy profile: $7m in 1980, when Publitalia was founded; $750m in 1985; 1,200 advertisers, with 250 of them providing 85 per cent of the accounts. The crown of Fininvest's success is worn by its president, Silvio Berlusconi, but another name also figures: Gianni Cottardo, director of the McCann-Erickson subsidiary, one of the largest agencies on the Italian market. Cottardo, after a period with the Italian group, returned to the American company and became head of one of its three regional offices in Europe. Chosen model: 'Madison Avenue, though blue serge replaced grey flannel', his successor told *Variety*, bursting with pride at taking over. [6]

The expert who hailed from McCann-Erickson not only founded Publitalia but also took control of Canale Cinque in the crucial moment when the private network was formed. Several spectacular coups can be credited to the Cottardo–Berlusconi duo in 1980–1. These include gaining support from members of the powerful MPEAA (essential source of programming) and the big advertisers, who were previously reluctant; the capture of sixty-four episodes of *Dallas* (kidnapped from RAI which showed the first thirteen episodes); the organisation and broadcast of the spectacular *Mundialito* which took place in Uruguay. After he left the Berlusconi studios, the advertising man remained a faithful ally. In 1985–6, during discussions between the private network and representatives of the advertising industry, he turned up as president of the Italian advertising agency association ASAAP.

In Italy, contrary to what happened in France, first there was deregulation, then they went looking for laws. One of the benefits of the situation is precisely that it shows rather more clearly how new rules of advertising conduct germinate in a context which combines commercial outbidding and a legal vacuum. While the Italian Parliament had still not discussed the need for a framing law in the audiovisual domain, the partners in commercial television signed an agreement for self-regulation, in order to insert some order into it. In February 1986, the two associations representing the agencies and the advertisers (ASAAP and UPA) agreed with Publitalia to limit advertising space to 16 per cent during prime time, and to 18 per cent elsewhere. Each party moreover committed itself to observing the full range of provisions agreed. This is what the agreement said:

— The length of a commercial break must not exceed 2 minutes and 30 seconds. This limit does not apply to transmissions that last more than one hour. Two advertising breaks interrupted by channel identification or program promotion are to be considered one break.
— A single advertising spot cannot contain products which are competitive.
— When one or more spots are inserted in a context of crowding greater than 16 per cent, the agency will be entitled to a reduction in price as follows:

Crowding up to 17 per cent	10 per cent discount
Crowding up to 19 per cent	40 per cent discount
. . . .	. . . . . .
Crowding greater than 25 per cent	no cost advertisement.

For children's transmissions, the 10 per cent discount is applied to a 16 per cent crowding.
— When spots with competitive products are broadcast in the same advertisement break or when the advertisement break is longer than 2 minutes 30 seconds, the advertiser is entitled to a reduction of up to 25 per cent on the agreed price.
— Publitalia agrees to limit the number of its . . . sponsored promos as well as the number of its own program promos and agrees to insert not more than one promo per each advertisement block. . . .
— This agreement will automatically be renewed annually.[7]

In short, the parties agreed on maximum limits for crowding commercials together. Beyond these limits, the alarm sounded: too much advertising would kill it.

In this pact, which *Variety* cheerfully called an 'anti-clutter' agreement, there was no allusion to the viewer who, notwithstanding, is the subject of this obsession with saturation. Yet the evidence is there: as an executive in J. Walter Thompson's Italian subsidiary put it, 'No one could expect the audience, general or target, to understand, absorb, remember or even watch the multitude of break times and overcrowded spots within them.'[8] There was no mention either of the cuts habitually made in the films transmitted, a practice denounced by film directors like Federico Fellini. The pretension to self-legislation and self-regulation is out of all proportion to the poverty displayed in these articles of agreement.

In 1987, the crowding of commercials got worse. It became overcrowding. Fininvest's networks transmitted 320,620 paid spots, that is, an increase of 31.2 per cent over the previous year. RAI transmitted 63,329, or 3.9 per cent less.[9] This flood of advertising chased the viewers away. During the 1987-8 season, the leading channel, RAI I, streaked ahead of Fininvest's leading network, Canale 5, taking 56.3 per cent of the audience to the latter's 22.5 per cent. The supremacy of the public service extended to all parts of the schedule. Even in prime time they had 52.9 per cent.[10]

In June 1988, twelve years after the historic decree of the Constitutional Court authorising freedom of the airwaves at the local level, the Council of Ministers of the Italian government considered the outline of the first law for the regulation of the audiovisual landscape. 'Zero Option': to ratify existing conditions. If it was intended to prohibit multiple ownership of printed and audiovisual media, the law placed before Parliament allowed a single group to control three national networks – precisely the case with Silvio Berlusconi. It guaranteed RAI 50 per cent of the global turnover of Italian television (advertising and licence fees). Two-fifths of these revenues were to come from state funding, the rest through advertising. Advertising quotas stand at 4 per cent of weekly air-time (12 per cent during peak viewing hours) for RAI, and for private television at 12 per cent (18 per cent during prime time).

That same month of June, at the television festival of Chianciano, Fininvest presented the first three television movies made under its aegis: *Due Fratelli* by Alberto Latuada, *Amori* by Dino Risi, and *Gli Indifferenti* (after the novel by Alberto Moravia and starring Liv Ullman and Peter Fonda) by Mauro Bolognini. The new producer revealed the group's ambitions: to increase the current production budget of 70b lira to 200b, and place it at the disposal of quality films for television by the best film directors. What lay behind this move? Was it a policy of prestige production to compensate for the plainly commercial rationale of the overall programming? If declarations made by a representative of the private network spared the susceptibilities of the film-makers, they were no less fixed upon the principle of advertising: 'We thought', he said, 'of following the American model and writing commercial breaks into the script. But we arrived at the opposite solution: this way, one avoids imposing artificial rhythms which would affect the whole work. The only thing we could do was to let the film-maker decide, once the product was finished, where the breaks should be inserted.'[11]

In 1989, the number of spots was so excessive that Berlusconi agreed to reduce commercial breaks from a maximum of 20 per cent per hour to 16 per cent during late-night programme hours (10.30 p.m. to sign-off). In March 1990, to the stupefaction of Italian politicians, a majority of Members of Parliament reviewing the law on television approved an amendment proposed by the Communist Party prohibiting the interruption by commercial breaks of all cinema films, plays and operas. The vote was 148 in favour, 84 against with 4 abstentions. The campaign slogan used to argue for the regulation of television advertising was 'You can't break a story into pieces, you can't interrupt an emotion.' But such are the subtle complexities of Italian politics under the hegemony of the conservative sector that in July 1990 this vote was reversed.

HOME INVESTMENT

The evidence is international. In January 1988, an opinion poll in France revealed that 84 per cent of people polled believed that advertising had reached saturation level; 67 per cent were against the interruption of films, 41 per cent found the breaks in the news irritating. Another poll five years earlier reveals a definite growth of disapproval and hostility to advertising: the number of viewers who watched the commercials attentively was going down (from 35 to 28 per cent). Channel jumping (what Americans call 'zapping') went up from 18 to 29 per cent (in five years the number of French homes with remote controls went up from 20 to 50 per cent). But the real surprise was the growing allergic response, which consists in leaving the room, or in lowering or cutting out the volume (41 instead of 23 per cent).[12]

Beyond the British Isles, the widespread experience of commercial television in Europe was forty years behind America. In a very brief lapse of time, countries like France were precipitated headlong into a different televisual culture. From the evidence of the chatter of people who saw the televisual diet handed over to the logic of advertising, they had a real live experience of deregulation, in which the memory of public monopoly was relegated to the darkness of night. According to a Parisian advertiser in 1988:

At the time of the monopoly, the scarcity of space was conducive to a certain quality in advertising. The advertiser sought above all to seduce. Now we're drowning in spots and advertisers have only one anxiety: to pound the message home in ever-shorter commercials (because ever-more expensive), which has a disastrous effect on the viewer.[13]

With the privatisation of the main public channel, TF1, in 1987, advertising space authorised by law has increased from 18 minutes a day to 12 minutes per hour.

Privatisation of public channels, creation of private ones, the launch of offshore broadcasting operations: Europe's airwaves and cables have been catapulted into the age of competition. The Last Mohicans who resisted the introduction of advertising on the small screen had to give in. Following Belgium, Denmark gave the green light in 1988, though with various restrictions. In 1989 the Netherlands removed the obstacles to the massive introduction of television advertising, by repealing the existing law which restricted it to 5 per cent of air-time and prohibited it on Sundays. Federal Germany remained protectionist. The timid deregulation of April 1987 lifted the prohibition on Sunday and public holiday advertising, and also on sponsorship, but advertising is only allowed before 8.00 p.m. While television has already captured around half the advertising receipts in Italy, Greece and Portugal, and around a third in Spain and Britain, the share in the Federal Republic, the world's fourth-largest advertising market, does not exceed 10 per cent. At the end of 1988, only Sweden and Norway had not authorised advertising on television. As these television systems are being restructured, the geo-advertisers are turning their eyes towards this European transformation. Between 1980 and 1987, total European advertising expenditure increased by a massive 103 per cent in real terms. Television showed a growth of 181 per cent over the same period.

If total advertising investment in Federal Germany has not increased more than 3 or 4 per cent annually, in Italy and Spain it has jumped by 20 per cent and sometimes more. In 1988, France registered an increase of 15 per cent, ahead of Japan (12 per cent), the Netherlands (11 per cent) and Britain (10 per cent). This forced march of European advertising contrasts with the low levels found in other latitudes: Canada (5.5 per cent in 1987, 0.5 per cent in 1988), Australia (zero growth), Brazil (down 5 per cent in 1988, down 10 per cent the previous year). Growth has been scarcely any better in the United States, where advertising expenditure went down nearly 5 per cent in 1987, and only the offshore growth of their networks by 37 per cent has enabled them to compete for the reduction in the internal market.[14] For the first time since 1975, the projected growth of US advertising expenditure for 1989 failed to keep pace with the GNP.

The distribution of mass advertising in the countries of the EEC in 1990, according to the AACP (Association française des agences-conseils en publicité): Britain, 24 per cent of total investment; Federal Republic of Germany, 20 per cent; France, 16 per cent; Italy, 15 per cent; Spain, 11 per cent; Netherlands, 9 per cent; other countries, 5 per cent.

In this Europe with its expanding advertising industry, there are also ups and downs. In Britain, after continuous expansion in which advertising spend increased threefold in ten years, the rate of growth has collapsed. According to the Advertising Association (AA), real growth in 1990 would fall by 4 per cent, with no recovery expected before 1992. The effects are suffered by television and the magazine press, which has also seen a fall in readership. At the same time, agency flotations and profits have plunged. A sector which had only known euphoria now faces new conditions. The boom of the early 1980s with its low interest rates, liberalisation of credit, rise in consumption and supposed fall in unemployment – all signs of the success of neo-liberal policy – have disappeared. Conditions are far from the slogan which Saatchis once conjured up to help the Tories roll to victory: 'Now we've the fastest growth of any major economy in Europe.'

THE ADVERTISING LOBBY

True, the weakest amongst us believe that they have almost to excuse themselves for the role of advertising in the economy and society. This is not the way we see it. Certainly there exist powerful forces which entrust the control of goods and services to the state, thus destroying our market economies. Attacks against free enterprise may be openly inspired by Marxism, or else more subtle: when it consists in crafty attempts to exploit the legitimate concerns of the consumer movement, or sensitive/delicate issues such as children's advertising with the aim of attacking the market economy on its weakest flank. Whatever form it takes, every attack on free enterprise constitutes an attack on free speech and freedom of choice. To lose a battle can mean for us to lose a whole market. Remember a moment: the advertising market for alcoholic beverages in Germany, last year, represented DM500m. . . . We support advertising and commend it, whether it is undertaken by the government, the municipalities, retailers, the professions. All contribute to enlarging the advertising cake, which the Marxist mice nibble on.

[Information Bulletin of the EAAA, 1984)

European advertisers have learned, over the 1980s, that advertising was too serious to be left to the uninitiated. They therefore arranged to be present wherever new regulations were under discussion or decisions were being taken which affected the institutions of the media in the immediate future. Their short-term objective was to push back the limits of the spaces closed by law to advertising investment. Their longer-term hope: to make the principle of self-regulation generally acceptable, the combination of agency self-discipline and the discipline of the market, to convince the state and civil society of the cogency of this philosophy of action.

The principle of business self-regulation as an alternative to public policy controls is not new, but is already there in the cradle of the modern advertising industry. What is novel is the creation of permanent institutions representing professional interests and actively promoting the operation and defence of the principle. It was effectively British advertisers who were the first to feel the need for a strong corporative organisation. This is what they brought about in 1961–2 when they proclaimed their code of self-regulation and created an organisation for the self-vigilance of the profession. The creation of these professional bodies on a national level is the first unified response of the advertising industry to the growing pressures of the consumers' and environmental protection movements. The year when the Advertising Association (founded in 1925) took the initiative coincided with promulgation by the government of the Consumer Protection Act, the first general legal text to define the rights of consumers. It was only ten years later that US advertisers created an operational body for self-vigilance in response to consumer pressures: the National Advertising Review Board (NARB). There, as in Britain, the centre of the debate was the question of 'false, misleading and deceptive advertising'.

It took until the second half of the 1970s for this corporative conscience to acquire a European dimension. The occasion was furnished by the firm attempt at regulating advertising practices by the General Directorate for Consumer Affairs of the European Community. Again – but this time on a European scale – the initiative took off in response above all to proposals to define and put a check on 'misleading and unfair advertising'. These first skirmishes with the 'Eurocrats' gave birth in 1980 to the Tripartite, or EAT (European Advertising Tripartite), which brought together representatives of advertisers, agencies and support media. One of the most active partners in this horizontal structure is the European Association of Advertising Agencies (EAAA), founded in Oslo in 1959 by a group of full-service agencies from the Nordic countries, France, Britain and the Federal Republic of Germany, and which included the principal networks operating in Europe. The leading role in the Tripartite has been played, since its establishment, by professionals from Britain. This is how, thanks to close co-operation between the latter and the Advertising Association, the first compatible statistics have been provided for countries of the trilateral zone. It is also the experts of the London agencies who have most often been called to defend the cause of self-regulation in the face of Community actions.

Accredited before the EEC and the Council of Europe, the EAAA and the EAT are dedicated to lobbying. This is how the former association describes the function in one of its information bulletins:

> The EAAA may submit its observations on all subjects related to advertising and has the right to formulate amendments before any parliamentary debate. Thus, during the meeting of the Ministers of Health, advertising was one of the few industries to be represented. In this way – and this continues – it was possible to ward off certain

laws or limit their effect. It would not be wise to boast about our lobbying, for this would compromise our friends and our future success. But even so we can cite two examples which show that lobbying by the EAAA has been, and continues to be, pertinent, pointed and efficacious. First example: the Council of Europe proposed to prohibit *all* advertising for *all* tobacco and alcohol products; thanks to vigorous activity by the EAAA, the proposal now only speaks of the *limitation* of this kind of advertising; favourable amendments of the same kind have been obtained in the case of the advertising for pharmaceuticals and food products, as well as advertising aimed at children. Second example: the EAAA has provided crucial assistance to the Italian agencies' association in opposing the introduction of an advertising tax. Together, we won our case.

If these triumphant bulletins attest to the reality of pressure groups in the debates about the future of European media systems, the least that should be said is that they conjure away the real complexity of the issues.

CEILING

Two projects for the regulation of audiovisual space in Europe have been prepared by Community bodies. The EEC proposed a 'directive'; the Council of Europe a 'convention'. The theme of advertising occupies in these documents one of three chapter headings alongside the question of programme quotas and that of authors' rights and related issues. The main focus of the regulations are: the separation of advertising and programmes ('advertising must be clearly recognisable as such'); sponsorship ('enterprises must not exercise any undue influence on the parts of the programme free of advertising'); a prohibition against targeting of the audience in countries receiving offshore transmissions; a fixed ceiling for daily advertising air-space; limitations of advertising on certain products (cigarettes/cigars, alcoholic beverages, medicines) or to certain groups (protection for children and young persons or minors).

The proposals of the EEC directive were preceded by a voluminous study published in June 1984 under the title *Television Without Frontiers, Green Paper on the Establishment of the Common Market for Broadcasting, Especially by Satellite and Cable*. The *Proposal of the Council Concerning the Activity of Radiodiffusion* was adopted in April 1986.[15] The EEC places emphasis on the need to respect the articles of the Treaty of Rome (the founding document of the Common Market), which guarantee freedom of access to the activity of advertising and its exercise throughout the Community. It therefore encourages member states to enact general legislation for broadcast advertising, and insists on the adverse effects of restrictions in member states who do not allow free flow of advertising at a moment when a market for broadcast advertising is in process of formation on a European scale.

The origin of the proposals in the directive was not the Commissioner responsible for culture and audiovisual production, with his experts in the media and the culture industry, but the Commissioner for Consumer Affairs with his team of lawyers. That is to say, the same office which in the preceding decade had been subjected to every type of pressure from the corporate networks and had arrived at a certain *modus vivendi* with them. There was also a certain objective: television without frontiers, a theme introduced by the representatives of the Grand Duchy of Luxembourg, the only European territory at the beginning of the 1980s to harbour international transmissions. For these specialists in the laws of consumption and competition, with little experience in the cultural complexity of audiovisual systems, this initiative aimed at the regulation of television without frontiers rapidly turned into a Pandora's box. For some, the theme of offshore television became a subterfuge for raising a debate accompanied by activities aimed at breaking the national monopolies. The choice of negotiating partners reflects this heavy trend. Crucial institutions like the European Broadcasting Union (EBU) – which incorporates most of the public radio and television stations – found themselves marginalised during this first phase, as did the industry's labour organisations.

It is hardly surprising, then, that this sense of frustration should reappear during the deliberations of the European Parliament, which began to examine the proposals of the directive in June 1987. The MEPs who formed the working party on a report by the Italian member R. Barzanti, extensively amended the text of the proposal. In April 1988 the EEC incorporated a number of these parliamentary amendments in new proposals. Among other things, these amendments re-established a minimum of democratic rights, especially in regard to the right to reply in the case of news. Also, an addendum was included which expressed disquiet over 'dominant attitudes which impose limits to pluralism and freedom of information in broadcasting and in the informational system as a whole'. Another modification was the introduction of a definition of a 'European' product – an important question in relation to quotas – which the proposal defined solely in terms of production capital but which the amendment defined in terms of the European character of the authors and workers involved in the production. As for advertising, in April 1988 the principle of a ceiling was established (15 per cent in the day and 18 per cent in any hour), and the regulation of sponsorship was considered, but the question of breaks was left undefined, as was the question of the moral rights of the author.[16] However, this version of the amendments was not the last. But in order to understand what happened

111

to the directive afterwards, one must first know what happened with the 'Convention'.

The European Convention on Television Without Frontiers, which got down to work in Vienna in 1986, has also been the object of several redrafts. None the less, in the absence of a minimal consensus, it was still not ready for signature in the autumn of 1988, when the Council of Ministers met in Stockholm. One of the seeds of discord was Article 14, which proposed only one break in a feature-length film; one break in 45 minutes in television films, magazines and documentaries longer than 45 minutes; no breaks in programmes shorter than 45 minutes; no breaks during the news, current affairs programmes, religious programmes, and children's programmes of less than 30 minutes' duration. On the eve of the meeting in the Swedish capital, the positions were divided as follows: *those considered inflexible* (West Germany, Austria, Belgium, Netherlands, Switzerland, Liechtenstein); *those open to compromise* (France, Portugal, Cyprus, Turkey); the *neutrals* (Italy, Greece, Spain, Iceland, Norway, Denmark, Sweden); *those against* (United Kingdom, Luxembourg, Ireland, Malta). Then, in Stockholm, the British managed easily to back a surprise amendment. To compensate for the hourly ceiling (an average of 15 per cent of air-time and 20 per cent in any given hour) which was vigorously denounced by the corporative organisations, London's proposal provided for multiple breaks, especially during feature films and television films (three breaks for a feature-length movie of 110 minutes). Other concessions favouring the Grand Duchy and the private Italian networks included the right for transborder television transmission of advertising specifically aimed at neighbouring countries, and a prohibition against a country interfering with the reception of a station for the mere fact that it violates its own advertising norms.

While Britain refused to sign the original version because it was insufficiently liberal, Belgium, on the other hand, opposed it because it was too concerned with lifting obstacles to the circulation of programmes – which consequently made it impossible for countries to establish their own regulations for the entry of foreign stations – and was not concerned enough about audiovisual creation, thus underestimating intercultural relations in a Europe composed of national and regional communities with unequal potential for audiovisual production (and advertising receipts).[17] In this dialogue of the deaf in which the single word 'cultural' made the delegation of the neo-liberal government in London jump, the representatives of the socialist government of France, ardent defenders of 'European cultural identity', had to soften their position. In spite of this backward step, the Parisian theses were only accepted with strong reservations. Concessions essentially concerned the delay between the first screening of films in the cinema and their diffusion on television (two years in place of three) and the obligation for transborder television to transmit a certain quota of European productions (France urged a minimum of 60 per cent; the amendment submitted for approval referred to a 'majority', and the obligation was only to be applied 'progressively and on the basis of appropriate criteria').

On this point, the April 1988 version of the EEC directive is much more constricting – as indeed for other provisions too. It proposes a quota of 'at least 60 per cent of air-time, apart from time given over to news broadcasts, sporting activities, games, advertising or teletext services'. Moreover, it proposes that stations 'reserve at least 5 per cent of their programme budget for community productions by independent producers', a target to be progressively increased to a level of 10 per cent. If French concessions to the Council of Europe accommodate countries like Portugal which refuse to give up *Dallas* and other soap operas in favour of French series like *Châteauvallon*, they are far from satisfying Gallic authors and producers who fear the erosion of the protection which they currently enjoy.[18]

A new episode in March 1989: the proposal for the directive, as amended in 1988, suffers a reverse due to the less constrictive terms advanced by the Council of Europe in relation to quotas. The obligation for television stations to transmit a minimum percentage of European production was renounced. The member states most opposed to the imposition of quotas (Britain, West Germany, Denmark) managed to win over a majority of the Twelve against the proposals of France, Belgium, Luxembourg and Spain.

Hollywood sighed with relief. These were the comments of the vice-president of Merrill Lynch & Co, one of the leading securities companies specialising in the communications industry:

> For the two contending parties, this is the best solution. Both the viewers and the media in Europe have need of our product, which in turn needs a public. It is therefore a rearguard action which the French government has been leading for the last few months. A battle lost in advance, as anachronistic as the Russian rejection of information technology which they have finally had to accept. In short, a useless struggle, because the Americans, with or without quotas, and following the example of French stations who know how to dodge the legislation, have managed to sell their programmes either by setting up companies in Europe or through coproduction.[19]

Finally, after many negotiations, the Twelve gave final approval to the directive on 3 October 1989 – with Belgium and Denmark voting against it. Article 4, taken from the Convention of the Council of Europe, invites member countries when practicable to reserve the major proportion of transmission time in the case of fiction and documentary films for European productions. A joint declaration of the Council of Ministers and the Commission specifies that this is a political obligation. To put it another way, Article 4 cannot in any way be considered juridically restrictive. The directive, then, is a legal text, except that as far as quotas are concerned it is only a declaration of intent, of which lack of fulfilment becomes extremely difficult, if not impossible, to subject to the sanction of the European Court of Justice.

Other aspects of the directive include the recognised right of each state to establish quotas for European productions overriding those fixed in Article 4, and the obligation 'as far as possible' to reserve 10 per cent of programming for independent producers. As far as advertising is concerned, it must not exceed 15 per cent *in toto*, with a maximum of 20 per cent in any hour. Amongst other stipulations, religious programmes, news and children's programmes of less than 30 minutes' duration may not be interrupted by advertisements. As for feature-length movies and television films, the directive repeats exactly Article 14 of the Convention (allowing one break every 45 minutes, with an additional break if the transmission is longer). Advertisements for tobacco, medicines and medical treatments remain prohibited, and those for alcohol are heavily restricted.

Despite the concession which limits the status of Article 4 to a mere declaration of intent, the government of the United States reacted energetically, declaring that it would appeal to GATT (General Agreement on Tariffs and Trade) against the decision of the EEC to limit the volume of foreign programmes shown in member countries – a decision incompatible, according to them, with the obligations of the EEC not to discriminate against foreign products.

PLANETARY CONSCIENCE

'European advertisers must defend their industry', according to an official of the international board of SSC & B:Lintas writing in *Advertising Age's* international supplement in February 1979. This is not his only professional function: he also used to be president of the European Association of Advertising Agencies (EAAA) and director of the European zone of the International Advertising Association.

To counter the wave of criticisms coming from consumer and environment protection movements, this European expert urged the advertising community to engage on all institutional fronts where advertising activities were at issue. He continues:

> Given the fact that the nature of such attacks is political and not professional – one generally is forced into political dialogue, invariably in defence of the freedom for the manufacturer to market and advertise his products – it is not hard to see why creative advertising

minds usually have little interest in and even less time to marshal a defence.[20]

Under the guise of encouragement, he drew attention to the first successes obtained by the united front of European advertisers, agencies and media with projects for the regulation of advertising activities proposed by the Economic Community in Brussels. What we have achieved, he commented, is that 'instead of regulation, [the Community] is now actively encouraging the industry to introduce its own codes of conduct and control.'

In June 1979, *Advertising Age International* reproduced extracts from a speech by the new president of the Federation of Advertising Agencies of Central America. He made the same exhortation as the Lintas executive, but in a very different social context:

> If we don't raise our voices in defence [of the advertising industry], what right will we have to lament that others attack it? . . . Not a day passes without someone criticising what has been called our 'consumer society' – words pronounced with disdain as though it were something obscene or immoral. . . . The freedom of advertising competition, the free distribution of budgets among different communications media, distribution based on marketing, not political reasoning, play a decisive role in guaranteeing that society has a mass communications system which is absolutely free and independent of political pressure of any kind. . . . To grow you must produce. To produce you must consume. The wrong is in producing little. We distrust those who incite us not to consume. That's their way of telling us not to produce, and not producing leads to poverty, and poverty brings to power those who are enemies of free enterprise, enemies of democracy, enemies of advertising.[21]

There followed a regular attack against government restrictions on advertising for alcoholic drinks and pharmaceutical products as well as the obligation for agencies using spots made abroad to deposit at home a sum equivalent to the costs of production.

In December 1980, *Advertising Age* opened its columns to a member of the council of the World Press Freedom Committee. The author of the article energetically assailed the report by the commission, headed by the Irish Nobel Laureate Sean McBride, which had been appointed a few months earlier by UNESCO. His thesis was that beyond the threats which weighed on the freedom of the press throughout the world, the international organisation had decided to undermine the very concept of advertising and the firms which created and sustained it. The article ended with a call for general mobilisation: 'I challenge the industry to rouse itself so that the sound in response to UNESCO's challenge to

advertising freedom is not a deafening silence but a thunderous roar.' [22]
In May 1982, at the 28th World Congress of the International Advertising
Association (IAA) in São Paulo, the president of Young & Rubicam
opened the debate with a violent indictment of the theses ascribed to
UNESCO and the McBride Report for 'wishing to suppress advertising in
the third world' (sic). The same year the European Association of
Advertising Agencies, the IAA and the World Press Freedom Committee
took their common objections to the American delegation at the conference on cultural politics organised by UNESCO in Mexico. This was the
conference where Jack Lang, the French socialist Minister of Culture,
made his famous speech about cultural imperialism. In May 1983, the
vice-president of J. Walter Thompson returned to the attack on the
occasion of the 36th General Assembly of International Federation of
Newspaper Publishers in London.

In the era of interpenetration of markets and enterprises, professional
groups can only have a global awareness of their interests. There is no
way, then, to understand the debates developing in the context of the
European Community without taking account of the emergence of this
global sense through organisations which operate on a planetary level,
and without considering other ways in which the 'transnational system of
advertising' takes shape.

One of those which have become strategic in the 1980s is GATT
(General Agreement on Tariffs and Trade). The question of advertising is
not its primary concern, but belongs, along with other economic sectors,
to the heart of its deliberations on the service society.

It was in 1982 when this body, which regulates international exchange
and represents nearly a hundred countries, initiated a programme on the
service sector, which brings together activities as diverse as financial
networks, insurance, telecommunications and data processing, as well as
advertising, marketing, management consultancy and auditing. In
autumn 1986, the plenary meeting at Punta del Este (known as the
Uruguay Round) began a debate on the liberalisation of exchange within
this domain. A particularly sensitive subject, given the huge global
disequilibrium in the control of the various networks involved: four-
fifths of world service exports come from the developed countries, who
also make up the destination of three-quarters of the sector's imports. In
an economy where so-called strategic services are related to companies'
competitiveness and productivity, there is increasing pressure to allow
these networks to operate freely on a planetary scale. At the centre of the
debate is the question of access to third markets without constraint or
control. The nations of the Third World, newly industrialised or not, do
not understand it in the same way, and are extremely reserved with regard
to proposals to do away with legal barriers. For even if Brazil has
adopted, in relation to the transnational advertising networks, a less

voluntaristic policy than India, for example, both agree on the need to protect the services of their young informatics industry and thus defend their national sovereignty. Brazil went even further by including among the basic principles in its new Constitution the idea that the domestic market forms part of the 'national patrimony'. But in 1990 the new President, the neo-liberal Collor, proposed to put an end to a protectionist policy more than thirty years old.

For the advertising industry, the challenge in their negotiations, which are multilateral and bilateral at the same time, is how to leap over the restrictions which affect them: the installation of foreign networks (forbidden or considerably restricted in countries like South Korea, India, Indonesia, Malaysia, Mexico, Nigeria, the Philippines, Thailand and Turkey); the repatriation of royalties or profits (a restriction which operates in countries as varied as South Africa, Argentina, Belgium, Canada, Denmark, Spain, France, Greece, Japan, Lebanon or Peru); the circulation of foreign advertising material such as films or videos (Australia, Brazil, Indonesia, Malaysia, Portugal, Britain, Nigeria); utilisation of a foreign language (Argentina, France, Mexico, Peru, Taiwan, Thailand, Malaysia).[23]

WORLDWIDE PROFESSIONAL NETWORKS

Ineluctably present in all the representative chambers of the community of nations is a single corporatist organisation which unites executives in advertising, marketing and media: the IAA. Although based in Madison Avenue, three-quarters of its membership is not American but belongs to seventy-five different countries. Supported by some 2,800 individual members, the IAA brings together transnational advertisers, the major advertising networks, and global communications enterprises as diverse as ABC, CBS, Globo, Axel Springer and Reader's Digest. Created in 1938, it was nevertheless only at the beginning of the 1970s that it acquired, at the same time as its multinational dimension, its character as a spearhead of the profession's international community. Its political efficacy rests on its network of forty-five national member associations, the latest of them in Popular China.

Its baptism of fire in the field of deregulation dates from 1973, the year the IAA published the corporation's first white book on the freedom to advertise, under the title *The Global Challenge to Advertising*. The programme included the construction of a 'strategic response to the attacks of governments and consumers'.

The objectives of the IAA include especially the following: to serve as spokesperson against unwarranted attack on restrictions on advertising; to expedite the exchange of knowledge, experience and ideas among its members to enhance the individual skills of each; to initiate and reinforce

117

national systems of self-regulation; to co-operate with national and regional marketing and advertising organisations; to establish and improve educational and training programmes in advertising; to improve the quality of advertising in established educational institutions; and to initiate and distribute studies and analyses relevant to international advertising. More globally, the IAA encourages its members and the advertising community to respect codes of ethics and especially the code of advertising practice of the International Chamber of Commerce (ICC), the basic text for all national codes of self-regulation.

Among the studies commissioned and promoted by the IAA is a series with the generic title 'Forbidden or Severely Restricted Advertising Practices'. Composed of reports produced under the direction of university professors, usually American or British, this highly professional series traces attacks on the right of self-regulation throughout the world and informs the reader of international discussions on the subject. It also deals with the taxation of advertising, systems of agency remuneration, or indeed with sexism, and the advertising of tobacco, alcohol and pharmaceuticals.

Its experts deal equally readily with the problems discussed in the Council of Europe or the UN Commission on the activities of transnational corporations. As early as 1979 the IAA made its presence felt within the principal organisations of the European Community. As *Advertising Age* reported in March that year, 'among other signs of the growing role of the IAA is its recent appointment as an official consultative body by the EEC Commission services charged with drafting marketing and advertising legislation'.[24]

In 1979 and 1983, the IAA organised two major conferences in Brussels on public service advertising. Their success was such that the EEC engaged the IAA as consultant for its own advertising – a task it fulfils to this day in concert with other organisations representing the European advertising industry. To be chosen as communications consultant for an organisation responsible for the regulation of advertising: this is indeed a public relations success story!

Another worldwide professional organisation is very actively involved in the lobbying issues in both national and supra-national arenas whenever advertising is questioned: the World Federation of Advertisers (WFA), set up in 1953 on the initiative of four advertiser associations – from Belgium, France, Italy and Sweden – under the name International Union of Advertiser Associations (IUAA).[25] In 1984, the organisation enlarged its scope and gained in stature, changing its name to the World Federation of Advertisers. With headquarters in Brussels, it is the only professional body exclusively representing advertisers and acting as their international spokesperson. The WFA's world network is made up of thirty-one national associations of advertisers, plus nineteen corresponding members. It also has twenty-four corporate members including American Telephone & Telegraph, Coca-Cola, Heineken, L'Oréal, Mattel, Nestlé, Philip Morris, Procter & Gamble and Unilever. This worldwide network represents over $170b annual advertising investment. The WFA has non-governmental organisation status with UNESCO, observer status with the WHO (World Health Organisation) and the FAO (Food and Agriculture Organisation) and a special consultative status with the Council of Europe and the European Economic Commission. It provides the advertisers' representational component of the European Advertising Tripartite.

Among the sensitive issues which face this professional body: the new European regulations on transborder television broadcasting and advertising; the challenges to the advertising of certain specific products, notably tobacco products and alcoholic beverages; sponsorship activities; harmonisation of television audience research data (a question in which the WFA assumed a pioneering role to identify the need for better media data on which to base investment decisions); advertiser/agency relationships (proposal of a set of contract guidelines); media-buying groups; taxation of advertising.

In addition to these transnational questions, the WFA assists its member associations, on request, by an 'early warning system' of actual and potential threats. Among the countries assisted by the WFA in 1988–89: Brazil, Canada, Costa Rica, Netherlands, New Zealand and Singapore (on tobacco and/or alcohol advertising); United States (on tax advertising); India and Morocco (on the identification of key advertising issues in these countries).

Defending the advertisers' right to freedom of commercial speech and the concept of free markets and free competition, the World Federation outlines argumentation which could be used by its members. It also produces a philosophy of advertising commonsense on the world events.

During the last few weeks one word, more than any other, has dominated TV screens, front pages of the press and radio news programmes throughout the World. That word is 'Freedom' . . . . The starting point of Freedom is to be able to speak out freely . . . expressing one's views without legal restraint and retaliation. It is indeed this basic freedom which has motivated the popular uprisings which have changed, almost overnight, the whole political framework of Eastern Europe. But there is, in the minds of some people, one freedom which is not sacred – namely, the freedom to advertise. . . . To single out the freedom to advertise a specific product is to strike at the very core of accepted human rights and freedoms since it denies people . . . the right 'to hold opinions without interference and to seek, receive, and impart information

119

and ideas through any media regardless of frontiers' (Article 19 of the UN's Universal Declaration on Human Rights). If legislators are allowed to apply what can only be termed 'political censorship', what is there to prevent them extending this to other areas where, for one reason or another, it is deemed necessary to circumscribe freedom of choice? This kind of censorship and restriction is just what the people of Eastern Europe have been seeking, successfully, to escape from. Thus, if advertisers do not wish to see their rights eroded, they – like the people of Eastern Europe – must beat on the walls of bureaucracy and insist upon being accorded the same democratic freedoms as everyone else in today's society.[26]

7

CHANGING ROLES
The new marriage of advertising and fiction

THE FUTURE OF AN OLD COUPLE

The problem of the debates about television without frontiers is that the argument about the ceiling on commercials has obscured the new stakes in the audiovisual landscape: advertising is no longer where the rub lies.

The centrality of the modern world of advertising, the multiplication of the interfaces between media and agencies, such is the intensification brought about by the process of privatisation and deregulation of television systems. The dream of vertical integration, projects for production and programming, the search for new genres, the desire for sponsorship, dreams of the creator, all testify to this aspiration to escape from the single role of producer of the advertising spot. In 1983, the producer of *Dallas* acquired the agency Kenyon & Eckhardt: a big 'first' in the culture industry of the United States. On signing the contract, the director of the firm of Lorimar indicated how far these two segments of the media industry are naturally destined to back each other up:

> 'We're not just a production company,' says ... Lorimar's chairman. 'We see ourselves as a communications company.' Besides its advertising business, K & E meshes with Lorimar in other ways. Its overseas offices, he explains, give Lorimar a local presence in selling programming – both its own and that of other producers – to foreign broadcasters. K & E also gives Lorimar a role in the barter of advertising spots for TV programming.[1]

In 1988, at the height of its success on the small screen throughout the world, Lorimar was driven by bankruptcy into the lap of Warner, while the advertising agency recovered its autonomy and merged with another American network.

Such is the compulsion of complementarity. At any rate it is not the desire for integration which is lacking, as demonstrated in 1987 by the last-minute takeover bid for J. Walter Thompson by the multimedia conglomerate MCA, and the purchase of capital in Saatchi & Saatchi by the Fininvest group of Silvio Berlusconi in 1989. But the move towards integration is less simple, and until now, few have managed it. The only firms to escape this rule are not new. They are neither American nor British: one is Japanese, Dentsu; the other is French, Havas.

Since the end of last century, Dentsu, which Tokyo journalists call 'the big amoeba', has been at the heart of the Japanese media apparatus. Today under majority control of the country's leading press agency, Kyodo, Dentsu started out by exchanging press despatches for the advertising spaces which it offered to advertisers. At the end of the Second World War, it was Dentsu's administrators and Dentsu's capital which made possible the installation of commercial radio and television. It purchased shares in one of the five commercial networks, the Tokyo Broadcasting System (conceived in 1951 as an alternative to public broadcasting) and in numerous local stations. Some years later, the number one in advertising followed the same strategy of buying in to cable television and participating in various teletext and videotext experiments. Index of its production potential: Dentsu produces 40 per cent of its television commercials itself. It also controls Video Research, the Japanese specialist in audience measurement.

Dentsu today represents 35 per cent of advertising receipts in Japanese television (a television which absorbs more than 35 per cent of the national advertising budget). It is the necessary partner of all big events like scientific exhibitions, sporting competitions, international fairs. It produces films. It has 6,000 employees in more than one hundred divisions. With its motto 'Communications Excellence Dentsu', its philosophy is 'to open new opportunities in communications and fill communications needs wherever they exist'.[2] Total communication. Vertical integration achieved through internal growth of the company to embrace the commercialisation of space, consultancy and participation in the media and production.

In short, Dentsu is one of the indispensable actors in the audiovisual landscape in Japan, whether public or private. In April 1986, Dentsu became one of the partners of SogoVision, created by the public television network NHK together with the country's second advertising agency Hakuhodo, three of the largest film companies, leading groups in the press and publishing, the electrical company Mitsubishi and the National Telephone and Telegraph Company (NTT). The new company's objective was to plan, produce, buy and sell programmes in anticipation of growing demand. Above all, to allow the prestigious national channel NHK to turn the corner of commercialisation smoothly. According to *Variety*'s Tokyo correspondent:

NHK, while anxious to get into the commercial arena to fully exploit its production facilities and large library of programming, is hesitant to appear to be 'going commercial'. It is, after all, Japan's broadcasting face to the world. In characteristically Japanese fashion, NHK is pursuing commercial opportunities at two removes and in combination with several big companies. First, it formed NHK Enterprises within the last year to exploit production and program sales. Now it has formed SogoVision. NHK's participation in SogoVision is via the NHK Enterprises subsid.[3]

NHK Enterprises, of which the Japanese channel owns only half, is supported in its new production policy by three banks who are also shareholders: Dai-Ichi Kangyo, Fuji Bank and Mitsui Bank. The alliance between Dentsu and NHK in SogoVision also coincides with a reorganisation from top to bottom of NHK's international activities. The aim: to classify and catalogue the public channel's 300,000 programme hours; to dub the programmes selected for international markets and promote them in English, French and Spanish; to increase international sales over five years from $13m to $26m. Excessively centred on their national territory, NHK and Dentsu, together and separately, are thinking increasingly in international terms.

Since its participation in the production by RAI of the series on *Marco Polo*, alongside Procter & Gamble at the beginning of the decade, the Japanese agency has advanced considerably in mounting frontier-free operations. Its objective is to become an international film producer. In 1988, Dentsu coproduced George Lucas's film *Dun Huang*, shot in China and based on a novel by Yasushi Inoue, the action taking place in Central Asia in the eleventh century. It placed its whole apparatus of research into sponsorship, promotion and organisation at the service of the launch of the film, and used the Japanese actors and period costumes in commercials produced especially for the Mitsubishi Bank.

In 1989, Dentsu reorganised its management and personnel to create a new business division: the Visual Software Division. Film production, selected television programmes (including a popular historical drama, several quiz shows and the hour-long news programme *News Station* that mixes reportage with segments of light entertainment) and video marketing, are handled by this new division. A sign of new transnational ambitions, Dentsu and a consortium called AKS each holds 50 per cent of a Düsseldorf-based satellite TV broadcasting company which transmits programmes in German and offers this European air-time to Japanese client–sponsors.

In many respects the French firm of Eurocom-Havas can be compared with Dentsu. They have a similar history in their relation to a big press agency. It was not until the end of the Second World War that the 'information' branch of the company was separated from its 'advertising' branch, following the expropriation of the Havas agency by the state and its transformation into Agence France-Presse (AFP). Both have in common a widely dominant position over the media advertising market: according to detractors, Havas controls more than a third of the space; according to its directors, not more than 18 per cent.[4] On the other hand, what in particular distinguishes the Japanese from the French firm is that the former's degree of vertical integration – especially in the audiovisual domain – bears no relation to that of the latter. Other differences are that until recently, Havas was a company of mixed ownership with majority control by the state, while Dentsu was privately owned; and that the international history of the French firm is much older than that of the Japanese.

Havas is a powerful publishing group – second to Hachette; it is a tourist business; it holds a monopoly on the electronic telephone directory; it is one of the controlling companies of France's first pay-television (Canal Plus); it has exclusive control of advertising on RTL's transmitters. It is the foremost French group in outdoor advertising; the leading specialist press group in France and continental Europe; the leading company in newspaper and magazine distribution in the regions. In advertising, it is the leading French group of agencies along with Eurocom.

Considered until recently the only French advertising group with a capacity for international credibility beyond Europe, Havas received preferential treatment by the government of Jacques Chirac at the time of its privatisation in 1987, as confirmation of its political and economic role as a national institution. If the group was virtually excluded from French commercial television, it was not dismantled. On the eve of its privatisation, it was learnt that the state would retain a golden share in the company. This measure would keep inopportune investors away, especially foreigners, who, like Maxwell, might wish to swallow up the leading French communications enterprise. It means that until 1992, the state can prevent any shareholder taking more than 10 per cent of the capital.

It was not the grandchildren of the supporters of the Popular Front who, on this occasion, crossed swords with the 'Havas Trust' (a term dating from 1936), but its French competitors. Rising up against these discriminatory practices, three rival agencies created an association called 'Democracy and Communication' and launched out:

> For some, the struggle against concentration and the notion of restrictions comes from retrograde and provincial behaviour. For at a time when very large communications groups are being formed abroad, nothing should be allowed to hinder the development of French groups capable of confronting them. The seemingly impeccable reasoning [re Havas] is in fact fallacious. . . . It is essential to

build up big communications groups, this is obvious. That said, the end does not justify the means.[5]

Havas protested the defamation and initiated legal action against those of its competitors (RSCG, BDDP and FCA) who had orchestrated the anti-Havas publicity campaign. The courts dismissed the case. The judge considered that if indeed Havas occupied a preponderant position in the Gallic media market, the court could not pronounce on the essence of the matter. Deregulation also has its reasons of state.

NEW PRODUCERS?

'We innovate. We are in process of setting up a production unit for sponsored television programmes. European television needs programmes. We're going to provide them for free, ready made. It's one of the best opportunities the market currently offers.' [6] Thus a senior executive of Saatchi & Saatchi told the press in September 1987.

If the promise is fulfilled, it will be an astonishing reversal of history. Is it not thanks to the alliance of broadcasters and advertising agencies that the American radio networks adopted the first programme schedules, with the effect of creating a regular mass audience? After convincing advertisers of the cogency of sponsorship, the big American advertising agencies launched themselves into production. A significant step was the restructuring of the old agency of N. W. Ayer & Son:

Gradually, it developed a staff of workers especially trained and experienced in the work; and in 1928, when the possibilities of radio advertising were clearly established, this staff was separated from the firm's other publicity work and organized as an independent department. Its duties were to assemble information about all phases of broadcast advertising, build up programs, hire talent, direct production, and handle the leasing of station time and all other details connected with broadcast programs.[7]

In 1929, one-third of American homes were equipped with a radio set. The weekly production output of an agency like J. Walter Thompson was twenty-three hours of network programming, only recently initiated, with a daily average of two hours and a maximum of five and a quarter hours on Tuesdays. All this financed by eighteen advertisers.[8]

When the American networks set up their European subsidiaries in the 1930s, this new know-how was already part of their baggage. Consider the history of the British branch of J. Walter Thompson. After the Depression:

Companies . . . were beginning to realize that advertising could extend beyond the printed word and, with the introduction of Radio

125

Luxembourg's English service in 1935, the agency set about converting a basement swimming pool into a recording studio. Sponsored programmes were the order of the day and JWT produced a portfolio of dramas and light entertainment that ranged from *Dan Dare* (for Horlicks) through *Opportunity Knocks* (for Horlicks again) to what should have been the unforgettable *Singing Joe the Sanpic Man*. Commitment to radio at the agency was so great that at one point almost half of all commercial programmes heard in Britain emanated from that converted swimming pool under the Strand. . . . But while the nation's living rooms were preparing for the exploits of Commander Dare (Pilot of the Future) and his trusty sidekick Digby, pilots of the time were scrambling to teach the Hun a lesson . . . JWT lost many of its young men, and its recording studio, to the war effort. Bush House became the centre of the government's propaganda effort.[9]*

One big advertiser in particular preferred to take up the reins of production itself: the detergent company Procter & Gamble. Backed up by various advertising agencies like Compton Advertising, Dancer-Fitzgerald-Sample and Leo Burnett, which produced the pilots for its radio and then television series, the world's foremost soap company and leading advertiser became the pioneer of a new genre, the soap opera. Every day of the week, every afternoon, for more than fifty years on the radio waves and more than thirty on television, American listeners and viewers (especially housewives – the primary target) had the pleasure of following the tribulations of the Bauer, Lewis and Spaulding families of Springfield, Illinois, in the series *Guiding Light* on the CBS network. More than 10,000 episodes have been broadcast since its launch on the radio in the winter of 1937. It was not until the savage deregulation of television thirty years later that this programme, conceived for a profoundly American market, crossed the Atlantic and was seen on the Italian network of Fininvest, then emigrated to the first channel in France under the title *Haine et passions* (Hatred and Passion).

This model of production, the direct responsibility of an advertising agency or an *ad hoc* marketing department of a big company, would be exported to Latin America under the aegis of Colgate-Palmolive, Lever, Lintas, and many others. Through a complex process of appropriation, Cuba, Brazil, Mexico and Venezuela in particular created their own televisual genre, the *telenovela*, which conquered the crucial hours of prime time.[10]

These Latin American countries in fact succeeded where Procter & Gamble until now has failed. When at the end of the 1970s the audience

---

* Bush House is now the headquarters of the BBC World Service. [Translator's note].

for melodrama was eroded in the mother country, the American company tried to diversify into other genres. After an absence from Hollywood of more than twelve years, it reopened its office on the West Coast and looked for new partners. This attempt is evidenced by productions like *A.D.* and coproductions like *Marco Polo* (with RAI). But it was not easy for these programmes to cross from daytime hours to prime time. In 1987, CBS failed the candidacy of Procter & Gamble and its four pilot series. According to one of the detergent company's executives: 'P & G will continue to pursue prime-time development, both on its own and in various production partnerships, including one with Culver City, Calif.-based MGM/UA Communications.'[11]

The real difficulty of the conversion of fiction to peak viewing hours seems to indicate that the synergy of publicity marketing and television production is hardly plain sailing. At the very least, they appear to have a very different logic of production. To achieve a qualitative jump, perhaps it needs a communications giant with the breadth of the self-sufficient Dentsu, which in addition to its own potential, is the point of convergence of such multiple alliances (like the whole interlaced Japanese economy) that no one knows who's who, nor what they do.

BARTER

In April 1989, the big media-buyers and the transnational advertising networks arrived in force at the international television programme market at Cannes (MIP-TV).

If the product was still far from matching declarations of intent, one thing is nevertheless certain: advertisers and advertising agencies are showing increased interest in sponsorship and television programme production. Everything is pushing them towards it. To begin with, there is a new kind of programme distribution called barter. The principle is simple: a transmission is provided ready-made to a television channel by an advertiser or advertising agency in exchange for advertising screen-time instead of money. The agency uses this space for its clients.

It is through this system of the swop that, thanks to its long American experience, Procter & Gamble sold to Berlusconi's network those soap operas which had never before crossed the seas. The Italian entrepreneur signed an agreement with the detergent company as early as 1981. In exchange for advertising time in the afternoon, Procter & Gamble undertook to provide 250 episodes a year of two of its most famous soap operas, *Guiding Light* and *Search for Tomorrow*. Through the same procedure, the other detergent company, Unilever, granted rights to TF1 for the American game-show *Wheel of Fortune*, in exchange for advertising space worth 90,000Fr per day; while Procter & Gamble got 270,000Fr-worth for its two soaps.

The system is flexible and has many variants. It applies to the most diverse range of programming: games, sports, news, fiction. From a more structural point of view, the novelty – although it is not such in the US – is the new synergy it produces. In January 1988, the president of Lorimar explained what it meant from the perspective of the transnational producer of series and television films: 'Achieving the full potential of barter will require a company to align itself closely with multinational agencies – and advertisers.'[12] The tightening of links between producers, advertisers and agencies within the perspective of the global market – this, in effect, is the long-term innovation brought about by barter. To prove this, it is enough to compare the recent upsets which have come about in the networks of programme commercialisation in the United States.

In 1987, three big American audiovisual producers (Paramount; Coca-Cola Communications (owner of Columbia Pictures TV and Embassy TV); and ORBIS Communications) allied themselves and brought all their barterable time under a single company, International Advertising Sales. In less than a year, five groups of this kind intensified concentration in what the Americans already call the 'barter-sales industry'. According to a protagonist of these developments: 'You're seeing more and more concentration of enormous amounts of barter dollars in fewer and fewer hands.'[13] Practically all the big television production and distribution companies have had recourse to these alliances on American territory. The latest, in April 1988, includes Metro Goldwyn Mayer/UA Telecommunications, Group W Productions and D. L. Taffner Ltd. One firm among the six television majors has resisted, namely MCA Television, which continues to sell its own advertising time for the programmes it produces and distributes. To give a simple indication of the space available in this barter industry: during 1987-8, Lorimar had no less than 10,000 x 30 seconds. And as for the air-space accumulated under the umbrella of Paramount-Columbia-Embassy-Orbis . . .!

A few people are disturbed by this movement of concentration. Like the executive of an independent company who thought that 'a powerful combination will have the leverage that will allow it to sell shows the buyer may not want in order to get the shows it does want. . . . Having only four or five companies calling on me with barter instead of 87 makes my life much easier.' But this system, he added, runs the risk of a reduction in the quality of programming. Precisely the opposite argument is used by the supporters of concentration, who believe that 'as companies get bigger and join forces, they're in a better position to finance good programming.'[14]

The impact of this practice on the television market is best assessed in relation to other structural changes: in particular, concentration in the buying and selling of advertising space by the media-buyers we spoke about earlier. Rationalisation of trade in advertising space at its origin, rationalisation of the final stage in the production of programmes forming the supply to the support.

Speculation about the future of the barter system in Europe is rife. In 1987, a London consultant, specialist in mounting prototype barter projects, went so far as to venture that 'by 1990 there will be three or four high-quality, advertiser-provided television programmes and series in Europe scoring high viewership ratings.' [15]

At the moment, what kind of production is it? Game shows, game shows, and more game shows. And then sports programmes, the sector of the television industry in which barter has succeeded in gaining most advantage, and which in current thinking comes closest to the global scenario. The international market for this kind of programme is in the hands of a small number of companies which organise the events, find the sponsors, assure them coverage and sell the transmissions. They are firms which offer their management and marketing services to the sports arena and athletic competition. One rarely finds them in the fiction markets of Monte Carlo or Cannes. The biggest are International Sport Leisure (ISL – based in Switzerland, partners with the Japanese giant Dentsu and the sports equipment manufacturer Adidas) and IMG, property of the international management group Mark McCormack, and its television division Trans World International (TWI), with headquarters in the United States. Headed by the erstwhile head of sports at CBS, TWI has offices in thirteen countries and production centres in New York, Los Angeles and London. TWI's portfolio of events includes Le Mans, the French football championship, open golf tournaments, the world skiing cup, Wimbledon, the Australian and US open tennis championships. From these studios come anthologies of the most outstanding sporting events. The Seoul Olympics were theirs: the sponsors recruited by Dentsu and Adidas, the television rights negotiated by IMG.

In the field of fiction, in addition to the old Procter & Gamble and its soaps, EC Television (an Interpublic Group subsidiary) began to produce *Monte Carlo*, a pan-European soap opera and *The Alliance*, an action-adventure series. (Through Lintas, Interpublic is also adapting *Wheel of Fortune* and *Jeopardy* to local tastes.) As for 'quality drama', it costs too much. According to an executive of the French media-buyer Carat-Espace, which is owned by another specialist in sponsorship, the British firm Aegis: 'Such productions will never be entirely financed by barter. That is why we are looking for co-finance partners. Ambitious works of this kind are of interest to big institutions: banks and insurance companies who want to project an image of quality and solidity.'[16] But here uncertainty reigns. At least, such is the diagnosis of the promoters of entrepreneurial patronage in France: 'A worrying problem, relations with television. On the little screen, patronage is close to nil, hidden by sponsorship of a more commercial and penetrating kind.' [17] Sailing boats, the numbers on the backs of team members, racing cars, attract the sponsors better than cultural creation. And even more so when sport, while scoring points on the advertising circuit for both corporate image and notoriety, is also a direct means of cementing general goodwill inside the firm. A symbiosis is found between the aim of footballer, the jockey, the tennis player or the skipper and that of the new winners in competitive enterprise.

ADVERTISING FICTION

If in 'quality drama' the new advertising industry is still looking for its way, in the case of other genres it is like a fish in water. *Informercials, Advertorials, Pubbligiornalismo, Publireportage* and more: the range of mediatised genres – audiovisual and written – enriches all languages with hybrid neologisms. Terms which erase the demarcation lines between news and commercials, advertising and editorial, publicity and journalism, publicity and reportage, between promotional surface and editorial content, advertising and the programme. Terms that are witness of a decisive change: little by little, the advertising industry proposes and engenders its own formulas and matrices. Composite genres, more in harmony with the mode of advertising.

Where does the programme end? When does it spill over into advertising? It is easy to tell when the spot lasts only 30 seconds, more difficult when it extends to two and a half minutes. According to an agency executive speaking in September 1987 at a seminar on the future of television advertising in Europe (organised by EAT):

> Supposing I put out a two-and-a-half minute item. To you it may be a commercial. To the audience it may be treated as a programme even though the commercial element is plain to see. Real examples of these exist. One such example is a series of spots – or are they mini-programmes? – shown in Germany by Coca-Cola and called Magic Music. They consisted of weekly two-and-a-half minute slots bought as normal commercial air-time but carrying excerpts from the latest pop videos and clips from forthcoming movies – all held together and heavily branded for Coca-Cola. These proved so popular with the audience (even though they did not like the presenter) that ratings apparently rose to such a degree, as the youngsters tuned in specially, that other advertisers tried to buy spots around them!

A query about how it works: is this spot-cum-programme counted as part of the advertising quota? The expert's answer: 'This drawing of the line between advertising and programming which is assumed in most of the legislation I have seen in and across Europe is obviously based on an outdated view of programming content and avoids the reality of the current and future financing of programming.' [18] Enough said. . . . This interpenetration of advertising and programme – which also happens in interactive children's series – is also a response by the advertisers (and programmers) to the rise in the practice of zapping the commercials.

The 'fictionalisation' of advertising and the increasing presence of the advertising mode in the production of fiction: two processes which give each other mutual support and consecrate modern advertising as the paragon of mediatised modernity.

It is still too soon to say for certain where the shake-out of the new formulas leading European television towards commercial operation will end. However, to know more, one can look at other environments where this logic has metabolised in the day-to-day mode of television production. Not to search for an image of Europe's destiny, but to try and capture how merchandise calls to merchandise, and the ordinary commodity lives within a perpetual sale, and the way the miscegenation of advertising, fiction and reality is produced.

From this point of view, the case of Brazilian television is exemplary, as we have observed. Born under a commercial banner – and in the case of Globo actually conceived by advertising people – it is today one of the most advanced audiovisual industries in the world. And its production of commercials is the measure of its modernity. The Americans are almost envious. As a journalist wrote in *Advertising Age*:

> An American visiting Brazil for the first time might be surprised at the sophistication of this country's advertising. But it would be no surprise to anyone who has been to an international advertising festival, where Brazil consistently puts on an impressive performance. Brazil ranks among the top 10 at the Clio awards and the International Film & Television Festival of New York. And Brazil is always among the top five prizewinners at the annual advertising festival in Cannes. Last year, it ranked fourth, with one gold lion, two silver and five bronze awards. [19]

Obviously the question of comparison with American television arises. 'Often, Brazilian serial ads take on an inside-joke, telegraphic quality because of the special hold the media has over the public.' The situation is a quasi-monopoly:

> One TV network – TV Globo – reaches at times as many as 90 per cent of the country's 17-plus million TV households. . . . When you've got a captive audience, you don't have to go back to the beginning of your advertising story every time you tell it. One can

just imagine what frequency one would get if most educated Americans watched CBS every night from 8pm to 9pm. The result is advertising that is up-to-date and rarely stale, offering Brazilians the chance to become part of the latest trend, current event, fad or joke. Ads often refer to characters in the nightly prime-time soap opera, or to the latest about-face in Brazilian economic policy.[20]

Here are the essential elements for understanding the symbiosis, through the advertising spot, of the various genres which make up the programming. But there is one other element which is integral to the very mode of production of the national genre of the *telenovela*: merchandising.

MERCANTILE FUSION

What the Brazilians call merchandising is an operation which consists of inserting commercial messages into text and images (dialogue, setting and personalities), transforming everything which occupies the space of an episode into a support. This practice goes back to the first radio soap introduced by Colgate. But it is now highly refined and in this particular domain Brazil has acquired a superior know-how to the United States, where the practice meets with the resistance of certain sectors of the public and of consumers' associations. At the beginning, given over to the raw appetites of secret advertising and comparable to greasing the palms of authors, actors and technicians, the practice gave rise, on the part of the institution of television, to rigorous codification, which at the same time as defining the limits, assured it a certain legitimacy.

Codification does not entail transparency. In effect the practice depends on the seal of secrecy. While we know all about the prices of conventional advertising, we know very little about the rules which govern the tariffs charged to the various companies who request this kind of 'merchandising'. To deal with the resistance of actors, directors, camera operators and other crew members, a financial consideration is included for everyone involved in the scene in which the product appears. Globo has become the grand master of merchandising, setting up its own merchandising sales agency (Apoio) in which thirty people devote themselves daily to analysis of the interaction of text and commercial product, to contrive opportunities for inserting products in a subtle and inoffensive manner. Most of the information to be found in the press about merchandising tariffs indicates that it is 40 per cent more expensive than commercials. Again, one must add that the cost varies enormously according to the brand, and a little-known product can pay up to five times more than an established one. And while advertising is strictly controlled by the law (fifteen minutes per hour), there is no legislation to act as a brake on the institution of merchandising.

The context in which merchandising has prospered is precisely that of a total legal void. It was only in 1978 that various organisations representing the media, the agencies and the advertisers agreed a code of self-regulation for advertising to try and remedy the situation. Two years later, the advertisers, agencies and media created an executive council for self-regulation (Conselho nacional de auto-regulamentaçao publicitaria, or CONAR). The inspiration for this code came from various sources: the International Chamber of Commerce (and its code of 1937, revised and corrected in 1949, 1955, 1966 and 1973); the directives of the IAA; the national code of ethics of advertising professionals adopted in 1957 at the first Brazilian advertising congress); and a group of recommendations put forward at colloquiums and seminars over the preceding years. The Brazilian code could not be more liberal. It authorises what is forbidden or strictly codified by the law in most of the market economies, particularly in Europe. It is thus overgenerous towards comparative advertising and alcohol and tobacco advertising, the only limitations being very general and moralising (prohibition against using children in alcohol advertising, not portraying the strength of the alcohol, etc.). If the code stipulates that the commercial and the advertiser must be clearly identified, and that advertorials must be identified as such so as 'not to deceive the consumer', there is only one mention of merchandising. It occurs in the appendices under the rubric 'alcoholic beverages'! It reads: 'Messages of a different kind which comprise what is called *merchandising* via television may only be transmitted between 9 p.m. and 6 a.m. with the exception of special sponsored events whose scheduling is not under the control of the media or the advertiser.' [21] In 1988, the Council for Self-Regulation of the Advertising Industry invited representatives of the artists to take a permanent place on this supreme organ of the advertising professions.

Asked about the practice of merchandising, the writers of *telenovelas* and series adopt three kinds of attitude or resort to three types of argument which indicate the diversity of attitudes.

The majority accept it as a constraint which derives from the very nature of the genre and its inscription within the market economy: the commercial environment of the *telenovela* only reproduces the day-to-day environment of the public, its immersion in the universe of consumption. Comments of this nature are at best accompanied by recommendations for discretion and subtlety. The strongest argument rests on the fact that, for the writer, merchandising represents part of the production costs.

The second position points out that if merchandising promotes consumer products, it could also promote 'community services': it could serve, for example, to show the population how to address letters correctly, or teach them new habits in matters of hygiene. It can serve ecological ends, like the preservation of the flora and fauna, or can publicise institutions which serve the public interest.

The third argument is more rare, even exceptional. Very few writers in the history of the *telenovelas* have refused to practice merchandising. One of them is Carlos Eduardo Novaes, author of *Chega Mais* (1980), in which he refused to have any truck with merchandising. Interviewed afterwards, he explained well the influence it could have had on the production: 'One of the reasons why the quality of the *telenovela* is so low is the excess of merchandising. My *novela* has none. I resisted because I would otherwise have had to make a series of concessions which imply the alteration of the characters.'[22] (It had been suggested to him that one character, proprietor of a fumigation business, be changed for a photographer, because Apoio had a contract with a manufacturer of photographic apparatus. Another suggestion was to introduce a dog because a dog-food manufacturer also had a contract with Apoio.) Novaes did not accede. But Globo placed various advertising slogans around the decor (and the author was deprived of dividends). Needless to say, the channel concerned has not shown a second *novela* by the same writer.

LEGITIMATE PLEASURE

The hurry of the advertising industry to assume the role of originating cultural products sometimes engenders strange projects. In 1984, the research group of a Parisian advertising agency received a request from a big publisher in the capital for a study on the development of a project called 'top-sellers' (a term adopted to distinguish the new concept from the established idea of the 'best-seller'). Through a semiological analysis of successful novels published over the preceding few years, complemented by a poll among readers, the idea was to discover an archetype which might become the matrix for a new fictional genre: a novel which would locate itself somewhere between the domain of 'literary creation' and that of the 'popular novel', the latter corresponding to romantic novels of the Harlequin type (similar to Mills & Boon in Britain), triumph of marketing and example of the book as consumer product *par excellence*.

Developed through testing, computer programs and even, according to precise rules, serial literature, the modern pink novel published by Harlequin – with its headquarters in Toronto and subsidiaries around the world – represents 215 million copies in ten languages, of which 45 per cent are sold in North America and 25 per cent in French-speaking countries. In 1985, 21 million were sold in France alone, with a life-span and distribution system the same as for romantic magazines. Sales in Spain reached 3 million in 1988, in the form of two series aimed at children and two others with more spice and excitement. To celebrate its fortieth anniversary in 1989, the Canadian multinational planned the simultaneous launch in no less than eighteen languages and a hundred countries of *A Reason To Begin*, the latest creation of one of the stars of its stable, Penny Jordan, author of some sixty novels with a sale of about 10 million copies.[23]

The 'top-sellers' project thus nourished the ambition to escape at one and the same time from the singularity of the 'literary creation' and the out-and-out serialisation. The chosen model for semiotic screening: *La Bicyclette bleue* by Régine Desforges, subsequently attacked for plagiarism by the heirs of Margaret (*Gone With the Wind*) Mitchell. Three other novels were selected to test the hypotheses extracted from the best-seller: *Le Roi vert* by Paul-Loup Sulitzer (defined as a 'mixed best-seller of masculine tendency'), *La Chambre de dames* by Jeanne Bourin ('feminine best-seller'), and *The Thorn Birds* by the Australian Colleen McCullough ('mixed best-seller of feminine tendency', which was turned into a famous mini-series on television).

Current practice in the French advertising milieu, this feasibility study for a new genre seeks to legitimise itself by reference to academic paradigms: it borrowed from the concepts of the linguist Vladimir Propp and his *Morphology of the Folk Tale* (used to identify the functions of the characters) and the sociologist Pierre Bourdieu (and various considerations of his on the economy of symbolic goods).

The reader of the 'top-seller' has two expectations: the expectation of pleasure and the expectation of enrichment. Two demands, two needs which are difficult to combine. The key to success is nevertheless their combination. The basis of the project was the following scheme:

Research into pleasure and the evasion of daily life	Research into enrichment of information organised according to a given scheme
But difficulty of accepting gratuitous pleasure an evasion	But what scheme? What authority? What knowledge?
A pleasure legitimised by:	A legitimate story

Syntactical advice to authors: use short sentences (never longer than five lines); highly simplified course of action; a breathless tone which connotes the imminence of a dramatic event; simple conjugation (imperfect, simple past); direct dialogue in the present tense; no preambles, no transitions, no oratory precaution; a dry style in the manner of cinema and even the television series, to allow for ready substitution between book and screen; easily imaginable decor; linear narrative continuity, with no backward turns or flashbacks; little punctuation.

How then to resolve the contradiction between expectations of enrichment and of pleasure, the tension between 'serious' and 'entertaining'? In short, how to legitimise pleasure? Answers: at the level of form, through what advertising people call 'indicators of authenticity' (quotations and references, and the legitimacy of the author); as for background, through 'true references, consensual values, symbolic exchange'; so that enrichment occurs in counterpoint with pleasure accomplished in the form through 'the principle of suspense, the system of implication', and in the background through 'participation, emotion, escape'. The result of the combination is 'pleasure in stories authorised by the truth of history'.[24]

The reference to history is omnipresent. The proposals are accompanied by the following advice:

> Historical references facilitate filching at the same time as the promotion of verisimilitude, historical culture and the seriousness of the book as an object. It is what links the book with a documentary code while lending it the appearance of a *feuilleton*. This is what differentiates a Harlequin from a top-seller.[25]

The recourse to history as legitimating agent is clearly recognised and underlined in the eventual design of the series' launch campaign: 'The label "top-sellers" guarantees pleasure in history and honesty of content'.[26]

'Legitimate pleasure' is the leitmotiv found at all levels of analysis of this marketing strategy for the creation of a middle-brow series. A cultural alibi – *exoneration* of the reader's guilt in the pleasure of reading (underlined in the text) – tells of the interplay between two legitimate purposes which each need the other: the pleasures of low culture, or mass culture, can be justified only through 'elevation', achieved by appropriating elements which indicate its other, 'high culture' ('legitimate enrichment: the pleasure of reliving an enriching story').

The apprentice producers of a new type of novel do not disguise the requirement of consensual values, aimed at guaranteeing the widest possible target audience:

> Its terms are as general, as legitimate, as possible. . . . The sense of the story and its moral must always relate to the existing social consensus. The book must justify this, argue it, reinforce it, to allow the reader to make it his own. Relationships between the characters must also be motivated by a morality which is only a reflection of the dominant morality. This is what confers legitimacy on the book as an object of social interchange.[27]

The conclusion which this inventory of common values required by the top-seller leads to: the book's educational and moral value. For this literature which borrows legitimacy from high culture at the level of the simulacrum, does so 'to allow the reader to make this morality his own'.

The document is a remarkable example of the paranoia of top advertising people, so to speak, and the case is unusual in a country where the long tradition of literary creation is far from legitimating such an approach. Does it happen in specially vulnerable sectors like children's publishing, for example, where prestige houses do not hesitate to entrust new series to advertising people? Be that as it may, it underlines what is normal in initiatives of this kind. This normality, to which intellectuals have rarely lent their attention, depends on the way in which concepts developed in academic research cross over into the field of marketing expertise. The way they serve, to paraphrase the language of these philosophers of advertising, as 'super-authenticators'. Here, in this paradoxical alchemy, and without the cognisance of the traditional intellectual, is to be found a crucial aspect of the interplay between 'high culture' and 'mass culture'.

Two centuries after the utilitarian philosopher Jeremy Bentham proposed a 'catalogue of the pleasures' to establish a network of regulation by assent, weaving a completely transparent link between individual, pleasure, community, calculation and legislation, the advertising industry has made progress in the old project of individualising pleasure.[28]

The logic which today claims to animate the management of the market for cultural goods (as manifest in the intentions of the emerging cultural-advertising producer) tries increasingly to reduce the margin of chance by attending as closely as possible to 'public expectation'.

With new encounters in every direction between advertising and the media world, one may ask if we are not approaching a new state of industrialised cultural production. The 'programme industry' is already singing a requiem for the old ideas of the 'production' and the 'work'. We have the management and adjustment of formats and formulas. With the introduction into the programme industry of the know-how of the advertising agencies, we get more measurement, more calibration, of product and consumer: in short, we get a little closer to the world of opinion polls.

A last word on the subject: there was a time not so long ago when advertising was a profitable business with no risks. It consisted basically in selling dreams (*pace* Jacques Séguela), with income determined by contract or the cost of time purchased from the support. One may ask if this irresistible desire to launch headfirst into ready-made cultural production is not likely to alter this simple scheme. Because the key, when considering this kind of product, is the public verdict. A sanction which until now the advertising industry has always managed to escape. Advertising as a high-risk business: this is what is on offer.

ARTISTS' ENTRANCE

The advertising industry possesses the financial resources required by its ambitions. Its audiovisual productions turn over huge sums of money. In the deregulated Italy of 1986, the contribution of advertising to the film industry was 280b lira, while the budget for the fiction film business was no greater than 200b. In Brazil in 1988, the difference was seven to one. The cost of a thirty-second commercial for McDonald's was equivalent to an average Brazilian feature film: $400,000.

Some 35,000 advertising films were shot in the United States in 1988, 7,000 in Britain, 2,000 in Italy, under 2,000 in West Germany, about 1,300 in Spain and 1,100 in France. The relative productive forces in advertising and feature production vary greatly from country to country. In France, film advertising represents 50–60 per cent of feature activity (in terms of numbers of days worked by technicians, use of materials and sums involved). In Britain, the proportion is very different: production activity in advertising is six times that of feature production.[29]

Matching the sums involved, the production of advertising has also become the privileged locus of experiment in synthetic animated computer graphics. In 1987, the cost of a second of synthetic image ranged between $8,750 and $52,500, depending on the complexity of the project.[30] The advertising industry has thus added a new role to its various attributes: that of the main mediator of modes of representation of modernity through new audiovisual technologies of image simulation. It was on the wings of a commercial for Michelin tyres that viewers in Britain – the country which has played a special role in Europe in developing the whole range of synthetic images – first became acquainted with this kind of commercial, made in 1983 by Digital Pictures. It took five months to do the job, but by 1987, infinitely more complex projects required no more than a week or two. In 1984, the Mitsubishi Space Wagon and Renault's 'Car of the Future' brought a qualitative leap to the commercial with films of richer meaning. In 1988, the winners of the advertising category of the Pixel-Ina prize, devoted to the best computer image productions, were Britain (which received two awards), Japan and Spain.

If the advertising industry is a hub for the development of programme formulas and matrices, it is also an important platform of work for artists, technicians and directors of films and television series.

'The commercial has saved Cinecittà' read the headline of the Italian journal *Communicare* in June 1987. In four years, the new team of managers had managed to save the huge cinema factory inaugurated by Mussolini in 1937 from destruction by attracting the producers of advertising films. Between 1983 and 1986 their contribution to Cinecittà's turnover rose from 10 to 30 per cent. The reverse of the United States, where 35mm film represents only 20 per cent of advertising production, in Italy it constitutes nearly 60 per cent.

Bit by bit, the arrival of these new clients is redrawing the map of audiovisual professionalism:

At the start things weren't all rosy. Here in Cinecittá, they were not accustomed to working on our type of product: a product that needs extreme attention to detail. A situation where everything has to be polished, practically like lacquer. You have to go beyond the papier-mâché image of cinema decor. In a feature film, nobody pays much attention to an ill-fitting door, and at first these technicians, who are the best in the world, got impatient with fulfilling our demands.[31]

The profusion of money and techniques has not succeeded, however, in banishing the old segregation. Another producer, who has shot more than half his commercials at Cinecittá since 1982, complains:

Italian cinema still entertains a provincial refusal to consider advertising an integral part of the film industry. It continues to think of it as like B-movies. This attitude persists in spite of the fact that the Italian advertising industry is now larger than feature production. They answer that it is not a question of quantity but of quality. . . . We are perfectly aware of the value of the film tradition represented by Cinecittá, whose heritage is one of the richest in the world. But we believe we bring a blast of pure, clean air. . . . The cinema of the future can only be born of a marriage between the traditional cinema of superior value and the cinema of professionalism, which is represented by the film advertisement.[32]

Few of the artists, technicians and film-makers turn up their noses, however. Many are happy to earn their living from advertisements, some enjoy shooting commercials for the pleasure of experimentation. As the actor Peter Ustinov remarked, 'I always have a strange feeling at the thought that in four months' acting on stage, one earns less than you get from a morning's commercial. The great Italian painters had the Church to subsidise them; today's patrons are businessmen.'[33] In France, for a well-known director to shoot a 30-second commercial can bring in 300,000Fr ($50,000); not counting the monthly retainer which directors charge for an exclusive contract from a particular producer. In the United States the rate fluctuates between $7,000 and $20,000 a day. A British director of photography gets almost £1,000 (around 8,000Fr); the French equivalent a bit less (6,000Fr) but rakes in another 3,000Fr in special charges. On the other hand, in these three countries the technicians, designers, hire firms, stunt men, make-up artists and actors are the most expensive in the world. Doubtless because, unlike other countries where most professionals in advertising come from television and photography, in Britain, France and the States they come from the film industry, where salaries were traditionally very high.

These costs of production are one of the factors which explain why French producers are deserting the country and shooting their commercials abroad; a reason no less important, however, than meteorology and the search for 'virgin landscapes'. Hollywood Chewing Gum vintage 1988 was shot in Venezuela, Orangina was shot in Puerto Rico, Four Roses in Australia, Belle des Champs and Cleopatra in Czechoslovakia and Hungary, Gervais in Morocco, and Cicatryl in Tel-Aviv Airport, while Vittel took to the New Zealand countryside to advertise its Eau des Vosges. The investigation by a journalist from *Communication/CB News* in June 1988, of the Cannes International Advertising Film Festival, illustrates perfectly this little-known development in the internationalisation of this increasingly determinant sector of the image industry. What are producers looking for abroad?

Mexico: Good climate, good laboratories, good technicians, an infrastructure as efficient as in Europe or the United States. Only the casting is restricted. Still there is a risk: there are so many commercials shot in Mexico that they have started using the same landscapes. This is why more and more producers are turning to Venezuela.

Venezuela: Well equipped while it was still a rich oil-exporting country, in the last few years its technical infrastructure – and competent technicians – have become available at interesting prices which attract producers from all over the world. A significant indication: while Paris has only three laboratories, in Caracas there are seven.

Brazil: With an audiovisual landscape of planetary dimensions, you find everything you need here: coproduction, excellent equipment (often new, which saves on the import duties incurred by having to bring it in) and superb casting, which even includes blondes!

China: Apart from a very good Technicolor laboratory, the country is technically under-equipped; but the amount of labour available, and the happy disposition and ingenuity of the people, means everything it lacks can be overcome. For instance, for the Citroën AX commercial, the Chinese did not balk at carrying cars up onto the Great Wall, on their shoulders, at night.

India: The world's biggest feature-film producer, India offers the entire infrastructure needed to do good work at low cost. An inconvenience, however, is the difficulty in obtaining permits for filming. It is therefore useful, there more than elsewhere, to shoot in coproduction with local companies; otherwise the law requires the presence of a government controller on location.[34]

Another face of internationalisation: the diversification of producers across the world. As evidence, the 1989 Cannes International Advertising Film Festival. Although Anglo-Saxon hegemony is still real (810 American and 480 British entries out of a total of 3,700 in the whole competition), other hubs of production are emerging, like Spain, with 246 entries; 325 from France; 267 from Japan; 216 from Italy; and 198 from Brazil. Britain won 36 'Lions', America 32, Spain 25 and France 20. The top award was given to the campaign by the Madrid agency Contrapunto on RTVE for Pippin, made by Nebraska-Perkins & Partners of Britain. For the first time, prizes were given to productions from Zimbabwe and Singapore, and even the Soviet Union sent three entries. Altogether fifty countries participated in this international festival founded in 1953 and organised by the Screen Advertising World Association, based in London.

Has the privatisation of public television perhaps accelerated national advertising production? Nothing seems less true, if you take the case of France. In 1988, one commercial in five was a direct adaptation of a foreign campaign, as against one in twenty, four years earlier.

CONFUSION OF GENRES

Everywhere agencies command the wallets of prestigious directors. Madison Avenue shoots with Robert Altman, John Schlesinger, and more recently, Nestor Almendros, who devised the commercial for the perfume Obsession. Spielberg has pastiched his own *ET* for Atari. In France, Roman Polanski has filmed for Kronenbourg beer and for *Marie-Claire*. Michelangelo Antonioni, Sergio Leone and the Taviani brothers filmed the Renault 9 and 18 advertisements, Claude Chabrol did the Renault 5, while the Citroën AX at the Great Wall was shot by photographer-director Raymond Depardon. Pierre Étaix and, a few months after finishing *Brazil*, Terry Gilliam took turns at shaking the Orangina bottle. For some directors, shooting advertisements during the long periods of hibernation between features has even become a habit. Chabrol, for example, has added to his filmography Crédit Lyonnais, Gervais, Weill, Winston, etc.

The opposite trajectory is also possible. For lack of other opportunities, young directors begin by flexing their muscles in advertising. For the new audiovisual generation, from Brazil to Italy by way of Spain, this does not even pose any problems, and the schizophrenia of their elders is a distant memory. In dictatorships like Chile before 1990, working on advertisements is the very condition of survival for many committed filmmakers, and the condition which makes the parallel survival of a national cinema possible. It can even be said that this apprenticeship within the world of advertising was of great assistance to the supporters of the *No* during the campaign for the plebiscite of 5 October 1988. The Chilean opposition, although divided and riven by contradictions, managed the media with greater facility than did the followers of Pinochet, and won the battle of the image. Faced with the heavy-handed propaganda of the *Yes* supporters, the commercials of the dictatorship's opponents, slim in means but full of emotion, astonished a military power which had consigned the left to the category of 'backward'.

But, above all, there are those who become celebrated because they have made brilliant débuts in cinema after many years of practice in an advertising agency: Alan Parker, Tony Scott, Ridley Scott (top prize-winner at the 1976 Cannes advertising festival for a commercial he made for the French magazine *Elle*) – in short the whole group of British film-makers, who before disembarking in California were only known for their commercials. A famous example, quoted and quoted again on Madison Avenue, is that of Adrian Lyne, also British, scion of J. Walter Thompson, and his film *Flashdance*. Dancing life: product of advertising, the musical comedy returns to advertising, inspiration for a line of commercials for jeans and fizzy drinks. These transformations are probably becoming more frequent, for times indeed have changed. 'Hollywood buys the advertising concepts', declares one of the top American directors of commercials, seduced by the seventh art:

> When I arrived in this city, they told me: 'You're from commercials? Out!' . . . But today it's changed. Out of commercials and MTV came a new film glamor that audiences see everyday. Audience responses to 'hot visual stuff' forced Tinseltown's powers-that-be to appreciate a commercial director's ability 'to put glitz on film' and handle a camera.[35]

The magazines of corporate advertising do not cease their praise – in every kind of language – for those who have given the commercial these new titles of nobility. Those who have managed to link the 'creative' image with that of the artistic creator. If the film-makers who have gone in for commercials remain more than discreet about this grey market of audiovisual production, the directors of commercials who have taken to cinema are gushing about the virtues of an apprenticeship in the agencies. 'Advertising', claims the Frenchman Étienne Chatillez, who spent fifteen years in commercials before directing for the cinema, 'is the most creative domain, the most daring. Turn on your set. Within three seconds you know where you are. A film, one sees something sooner or later. A television film? Hell with shitty lighting and awful sound. Nasty. Adverts? The height of ellipsis, collision. State of the art.'

In its sudden ascent, the advertising industry gets out of hand. Reportage, visual puns, cinema, montages of still images, burlesques, videos, homely vaudevilles, cartoon strips, musical comedy, mini-operas, animation. The self-promotion of the commercial as a crossroads of genre, support and the most diverse forms of aesthetic expression, with the wind in its sails. At risk of cruising straight out onto the high seas of megalomania.

The hypertrophy of the market can only sharpen the tension between 'creation' and 'creativity'. The multiple encounters of the world of advertising and cultural production have been extended to all forms of expression. The fabrication of images by the advertising industry tends to sow discord in the field of artistic creation. Here is an example and a testimony.

In June 1988, an unprecedented event: a French museum with a high reputation, officially dedicated to the plastic arts, opens its doors to photos and drawings by an advertising 'creative', the very same who just over a year later was crowned on the Champs-Élysées as mastermind of the pulsating carnival parade for the bicentenary of the French Revolution, broadcast to more than 700 million television viewers. In the preface to the catalogue of the exhibition reigned ambiguity: the flux between advertising and the plastic arts. Point of attack by the art critic of *Libération*:

> Let us be clear: art does not possess a superior value to advertising. Each responds simply enough to two radically different types of aim which are sometimes antagonistic. Whether it is better to be an artist or in advertising is a question of no interest. . . . It is time to remember that relations between art and advertising have existed for a long time. . . . Advertising assumes on its own account and for its own use a certain number of formal inventions produced by artists. The use of Magritte is the most significant case. Conversely, it happens that certain artists have been inspired to incorporate a message or image of advertising, assimilate or reformulate it in their own manner. One need only cite the example of Andy Warhol. . . . Artists can pick over advertising like no other source for their own needs. Advertising, on the other hand, at least certain people within it, believe they have need of an artistic 'plus' in order to disguise a little their mercantile activity. Must one insist that it is clearly no dishonour to gain a living by selling images? But it is the very development of advertising, its 'brand image' which promotes confusion. . . . How can one hope to familiarise the public with the complexities of ongoing research, if this incites the thought that wherever there is an image, there is necessarily art? This, at best, only gives evidence of incredible naïvety.[36]

8

AUDIENCE MEASUREMENT
Towards a bar-coded world?

OBSERVATION

There can be no advertising network without a research network, no media and no campaigns without a fixed apparatus of evaluation, both quantitative and qualitative, of audiences and targets.

The end of the era of rationed advertising space has upset established ways of conceiving the audience and its measurement. Media-buyers like the agencies must provide advertisers with sharper information in order to direct their investment in television more effectively. In the highly speculative context of an explosion in the supply of advertising space, data on audiences must justify the accuracy of this or that placement. Observation of the ebb and flow of audiences, programmes and products has therefore entered a new phase. To grasp this shift the better first requires a little archaeology, a review of the period which is now coming rapidly to a close.

The first media observers were set up in the 1920s, when the first private research companies got started. The founders were George Gallup, Claude Robinson, Daniel Starch and Arthur C. Nielsen. The patriarchal symbols are those of the Nielsen ratings, an international index of audiences, and Gallup, synonymous with opinion polls.

George Gallup started out on a university career in Iowa with a thesis on journalism. The subject was the extent to which readers of newspapers remember what they read, the first step towards the study of impact. Item by item, he tested samples of both news and advertising. In 1932, he quit teaching to join Young & Rubicam, which he left in turn in 1935 to set up his famous institute with Claude Robinson, a colleague from Iowa. Their heritage is the Gallup–Robinson technique, which registers the memorisation of a message by classifying recall according to whether the brand-name only is registered or the message as well ('reading and noting test').

Less well known internationally, Daniel Starch, doctor in psychology, also from the University of Iowa, started his own institute in 1923, and bequeathed to advertising the Starch technique: the classification of

144

magazine readers according to the degree of penetration of an advertising message. (Has it simply been seen? Appropriately identified? Carefully read?)

The year 1923 also saw the creation of A. C. Nielsen Co. Nielsen's first initiatives had little relationship to the media world, in fact they were performance surveys of engineering and other equipment, not unrelated to the time-and-motion studies introduced by Taylor. Nielsen's vocation for the media thus assumes the character of a diversion from his original focus. The first Nielsen Index responded to the needs of the pharmaceutical and food industries, for which representative panels of dispensaries and retailers were set up throughout the country in order to measure the flow of selected goods and thus build up a database on market share information. These were the Nielsen Drug Index and Food Index. Before the end of the 1930s, the same panel techniques emigrated towards the field of audience measurement, and in 1939 Nielsen began to employ the first mechanical listener-measurement devices – ancestor of the Audimat – perfected for the firm by the famous university institute of MIT (Massachusetts Institute of Technology).

Only Britain has a similar prehistory of audience research, with the establishment of the BBC's Listener Research Section in 1936, under the direction of R. J. E. Silvey of the London Press Exchange, who according to the historian Asa Briggs, built up 'a wide-ranging and effective listener (and later viewer) research organisation'.[1] Newspapers also gathered their own statistics, and further evidence was collected by the independent pressure group Mass Observation, who published a survey in 1939 called *Broadcasting in Everyday Life: A survey of the social effects of the coming of broadcasting*. According to the authors, broadcasting was 'so revolutionary a change in national and international communications', that it must be reflected 'in the everyday life and tastes and points of view of us all. There is much talk of the influence of wireless, yet very little study has been made to determine what that change consists in.' By contrast, the radio and television audiences in France only became the object of systematic study in the 1960s.

In 1929 comes a big first in US entrepreneurial history: the soap company Procter & Gamble sets up its own market research department. Its mission was to poll the reactions of consumers to feed its marketing strategy. The semantics of the time are still close to the terminology of police enquiry and the new professionals are called by the same professional title as FBI detectives: investigators. From this specialised department emerges in particular the method known as DAR (Day After Recall), developed jointly with Dr Gallup to measure the recall of an advertising spot. This measure of memory traces, twenty-four hours after exposure of the subject to the message, is directly indebted to a technique used for training pilots in the Navy in the 1940s. To the credit of Procter

& Gamble's new department was the diffusion in particular of a manager/ marketer model. A veritable school of hypermodern enterprise management, this high-quality model was to spread in the 1950s when the firm decentralised its research to its twenty-six foreign subsidiaries. Today, anyone who serves an apprenticeship with the detergent company is equally appreciated in big publishing houses and leading supermarkets.

ANTAGONISTS AND PROTAGONISTS

The emergence of a private apparatus for research and consumer investigation arose within a context dominated by what the historian Stuart Ewen has defined as 'mass participation in the values of the mass-industrial market'.[2]

The decade of the 1920s is effectively that of the process known as consumptionism, celebrated by Christine Frederick in a famous book published in 1929 under the title *Selling Mrs Consumer*:

> Consumptionism is the name given to the new doctrine; and it is admitted today to be the greatest idea that America has to give to the world; the idea that workmen and masses be looked upon not simply as workers and producers, but as *consumers* .... Pay them more, sell them more, prosper more is the equation.[3]

The official histories of the American advertising agencies agree, however, in considering the great depression of the 1930s to have played the decisive role in the real inception of private research in the service of advertising, advertisers and the media.

The worldwide crisis was particularly harsh for the agencies (several of which had only just internationalised themselves). In 1929, advertising expenditure fell by 25 per cent. It reached its lowest level in 1933, with the advertisers' budgets reduced in four years from $3.4b to $1.3b, that is, the same as in 1914. Two-thirds of the agencies disappeared from the scene over this period.

Additionally, the survivors had to confront the virulent criticism of the nascent consumers' movement. Emerging from this movement, a research organisation, Consumers' Research Inc., was established in 1929, which responded to activists by undertaking the first studies to test the value of different products and the veracity of advertisements. The organisation published its first report in 1932 under the title *100 Million Guinea Pigs*, the most effective of all attacks against advertising and selling of that time.[4]

Evidence of the effervescence and contradictions which play around consumption, a dissident movement was formed in the 1930s called the Consumers' Union of the United States. Its concern was 'the need for a pro-labor consumer organisation functioning on a broad social base, democratically controlled, and serving especially the worker, the low-salaried employee, and the housewife.'[5]

With the rise of new forms of consumer protest, the characteristic theory of the consumer as captive clientele was strongly shaken; namely, the theory which holds that the consumer has only the choice between two positions: to continue buying the accustomed product even if it satisfies less, or decide to purchase a competing one. The various consumer movements show that the dissatisfied consumer has yet another option: to speak out.

The multiple pressure of these movements opens a period of close intervention on the part of government authorities intended to control the activities of advertisers constantly inclined to claim the right to self-regulation. In 1938 the Federal Food, Drugs and Cosmetics Act is revised, and the basic law of control over marketing, selling and advertising is thus recast.

Summing up these times of tension on the threshold of the contemporary period of deregulation, *Advertising Age* admitted that 'the consumer movement and the anti-advertising legislation which flourished in the 1930s aroused marketing people to the need for documentation of advertising's social usefulness.'[6]

Indeed this period saw the creation of the Advertising Research Foundation, on the initiative of the advertising industry itself; its first activities date from 1937; its first patron was Mrs Alfred W. Erickson, widow of one of the founders of the agency McCann-Erickson; its first study was entrusted to a professor of advertising at the Harvard Graduate School of Business Administration. The project took four years to realise and in 1942 a report running to more than 1,000 pages concluded with the following diagnosis: 'So long as individual enterprise flourishes and a dynamic economy continues, advertising and aggressive selling will play a significant social role.'

Collaboration and interchange between the advertising industry and academic milieux in the United States began in the early 1920s, with the contributions of erstwhile university professors Gallup and Robinson. There was also the contribution in 1922 of John B. Watson, founder of behaviourist psychology and later vice-president of J. Walter Thompson, where he put into practice his ideas on the need to eradicate, according to his own statements, the social attitudes which resist consumption by proposing a formula of the satisfaction of needs by commodities – commoditised sensual gratification.[7] But also, and above all, the whole of functionalist sociology – standing in opposition to the European sociology inspired by Durkheim, Mannheim, Weber and Marx – found it entirely natural to lend its authority to the theorists of the study of the market.[8]

These first forays by enterprise for recognition of the idea of the universal democratic marketplace through the intervention of advertising and marketing were interrupted by the bombing of Pearl Harbor.

During hostilities, the advertisers and agencies associations lent their services to the Office of War Information, the American government propaganda bureau. They created the War Advertising Council and appointed an executive of Young & Rubicam as the first president of its administrative council. After Japan's capitulation, this organisation put on civvies as the Advertising Council. A non-profit-making organisation, this permanent body has since then brought together resources and talents from the three links of the advertising chain in order to offer voluntary campaigns of aid in the solution of major social problems: all the issues for which, in Europe, the state became the advertiser. Every year the council orchestrates more than twenty campaigns with a budget equivalent to almost a billion dollars in time and free space offered by the media, and lends technical assistance to a number of similar initiatives by other institutions.[9]

That, at any rate, was yesterday. The questioning of the Fairness Doctrine has affected precisely the obligation for radio and television stations to devote part of the air-space to causes of public interest. This places in doubt the early conquest of the first consumers' movement in forcing agency and advertiser to think socially.

DUOPOLY

In contrast, it seems, to the crisis of 1929–33, the flow of advertising investment has not dried up with the recession of the 1970s – proof that advertising is considered by more and more companies as productive long-term investment. This, at least, is what the official doctrine of the big networks and the major advertisers affirms.

According to Saatchis in its 1980 Annual Report:

For many companies this new approach has been the result of experience. The recession of 1974–5 saw many advertisers reducing the advertising support they gave to their brands – the long-term risk was often discounted by the short-term need for profits. US research has now quantified for the first time the long-term sales effect of different responses to advertising in a recession. This major study, of 468 US corporations spending $11 billion annually on advertising, showed that those companies which maintained their advertising investment in the last recession were rewarded by short-term and long-term sales growth significantly in excess of those companies that looked for immediate returns by reducing their expenditure.[10]

Moreover, maintaining the level of advertising expenditure goes together, in the case of the big advertisers, with the increased rationalisation of their budgets, as evidence the discussions of the needed deregulation of the current system for the remuneration of the agencies.

A significant illustration of this desire to exert more control on the other partners in the advertising process (agency, media-buyer, support) is provided by the Telescan episode. In February 1985, the FCC annulled the obligation on television stations to provide their clients with a complete listing of commercials broadcast, whereupon the Telescan company proposed to the market a new method of automatically monitoring television commercials. Each commercial was to carry an invisible digital code that could be read by a computer whenever it was broadcast. Using Telescan – the name of the proposed device – the advertiser could verify if the commercials were indeed transmitted both within the hours scheduled and complete, and if colour and sound were satisfactory. Other companies, like Nielsen, proposed similar services. The FCC approved the process despite heavy resistance by the television stations, who objected that the signals needed could degrade the quality of the images.[11] A process in which technological innovation and the restructuring of the private apparatus of research renders the new reality by refining its instruments of measurement.

The international industry of commercial research, and in particular that of audience measurement, is extremely concentrated. Two firms effectively control the world market: one is American and one British (as in the financial press). The first is A. C. Nielsen, with its two divisions: the Marketing Research Group (with offices in twelve cities in the US and subsidiaries in twenty-six countries); and the Media Research Group (eight US offices and five abroad). The company's international turnover represents around 60 per cent of its activities. This explains the weight Nielsen has exerted over sixty years, together with the multiple connections of the mother company because Nielsen, not long ago, lost its independence. The audience measurement specialist was taken over in 1984 by Dun & Bradstreet for the tidy sum of $1.3b, three times the price paid by WPP for J. Walter Thompson.

On the strength of massive investment in technology and successive acquisitions, the more than 140-year-old American company has progressively diversified to the point of metamorphosis into a paragon of the global information society. Dun & Bradstreet offers its clients strategic information, logistics and a whole range of services: credit, insurance, finance, energy, human resources, marketing, air transport, education, etc. Its National Business Information Centre holds information on more than 7 million firms updated daily 'to ensure that decisions affecting tomorrow's profits are not based on yesterday's data'. Dun & Bradstreet owns the travel agency Thomas Cook; they publish the official airline timetable and the *American Journal of Cardiology*, not to mention a range of technical magazines and the famous Moody's Investors' Service, indispensable instrument for every self-respecting financier.

Nielsen's English competitor is AGB Research. Founded at the beginning of the 1960s, it has almost 3,600 employees in more than twenty countries. Its main activity is market studies. But the company also publishes some thirty magazines on security, office equipment, commercial fishery, the transport industry, etc. Some 46 per cent of its turnover is in Britain, 23 per cent in the US (with its subsidiary NFO), 16 per cent in Europe and the rest in Australia and the Far East.[12]

Seven out of the ten biggest commercial research companies are American. The others, AGB apart, are German (GFK-Nuremberg and Infratest). The Dentsu subsidiary Video Research comes a little lower on the list. Notice the separation: the turnover of Nielsen in top place was ten times that of number ten, and more than five times that of AGB. Obviously not all these companies are specialists in audience measurement: on the international market the two main rivals are Nielsen and AGB; in the American market there is also Arbitron. But none of these firms is exclusively dedicated to this job alone. On the contrary, all these bureaux are closely related to the media and advertising industries. On the one hand, they form the base for the opinion poll business and for this reason connect with the most diverse sectors and themes. On the other, several of them feed the advertisers directly or indirectly with information concerning the effects of their investment in advertising on the movement of their products.

The ownership structure of these marketing and opinion poll research bureaux is extremely mobile and many have changed mother company or status over the last few years. To attempt a typology of the main features of their links with the information and communication industry, among the top twenty companies we find:

—— three advertising agencies: J. Walter Thompson-WPP and its MRB division; Ogilvy & Mather, which in 1987 bought Unilever's subsidiary Research International with its network of offices in twenty-nine countries; and Saatchi & Saatchi, which in 1985 acquired the American firm Yankelovich Clancy Shulman;

—— three media firms: (i) Time Inc., proprietor since way back of SAMI, which in 1986 bought out Burke and its international network in twelve countries (Japan, Argentina, Brazil, Australia, Canada, Belgium, Denmark, France, Britain, Italy, West Germany and Sweden). In 1987 SAMI/Burke became partners with Arbitron, owned since 1967 by the computer firm Control Data, but in 1989, Arbitron sold Burke, which in 1990 entered an alliance with IRI; (ii) the ABC/Capital Cities network, which has controlled Chilton Research Services since 1979;

(iii) the press group Gannett, owner since 1975 of Louis Harris & Associates, one of the most internationalised (43 per cent of its turnover comes from abroad; with its main offices in Paris and London, the firm also has a presence in half a dozen other countries).

Of the leading companies in the US, only IRI was still independent in 1988, the year in which Gallup, then relegated to thirtieth place, lost its autonomy. Evidence of the restructuring going on in the international research industry: in that same year the press baron Robert Maxwell, while failing in France in his attempt to infiltrate Havas, succeeded on the other side of the Channel in acquiring AGB, and reached agreement with Dun & Bradstreet to take over the Official Airlines Guide; in 1987, Dun & Bradstreet had unsuccessfully launched two savage takeover bids against AGB and IRI. Worried about the elimination of competition, the Federal Trade Commission blocked the IRI partnership with Nielsen. In 1988, they bought out the third-largest research company in America, IMS, founded in 1954 and, with some sixty offices abroad, an international specialist in information on the healthcare and pharmaceutical market. There is no more evidence needed, then, of the synergy circulating between the research industry and global communications.

Two factors in particular are currently stimulating the internationalisation of the network activities of the major research companies in the 1990s: the growing demand for pan-European research and the need to monitor the buying patterns, behaviour and values of the uncharted consumers of East European and Soviet markets. An example which illustrates the first of these trends is that of Nielsen, the European market leader. After buying up several research firms in Britain, Italy, Finland and the Netherlands, it opened an office in Lucerne in Switzerland specifically to deal with so-called multicountry research. Its first subject of pan-European study, Quartz, provides simulated market tests for marketers preparing to launch a product. Nielsen was also awarded the contract for pan-European TV audience measurement in eleven countries by Pan-European Television Audience Research (which includes the BBC, RAI, Sky Television and two German-language satellite channels). Its rival AGB, Europe's third-largest market researcher after Nielsen and IMS, has launched a European Market Measurement Database with its partners in the Europanel consortium, GFK and Secodip.

As for the call of the markets of the East, there is the offensive by the Gallup network, which has carried out the first surveys of Soviet consumers, while Nielsen has concentrated its efforts in East Germany, and the German firm GFK has undergone accelerated expansion in East Germany, Hungary and Poland. Young & Rubicam has such ambitions in the Soviet Union that it has appointed a full-time Soviet research director, formerly a researcher with the Institute of Sociological Research of the Academy of Sciences, and has offered to restructure the information held by the Soviet Chamber of Commerce and Industry and Goskonizdat, the official ministry for data collection, into a database.[13]

BAR-CODED WORLD

'Over the past five years', confided the research director of Procter & Gamble in 1987, 'new ways of reading consumer behaviour have emerged, and most are electronic; that will continue. That provides people who study consumer behaviour with an immense, rich new database.'[14]

Infoscan, Behaviorscan, Scantrack, Scantrack-Plus, Scan-America, Samscan and a whole lot more: the language of the scanner has moved out of the hospital and the clinic to invade marketing and private research on the media. It designates, in the first place, this new electronic brain which, attached to the television receiver, registers the presence of an audience, the channel being viewed and the length of time, given the viewer's complicity, since each member of the household signals their presence by pressing their own identification button. As well as these audience measurement devices, it also designates the new optical bar-code readers used to register home purchases. This was precisely one of the aims of the takeover bid launched by Nielsen's mother company for IRI: to bring the two measurement specialists under one banner, to force the marriage of the first company's 'Peoplemeter' (a push-button device to measure the audience individually) with the bar-code reader of the second, thus to relate exposure to advertising messages to purchasing behaviour. This intermix can only intensify, precisely to the degree that the number of retail outlets equipped with bar-code readers is extended: 20% in Europe in 1989 (ranging from 5 or 6 per cent in Italy to 33 per cent in France), compared with 60–5 per cent in the United States. Projection for 1993: an average of about 40 per cent in Europe. The logic of the intersection of audience flux and the flux of purchasing behaviour was never perceived so crudely until Berlusconi took possession of one of the biggest supermarket chains in Italy, Standa, in 1987.

The big boys are positioning themselves to enlarge their share of the individual television audience measurement market. There were victories celebrated by the British company AGB in its annual report for 1985–6. In the Netherlands, its subsidiary Intomart had obtained a five-year radio and television research contract. Its mission: to install 4,900 push-button audience meters (AGB model), adapt the apparatus for cable television which already reaches 70 per cent of homes, and measure viewers' appreciation of the programmes. In Italy, it has carried off the five-yearly contract awarded by Auditel, an organisation of television station proprietors, agencies and advertisers. In the United States, AGB tried to purloin part of Nielsen's quasi-monopoly, an attempt which was doomed to failure. In South-East Asia, research contracts and acquisitions have given AGB a dominant position in the region, and it has even acquired a majority share in the Japanese market leader ASI Market Research of Japan. And revealing the general preoccupation with frontier-free operations, the British company was engaged to carry out the first investigation of the pan-European audience.

In the race for contracts, every kind of tackle is allowed. AGB thus circulated a letter among agencies and the media in France openly denigrating the services offered by its American rival, who naturally replied by taking legal action.[15] But it served for nought, since a third contender carried off the French television contract. Supported by the main advertising groups, the private institute of Médiamétrie eliminated AGB, despite AGB winning the first round, as well as the Franco-American tandem Sofres-Nielsen. A Swiss process, Télécontrol, already installed in Switzerland, the Federal Republic of Germany and Belgium, took preference. But this did not prevent Sofres-Nielsen installing its own competing Peoplemeter network in parallel.

The obsession of the quest for increasingly sophisticated audience measurement is this: to leave behind the simple counting of heads and go further in counting levels of attention. But the smallest grain of sand, the smallest non-programmed gesture, jams up the whole apparatus of calculation. Since most of these indices require the active participation of their sample – they generally employ a push-button remote-control – the measurement process still depends on the viewer's co-operation. According to a report by Nielsen on the use of .the Peoplemeter, one of the problems is that 'children do not consistently push the buttons they are supposed to when watching television'.[16]

It isn't only children who fail to behave the way advertisers imagine. In 1989, a new British agency, HHCL (Howell Henry Chaldecott Lury) dared to challenge the credibility of the whole system of audience research operated by the British Audience Research Bureau (BARB). A self-advertisement for the agency in the *Financial Times* showed a couple making love in front of a television set, with the legend, 'Current advertising research says these people are watching your ad. Who's really getting screwed?' Thames Television was so appalled that they withdrew their £5m account with the firm.

'It is absurd to assume people *watch* TV if they sit *in front* of it', said one of the firm's directors. People have the television on in the background. 'Numbers give a false sense of security.' The same is true of readership surveys which do not reveal whether the reader has really read the paper, rather than just glancing at it. HHCL argues instead for qualitative research: in-depth, carefully targeted, discussion-type interviews with potential customers as the basis of research. This approach has won the agency major contracts from such companies as 3i, Fuji, Exchange & Mart, and Midland Bank's First Direct.[17]

ANSWER WITHOUT QUESTION?

In other places, with other audiovisual landscapes, other ways have been developed to mitigate the logic of numbers by a cross between modern poll and rating methods and the ruses of artisanal know-how.

Brazil is again a representative case in the field of audience management. In the early days of its audiovisual system, it refused to place itself in the hands of Nielsen and instead created its own institute, the Brazilian Institute of Public Opinion Studies and Statistics (IBOPE), founded in 1942 by a local professional. Today, IBOPE is an index as famous in Brazil as the Nielsen Index is in the United States. This has only been the case since 1970, when Brazilian television was truly modernised under the emblem of the Globo network.

The essential difference is that while the hyper-competitive audiovisual landscapes of deregulated Europe in the 1980s were unquestionably dominated by an obsession with distribution, in the Brazil of the 1970s with its captive audience for private television, the main concern was production: to connect the management of the audience with the development of their own television genres. The history of audience measurement in Brazil is that of the progressive construction of social links. In this television system where the main genre, which may well run to 150 episodes, is inconceivable without the continual feedback of the various sectors of the population, IBOPE is at the heart of an apparatus with several investigative branches.

Various kinds of feedback enter into the production of the text, and here, no doubt, lies the deep singularity of this form of dramatic creation. The first kind is provided by the opinion institutes, and especially the research and analysis division of Globo. Among other things, groups of viewers are regularly invited to give their opinions on the script and the characters. These measurements of opinion, some of which are highly technical, are accompanied by an analysis of the abundant correspondence received by the channel and the author. The author completes the feedback with his own system of response, rather more personal, day to day and do-it-yourself in form. According to the scriptwriter Aguinaldo Silva:

> My daily help returns every evening to her home in the *favela*. She tells me every day of the reactions of the passengers on the bus and the people in her neighbourhood to the previous evening's episode. Yesterday, for example, they asked her to tell me that it wasn't

necessary to send the leading character, Roque Santeiro, away from the city.

The originality of this mode of writing lies in the fact that the author continues to produce the text while it is already being screened, and can incorporate the reactions of the public, make changes and corrections, etc. In this special temporal reality of the *telenovela*, the author counts on its continuation to develop the characters. The creativity of the actors can induce him to modify the initial line of certain characters, according to the new dimensions which their interpretation reveals. However, an important reservation must be made: the genre is highly codified. Almost invariably the heroes meet each other in the thirtieth episode and spend the remaining 120 resolving the obstacles which get in the way of their love. But to a great extent, the public guides the dramatic evolution. Its reactions inflect the situations, the characters and the course of the narrative.[18]

Technology follows technology, it is said. Yet nothing is less true when it comes to the present state of audience measurement techniques in Venezuela. This country, with a television and advertising industry no less powerful than before, was still in 1988 debating what kind of audience measurement technique would suit the growing needs of the advertisers. At the beginning of that year the agencies and advertisers and television companies still had no fixed system. J. Walter Thompson offered a periodic qualitative study carried out in 860 homes (3,000 people) in Caracas by its own investigators who went from house to house leaving questionnaires which they collected a week later. Also the company Datos offered three types of measurement: TV Check, the oldest method going back twenty years, carried out four times a year and measuring when the set was turned on and the preference for one channel or another; second, a periodic telephone investigation (12,000 phone calls between 6p.m. and 10p.m. over a week and limited to the capital); and last a study called 'Recall' (1,200 interviews on a national scale). This is a panorama of devices which takes us back to the time when French television had not yet entrusted fixed audience measurement to the French firm SECODIP, with its Audimat meters.

For lack of agency interest, the introduction of audience meters in Venezuela at the start of the 1980s met with failure. And yet in those years a local firm had approached SECODIP and tried to link the participants in the advertising process in a project to assemble the French devices in the country.

In 1988, an electronic engineer at Simón Bolívar University had proposed his own audience meter. He evaluated the audience not in terms of individuals (like the Peoplemeter) but in terms of homes: the method employed by most of the European systems until recently. The installation of this national audience meter in some 100 homes began in June. A problem: the lack of telephones. According to the engineer, his device offered two choices: it is either linked to the telephone in the home, 'or if there is no telephone, to a recorder on the side of the set . . . . In Caracas there are 513,000 homes with telephones (63 per cent penetration). Difficulties are found at the D/E level', i.e. in the lowest social classes.[19] The problem lay in how, faced with the lack of equal opportunity for access to a telephone or recorder, to guarantee the democracy of audience measurement?

It is too easy to ascribe the problem to the South. Are we so sure this is the right question to be asking? Far from it if we turn back to the Europe of deregulation. Because there, the whole experience of technological progress scarcely conceals its sociological inconsistency.

This takes us back to debates which took place in the United States in the 1960s and which did not receive satisfactory answers. Those years opened an era of suspicions. In the dock there were two firms, A. C. Nielsen and Arbitron, which shared the audience measurement market. The charges were the refusal of A. C. Nielsen to furnish details on its samples and its weighting procedures; the impossibility, therefore, of verifying the accuracy of the indices produced by the quasi-monopoly. The courtroom: Congressional Hearings, a democratic institution unique in the world, in which American parliamentarians summon and question witnesses to investigate different issues, from the government's cultural foreign policies to the life of the country's biggest enterprises and groups. In the course of the hearings in 1961–2, testimony was taken from numerous experts from within the advertising industry, from ordinary citizens and from university media scholars. The conclusions made clear the lack of methodology applied by the two firms in their television audience measurement.

In 1975, concerned by this loss of legitimacy, the Advertising Research Foundation proposed a project comparing the methods used in television with the techniques used for magazine readers. No one in the sector voted in the project's favour. 'Apparently, there was less interest in exposing error than in maintaining an uninterrupted flow of data to justify advertising media decisions.'[20] This is the lesson flourished before us by Leo Bogart, one of the fathers of American sociology of public opinion and a researcher for several years now for the Newspaper Advertising Bureau of New York.

In an article entitled 'Mass advertising: the message, not the medium', published in the *Harvard Business Review* in 1976, Bogart expressed his concern over the power of life or death which these measurements had over the programmes. A discretionary power, so that in 1975, for example, three series programmed in prime time at the start of the season had disappeared from the small screen by the following spring without having had a chance to find their public.

A good many years afterwards, his comments have a special resonance:

Changes in the media, with all their tremendous consequences for the flow of information and the character of public taste, are not made by popular request. They do not reflect the 'democracy of the marketplace'. Rather they result from the decisions made either directly by advertising buyers or by media managements anticipating advertiser demands; they are decisions made by the numbers . . . . The percentages in most media research no longer represent real people whom somebody actually questioned; they are percentages of IBM cards. This change in procedure qualitatively transforms the relationship of the research analyst to his data. At any rate, most of the people who deal with media research statistics are not analysing them; they are quoting them, either to sell advertising or to justify their purchases of advertising to their clients or employers. Users of the numbers don't want to be bothered by what they regard as trivial technical matters, and so, for a quarter of a century, since the beginning of regular syndicated research, they have been sweeping the details under the rug . . . . The mistakes made as a result of this process may not hurt the advertiser, since his competitors are probably making the same mistakes, but they do have serious consequences for the mass media, and for society.

Without reaching this level of discussion about the relationship of audience measurement to society, at the end of the 1980s the polemic was renewed within the professional milieu more strongly then before when it emerged that the Nielsen ratings were unable to evaluate the phenomenon of zapping. Geared to quarter-hourly figures, the observation of this viewing habit which occurs in the main at intervals of less than five minutes, escaped the American firm. On the horizon this time was a greater worry: how to weave an operative link between audience measurement and the elaboration of strategies of programme production capable of putting a brake on the zapper's slalom-ride.

Another contentious issue weighs on the search for more concise statistical tools to evaluate the performance of newly segmented media. But beyond the questions raised about fixed audience measurement, which deals primarily with the mass public, a further suspicion has arisen about the real effect of mass advertising. The world's foremost advertising market is confronted by a decline in advertising investment in the major networks. In the course of the decade, their audience has fallen in favour of cable and video. In the evening, during prime time, it has gone down from 92 to 67 per cent; and in the afternoon, from 77 to 57 per cent. For 1989, the estimated rate of growth for advertising on cable and local television was 25 per cent, against 1 per cent for the networks. To counter the fall in the audience, the networks have refused to reduce their tariffs but offer shorter spaces: a reduction from slots with a duration of 30–60 seconds down to 15 seconds – with a growth in the latter from 2 per cent in 1981 to 38 per cent in 1989. The first who complain are the 'creative' staff, who with such an accelerated rhythm have great difficulty in establishing brand-name differences between the product they are plugging and the competition.

To reduce the element of chance, there is an outbreak of new methods of electronic research: experiments with samples of viewers through the installation of miniature cameras in their sets; the application and conversion of military detection systems.

The hyper-competitive European audiovisual landscape has become a laboratory, and has given birth to 'outsiders' in the audience measurement international market. The fruit of extensive investment and three years' work – in the greatest secrecy – the engineers of the French company of Bertin, specialists in optical electronics, have developed the Motivac. Placed beneath the TV set, the device is able not only to count the number of viewers, but also to recognise the channel viewed and video recorders in use, all without human intervention. With this instantaneous audience reading, advertisers and TV stations can trace the reception of a transmission, while Nielsen ratings are not available until the following day. The Motivac 'eye', a wide-angle lens focused on the viewers, 'sees' the fringes of nearby infra-red waves and captures all luminous sources in the room. To distinguish living bodies from lifeless objects, the apparatus analyses the variations in each source. Computer chips sort out the data. An expert system analyses the signals, memorises them and traces their variation in time. Clients for this system can extract data on, for example, the number of women aged between 30 and 40 watching a given channel at a certain hour on a certain day, or how many agricultural workers in a certain region were watching another, and at what time. In 1990, these passive Peoplemeters migrated from France to the United States by way of Arbitron.

The French company O'TV – an agency specialising in television advertising investment and a joint subsidiary of HDM and Young & Rubicam – has bought the rights to the British C-Box system. The system combines a receiver, normal in appearance but containing a minuscule camera, with a battery of recorders all software-controlled. The company then installed this spy-camera in a sample of homes in the Paris region, where nevertheless those being spied upon still have the option of not sending the investigators the tapes that have been recorded! As opposed to Motivac, this is not a fixed form of measurement but rather, one might say, a sample for an ethnographic study. This qualitative jump in audience investigation is helped by the appearance of new actors like the centralised media-buyers, hopeful of entering the field of production. This we learn from the new services offered to advertisers and programme producers by Carat-Espace. Thanks to a permanent panel of 1,000 people, liable to be questioned at any time, its subsidiary Carat-Laser offers instant analysis on public reactions, carries out tests, checks on schedules, evaluates transmissions, and measures the decline in the audience for any particular programme.

What yesterday still awakened democratic suspicions, because it was like the instruments of high surveillance of the private citizen, enters imperceptibly into commercial mores. The Taylors of consumption have appeared. And already certain 'Doctor Nos' imagine that they will soon be able to place miniature capsules into guinea pigs to monitor facts and behaviour.[21] Thus the absorption of the market in collective and individual life ceaselessly pushes back the limits of the intolerable!

9

THINK TANKS

The bestiary of 'lifestyle culture'

WAR GAMES

The era of planetary logic and savage takeover bids is peppered with military metaphors – metaphors which have long been present in the language of research about targets. It is almost trivial to observe that without this code of warfare, the mode of expression of advertising practices would be deprived of a large number of its guiding concepts: target, impact, penetration, strategy, campaign, etc.

Sign of the times: in September 1986, the Harvard-*L'Expansion* award was given to a work called 'Third-Wave Marketing' (*Le Marketing de la troisième vague*).[1] Its author, professor of the Faculty of Business Administration at the University of Ottawa, analyses the concepts of strategic marketing and their practical application according the principles of the art of war. To confront competition, he proposes to draw lessons from the great masters of military strategy.

The progressive shift to warlike reference began at the end of the 1970s. In March 1979, London hosted the first European seminar on 'The Marketing War'. With the slogan 'What works best in warfare, works best in advertising', the promoters were AMR (Advanced Management Research International) and the Marketing Society, two of the biggest corporate organisations in the American management and marketing industry. Taking the Prussian General Carl von Clausewitz as its guide, the seminar began by reviewing four types of belligerent conflict: offensive warfare, defensive warfare, flanking warfare and guerrilla warfare. Among the methods recommended for guerrilla warfare were those available to small companies, which take account of principles like 'duration of combat' and 'use of surprise'. Based on practical case studies, the seminar demonstrated how small companies could use speed and agility to compete in markets dominated by much larger competitors. One session was devoted to 'weapons of the future':

> The rapid development of micro-technology is providing an impressive array of computing-based weapon systems for marketing

warfare. Weapons for market surveillance, interpretation of market intelligence, and for the simulation of campaigns are available in profusion. The problem will be to match the weapons to the need of the organisation, and to train the [troops] in their effective use.

The keynote speaker was General William C. Westmoreland, and among the organisers were research executives from firms like Twentieth Century Fox, Playboy Enterprises, H. J. Heinz & Co., Playtex and Johnson & Johnson. A while later, a French version of the same event was held in Paris.

In the same way as the doctrine of globalisation, the enrolment of marketing and advertising in the war game was far from producing unanimous assent. Some even went so far as to say that its reduced vocabulary disguises the misery of strategic thinking, like the professor of enterprise management at Cornell University, Karl Weik, who readily affirms that the repeated use of military metaphors seriously limits our faculty of reflecting intelligently on the questions of management. This is because people resolve problems by analogy, and if they use a military analogy, this requires them to resort to a very limited class of solutions, and it consequently limits their creativity to a reduced range of organisational modes in the enterprise.[2]

Military semantics have close links with the original conceptual matrix at the basis of the advertising approach: the linear theory of information and its stimulus–response scheme. Still referred to as 'the theory of the hypodermic needle', it postulates that message X necessarily corresponds to effect Y. The Y effect, for the advertising industry, is the adherence of the consumer, measured in terms of the value of sales of the product advertised. The art of war and the linear theory share the same determinism. Both envisage the target as a passive recipient, a patient without defences. Essentially this is a question of detecting the traces which the message leaves in the memory. This presupposition has served to guide an important number of investigations into knowledge: not only the measurement of the audience but particularly evaluation of the 'memory factor' and noticeability. A group of problems first posed by Gallup, Robinson and Starch in the 1920s. In evaluating the prompted or aided memory, these techniques for the measurement of immediate impact combine with those which scrutinise the loss of memory over time, that is the remnant of a message, its medium- and long-term effects.

In their search for a method reliable enough to appreciate the effectiveness of advertising campaigns, advertisers and advertising studies have undoubtedly favoured questions of memorisation and brand reputation. The indices of memorisation have become indispensable tools: the measurement of brand awareness is used to predict the memorisation of advertising activities, and in the case of product launches, the development of sales. The chosen indicators were the first brand mentioned by people being questioned from among the brands corresponding to the product category; spontaneous awareness measured by the percentage of people capable of mentioning the brand unprompted; prompted awareness corresponding to the proportion who claim to recognise a brand from a list; advertising awareness, or identification of advertising campaigns (the proportion of interviewees who claim to have heard or seen the message as against the proportion who identify the brand correctly). The quantification of the remembered results of media exposure leads to knowledge of the limits of individual cognitive capacity for each category of product, and thus the adaptation of marketing strategy.

This battery of tools to evaluate the effectiveness of communication following a launch is complemented by the range of 'pre-tests', that is, tests prior to the launch, in which the envisaged advertising material is tested out on a sample. Here are some examples. First, laboratory tests, with the help of measuring tools such as the tachistoscope (for variable-speed exposure to an advertisement); reading tests (using a special 'eye camera' to record ocular movement, the movement of the eyeball back and forth with pauses and their length); linguistic and semiological tests (ease of reading, capacity to attract, analysis of vocabulary, and semiotic tests to track the phenomena of coding and decoding). Then come complex simulations involving a real campaign on a reduced scale. Last, there are interviews following prompted exposure; the 'folder-test' (using a set of different versions of the same advertisement which are tested on a sample group who are questioned immediately, or one or two days later); experimental review (insertion of test advertisements in real publications); and family tests (a short video including a programme and the advert is shown to a dozen families in their homes).

Doubtless these methods of evaluating the efficacy of advertising still have a great future before them. They are a necessary accompaniment to globalisation strategies. It is equally true that the advertising industry long ago abandoned the model of the conditioned buyer, known as the stimulus-response model, in the crude version put forward by the American Watson in the 1920s. Other models, equally linear and determinist, have taken over: for example, the models of the hierarchy of learning (DAGMAR, AIDA and several others*) which consider not only levels of knowledge or cognition, but also levels of sentiment or attitude. These represent successive stages which the potential buyer must supposedly go through before embarking on purchase.

Also, the times are changing. According to Saatchis' annual report for

---

*DAGMAR: Defining Advertising Goals for Measuring Advertising Research; AIDA: Attention, Interest, Desire, Acquisition.

1984, we are in another cycle. The implication of consumer brand respect is of another kind.

> When probed deeply, consumers describe the products that they call brands in terms that we would normally expect to be used to describe people. They tell us that brands can be warm or friendly; cold; modern; old-fashioned; romantic; practical; sophisticated; stylish and so on.
>
> They talk about a brand's persona, its image and its reputation – and this 'aura' or 'ethos' is what characterises a brand.
>
> The relationship that consumers enjoy with a brand is therefore a complex mixture of rational and emotional factors. The balance varies, brand by brand, product category by product category. In some categories, rational factors tend to outweigh emotional ones – in other words, the consumer rates functional values higher than emotional values. At the other end of the spectrum, there are many categories where the emotional relationship between the consumer and a brand is at least as important, if not more important, than the functional relationship . . . .
>
> The two elements of the relationship are completely interdependent – the emotional building on the functional, the functional underpinning the emotional.
>
> It follows that all brands, like all people, have a 'personality' of one kind or another. But like the strongest individuals, the strongest brands have more than mere personality – they have *'character'* – more depth, more integrity, they stand out from the crowd.[3]

A classic text if ever there was one, illustrating perfectly what Marx analysed with the term fetishisation of the commodity, or the process of personification of inanimate objects, which parallels that of the reification of persons. That, however, is not the crux of the matter.

SECRET LIFESTYLES

It was in the 1970s when the applecart was upset. The exponential growth rates of the 1960s disappeared, and with them the slick notion of a consumer carried forward by the idea of endless progress. This period of uncertainty and crisis destabilised in turn both the classical economic model of the rational purchaser and that of the purchaser conditioned by behaviourism.

Towards the end of the 1970s, an attempt to loosen the hold of such unidimensional visions produced the inverse notion of 'cultural variables'. This is the role of 'lifestyle' surveys, or in the French advertising tradition, the investigation of 'socio-cultural currents', which began in the US and have been adapted to the particular conditions of each environment where they are developed.

Their development results from the incapacity of the traditional tools of psychology (too subjectivist) and economics (too rationalist) to give adequate account of the phenomenon of the consumption of products or messages. A notable reaction, therefore, against the psychologism which underestimates or ignores the role of social determinants in behaviour. The project of 'lifestyle' studies is to define the coherent profiles and homogeneous typologies of consumers–viewers–listeners–readers which are brought together in individuals. A matter of logging socio-cultural mentalities as 'large ensembles of individuals united at the same time by their condition of life (habitat, social class) and a system of values, priorities, ideas and norms to which they adhere.'[4] These blocks are hewn into 'socio-styles' by playing with purely cultural criteria (consumption, mentality, values). Observation of the evolution of these social typologies allows 'flow' and 'currents' to be registered, without capturing either their origins or their causes.

On consulting these classifications one learns, for example, that French television viewers in the early 1980s could be grouped according to three 'mentalities': those of utility, progress, and reassurance. The first is sensitive to rigorous and strict advertising language, that is to say, discourse which is not quite advertising, as long as there is no seduction in it. As for adherents to the mentality of progress, the televisual image, precisely through its movement, is perfectly suited to satisfy their permanent quest for movement, and the fascination which comes from the use of the most sophisticated techniques is very useful. Because what it comes down to is catching and convincing those who believe in perpetual innovation. Lastly, there is the mentality of reassurance. The preferred language here is demonstrative and honest, stuffed with guarantees and assurances. Does that mean austere? Certainly not. Balanced between audio and visual, its obsequious, even sensualist language resorts by preference to signs, symbols, images and metaphors. All the better, then, for advertising which, in addressing their imagination above all, makes them dream a little more.

One can also learn that around 1978 there appeared the category of 'disconnected persons' (les décalés) and that 'rigorist' currents characterised the 1980s; that rigorist reassurance covers 'executives', 'conservatives' and 'moralists', while the galaxy of the disconnected is inhabited not only by disconnected persons but also by libertarians, activists, dilettantes, opportunists and the enterprising. One also learns that dominant currents have been succeeded by contradictory currents and the most pronounced tendency to emerge will be that of withdrawal, amongst many other things.

A new concept of study, a new form of organisation of work and the market, these 'lifestyle' studies tend to present themselves as precision instruments. Their promoters are thus obliged to provide new data at regular intervals in order to update their results and follow developments in progress. This trend towards building up professional databanks is rarely mentioned by their users, and it is appropriate to ask about this silence. In fact, in the framework of these macrostudies, the exploitation of information (and the technology it presupposes) becomes a greater budgetary cost than the collection of the information, despite the size of the latter. This produces a reversal in the habits of the profession which deserves to be signalled since, at the same time, the cost of fieldwork continually goes up.

In France, the size of the investment required to carry out these studies has led to the rapid creation of a quasi-duopoly between the CCA (Centre de communication avancée of Havas) and Cofremca. Effects on competition in this area are difficult to assess. The CCA possesses a databank with 35,000 variables, and questions a panel of 3,500 people every two months. The public, specialised or not, knows absolutely nothing about these methods, the detail of the figures and the investigations carried out ten years ago on which the classifications are based, which therefore makes debate impossible. This drove a sociologist to observe that 'the CCA achieves the tour de force of selling and popularising a body of knowledge whose existence has never been demonstrated.'[5] A different situation is found across the Channel, where the concept of 'lifestyles' was taken up by the press at quite an early stage in its development.

What is the balance that the French advertising industry draws from this socio-cultural 'mapping' (to use the expression employed by the CCA)? The answer is that right across the profession these studies have fulfilled a pedagogical function: the construction of a code common to the milieu, plus a lesson on the character of the social and how to talk about it. It is a description, according to one advertising executive, 'which at least had the apparent merit of putting forward a unified vocabulary throughout the chain from the advertiser to the advertising practitioner . . . . That is important when you know the gaps which can crop up in the chain of production in advertising.[6]

To which the marketing director for the French subsidiary of Nestlé adds:

Lifestyles are part of the search for an understanding of the consumer and help to expand it, giving better aim at the target through integration with an increasingly complex environment apparently without structure. In a society in full economic, sociological and ideological mutation, the avowed ambition, which consists not only in understanding and explaining but also predicting, can only seduce the marketing people that we are. But this seduction must be compared with the irritation, even exasperation, which the initiative also provoked; we don't like to remember the controversies it gave rise to (secret, esoterical language, fashionable trends) . . . . We recognise in lifestyles their help in having us reflect about communication, which has been much more enriching than mere socio-demographic criteria. We have moved from the portrait of a robot offered by the latter (woman of 35, living in a city of 100,000-plus, with 1.5 children, active, housewife) to that of the photo-novel (hedonistic, polysensual women, sexually liberated, who seek materialist pleasure and like living in convivial groups). The recent evolution of the lifestyle approach which combines customs, behaviour and socio-styles, seems to provide an image which is not so blurred, halfway between the rational and the emotional . . . . For the industry it is important, because of a double preoccupation with innovation and communication, to have a process of reflection and points of reference that introduce intelligible order into the flux of disparate information which inundates it.[7]

As might be expected, sociologists and political scientists dig into socio-styles somewhat more seriously: these studies offer virtually nothing new; even worse, they foretell the past. The sociologist Nicolas Herpin has ironic things to say about the social use of socio-styles: consulting specialists in 'social meteorology' is the equivalent of animal sacrifice prior to sea journeys carried out in antiquity, performing the function of psychological appeasement for decision-makers, and of demonstrating respect to the gods of the marketplace.[8] While the political scientist Érik Neveu tears to pieces the pretence of these studies to renew our knowledge of the social:

The bourgeois gentleman spoke in prose without knowing it. The experts of the CCA are in a comparable situation. They reject academic studies as dogmatic and impotent . . . . For whoever knows the forms of knowledge and the analytic tools which were forged decades ago by researchers of various sensibilities in Europe, North America and the Third World, the pseudo-revolution of the CCA can only leave them astonished. Astonished by the inspired imprudence of the promoters of the socio-styles enterprise. They almost persuade themselves they have reinvented learning when, in 1986, they come up with a translation of social logic and evolution analysed and scrutinised by others a long time ago. Astonished above all by what the success of this literature among decision-makers, advertising people and other 'modern' entrepreneurs seems to demonstrate. If the CCA teaches little about French society, it reveals a great deal about the sum of naïvety, prejudice and ignorance which characterises a large number of our economic executives, to the point where they take a simplistic card index for knowledge and believe the moon is made of green cheese . . . . Every thought can be bought at the take-away: even the sad demonstration of an increase in 'assistance mentality', references to Jean-Jacques Servan-Schreiber, praise of leaders, an absurd Anglo-Saxon jargon which crosses the marvels of modernity with those of erudite esotericism.[9]

If these studies first saw the light of day across the Atlantic, France is their promised land. Why? The need to legitimate advertising practice by means of a game-playing element within a hostile cultural environment. Also to construct a language of sociologese to oppose to the critical sociologies which were then predominant. With their appearance of worldly amusement, destined to impress and attract an audience made up of officiates and bosses, the multiple jargon of segmentation by socio-styles side-tracked both old beliefs about the persistence of social segregation and renewed thinking about new forms of social exclusion. Beginning under the auspices of the analysis of social determination in a France shaken up by the ideological seism of 1968, the work of the CCA reflects the falling trajectory of the idea of the collective social project. 'The social classes are dead. Long live lifestyles!' is the motto of the lifestyle professionals.

Something similar happened in England. In March 1988 a writer in *Marxism Today* summarised what he believed to be the thinking of advertisers, with whom it appeared he was in sympathy:

Cultural as well as economic splintering of what were in the 1960s and 1970s solid market blocs (the working class, youth, the house-wife etc.) calls for a rethink. The market has filled up with segmented consumer profiles both up and down the scale: C1 and C2s, yuppies, sloanes, the working woman, gay men, the young, elderly. A changed situation demands a different type of campaign. This is where the design input comes in. Lifestyle advertising, where the message is more 'emotional' than rational and informational, feeds off design and visual imagery. The idea is to create mood, where consumers experience their quintessential individuality in the product. Levi jeans, Saga holidays, Dr. White's, all work with this brief. Lifestyle advertising is about differentiating oneself from the Joneses, not, as in previous decades, keeping up with them.[10]

This was only the beginning of a polemic which was sustained by this journal over the succeeding months, which is still far from over, and which demonstrates the degree to which progressive sectors of society have been orphaned by the loss of traditional concepts of the theory of social classes.[11]

In the construction of transnational space, one thing is clear: the idea of 'lifestyles' is forging ahead among those who identify the strategies of segmentation in a pan-European context. 'Beyond 1992: lifestyle is key', claims a journalist in *Advertising Age* in July 1988 at the annual conference of the European Association of Advertising Agencies (EAAA) in Milan, where this theme was discussed.

Already in 1989, the French CCA brought out the first encyclopaedia of the Europe of lifestyles. To produce it took 24,000 interviews in sixteen European countries (the Common Market, Switzerland, Sweden, Norway and Austria), the analysis of 3,000 variables, a report of 20,000 pages. The result? A European bestiary. No sooner has an end to the jungle of the class struggle been decreed, than there appears the zoo of European lifestyles. Here, then, are the occupants of the cages:

Street cats: they live above their means; they spend on beauty products, excursions and leisure to the detriment of ordinary eating. They like 'Hollywood-style' advertising, brash and quadrophonic.

Herons: inclined to bourgeois accommodation, home management, big cars. To the detriment of clothes, ordinary eating, travelling and going out, beauty products (but not those for body care). They mainly read national quality daily papers.

Doves: mainly housewives aiming to achieve a comfortable standard of living. Good customers at the supermarkets. Highly demanding of product quality.

Elephants: highly attracted by small specialist shops which offer personal services; they pay above all for service and the shop. They mainly read news.

Foxes: attracted to products with the added value of small distribution (for reasons of fashion or selectivity, etc.). They mainly read the news and quality reviews.

Squirrels: attracted above all to added value products and the relation between price and quality.

Owls: attracted to basic products. They like classic, demonstrative advertising.

Sharks: these like Hollywood-style advertising and TV series like *Miami Vice.*

Gulls, Albatrosses: appreciate Japanese-style advertising, monochrome and spectacular.

Badgers: these love the advertising screen and sponsorship. And series like *Dallas.*

Sea lions: these like leisure and home magazines.[12]

Thus, while Europe chaotically pursues its audiovisual identity, the specialists in market studies announce that they are in process of providing the common denominators which unify the diversity of national and regional realities and modes of life.

BLACK BOX

The 1980s were no longer dominated by what had been since the 1960s the royal sciences of sociology, linguistics, structuralism and deconstruction theory.[13]

In the advertising industry, just as in the milieu of academic research, determinist theories about the *imperium* of structure (be they in the service of the system or against it) have hit crisis. The order of the day is the notion of interaction and synergy between different disciplines. The marketing director of Nestlé's French subsidiary writes:

> The old stimulus-response scheme has been superseded. Advertising does not fall into stages the way the DAGMAR and AIDA models would have it . . . . Until now we have had the assistance of disciplines like psychology, mathematics, psycho-sociology, creativity, semiology, sociology; while others, like history, philosophy, epistemology, biology . . . [what Georges Péninou, a researcher for Publicis and erstwhile student of Roland Barthes, called disciplines of the 'distant gaze'] could considerably enrich our understanding of the relations between man and his environment. It seems there exist at least two approaches possible in the future, a priori contradictory: investigation of the individual, and systems theory.[14]

The same vibrations were felt in the United States, where advertising's loss of credibility – brought on by merger-mania – and that of the networks, plus the rise of rebel practices by users, prompted a search beyond the beaten trail of explanation. Hence the allegations of the research director of the Saatchi/DFS Compton network in New York:

> Advertising generally looks at the consumer as conscious and rational, but obviously there are other factors at work. What is the emotional side of purchasing? Why do people say what they say and act as they do? There are people who face these same kinds of questions every day – clinicians in private practice, psychoanalysts, and psychologists. The idea was that, with their help, we could interpret consumers' conscious responses in terms of the unconscious.

The psychological approach worked, she said, 'but there was something missing. People don't consume in a vacuum. They do it in an environment which is our society, our culture.' That got her thinking about the cultural connections, and who was better equipped to investigate this, she thought, than anthropologists? Accordingly she hired specialists

169

trained in cultural anthropology to do original observational research in stores and homes, on the street, and in special sales situations like car lots. This psycho-cultural research has only just started. She admitted there was a lot of scepticism about their initiative. Many people don't even believe in psychoanalysis, so she asks them to suspend their disbelief for twenty minutes. Usually, when she finishes, they say things like 'you've just explained my business' or 'you've given me a completely new perspective on things'.[15]

Advertising research is caught in a schizophrenic double-bind: on one side, the solid factual logic of the determinism of global strategies; on the other, the timid emergence of relativistic theories. A French adman who comes from structuralist semiology observes as follows:

> As opposed to determinist theories (where subjects are passive 'receivers' of the message), relativist systems (where the message is not self-contained, because in parallel the reader brings his own culture to it, and feeds it with his own experience) are almost completely missing from our professional field, and have hardly given us any useful tools . . . . To talk, as we do, in essentially military-determinist metaphors . . . is firstly an obvious limitation in our vocabulary. But it is also a limitation of our very capacity to think about one of the essential components of communication, inscribed in the very heart of the word 'communication'; namely that of interchange, which is always present, even if the receiver's response is usually a silent one. To improve our approach to the phenomenon of communication, we too need to open up our vocabulary to other sources. I have suggested – borrowing from relativist theories – terms like *game, process, functioning, interaction, work, construction, halo, uncertainty, figures, circulation*. But this is only the tip of our iceberg. Everything still remains to be investigated.[16]

Marketing pursues its mad dream: to predict behaviour and maybe manage to control it. To penetrate the secret of the black box of the 'consumer'. For the future of the democracy of daily intercourse, one can only hope that the day on which they find the key and their schizophrenia disappears is far away. The repeatedly postponed prophecies of George Orwell and Aldous Huxley would otherwise run the risk of becoming reality. Like the ethnologist of daily life, Michel de Certeau, we should keep these 'curious and suspicious readings' made by the poachers of consumerism, in the domain of the poetics of everyday practices. And for as long as possible.[17]

That this should not be a case of wishful thinking, it is crucial that the intelligentsia confronts an essential problem: the growing professionalisation of the field of communication. The advertising industry

170

increasingly demands the participation of sociologists, anthropologists, semioticians, cognitive scientists, even psychoanalysts. This qualitative shift in the recruitment of consultants and experts undoubtedly suggests a new phase in the attempt to penetrate the secrets of the black box. This is noticeable not only in Europe, but especially in the larger Latin American countries, where until recently the social sciences were reticent to connect with the universe of the market, and resistant to give marketing assistance in improving its profitability.

ORCHESTRATION

They work neither in audience measurement, nor lifestyles, nor campaign impact evaluation. Even so they are everywhere. The reservoirs of grey matter of consultancy. The biggest come from the United States, but their foreign subsidiaries blend in perfectly with their various national landscapes. Among the most famous are Arthur Andersen, one-time target of Saatchis; McKinsey and his worldwide network of 1,250 consultants; and Booz, Allen & Hamilton with 1,800 specialists, who each year fulfil more than 2,500 missions for more than 1,000 clients in thirty-five countries, intervening in the most diverse sectors (from financial services to the chemicals industry), supported by a network of thirty-nine offices in the United States, six in Europe (Paris, London, Düsseldorf, Milan, Madrid and The Hague), two in Latin America (Mexico and São Paulo), four in the Middle East and one in South-East Asia.

When in 1986 the government of the Netherlands became worried by the invasion of the territory by pan-European programmes, it was the experts of McKinsey they called on. In 1988, when Margaret Thatcher wanted to develop a strategy for the deregulation of British television, it was Booz, Allen & Hamilton she turned to.

This last investigation team has carved a solid reputation in supplying services which it offers to its clients as 'the formulation of government policy in the audiovisual domain'. It is thus called on to carry out studies on the privatisation of the radio frequencies, to make proposals for new pay television channels, or to measure the 'profitability' of television advertising.

To formulate government policies means intervening in a whole chain: from the realisation of an economic study, to communication of the results to executives and the press, to government action. In the reality of pressure for European deregulation, this is above all to assume a new role, as producer of a discourse for the legitimation of strategy. This, probably without realising, is what the British journal *Business* meant by praising the team's study in July 1988: 'Booz, Allen & Hamilton . . . has re-written the intellectual debate – most influentially by arguing the case for more TV.' They had understood. The key area of the business is above

171

all the economics of television advertising, because in the near future the configuration of audiovisual systems will revolve around the elasticity of the market for commercials and sponsorship.

The decision of the 'Iron Lady' to destabilise British television strongly confirmed the image of the Booz, Allen & Hamilton team for efficiency. Not resting on their laurels, in September 1988 the company circulated to all leading European companies a proposal for investigation entitled 'Commercial television in Europe. Dangers on the horizon for 1990'. It invited the enterprises it had contacted to subscribe to a study commissioned by Mars, Kellogg and Heinz on the impact of new European legislation on television advertising. One reads in the preface:

> The new law currently being discussed by the Council of Europe represents a real danger of a considerable cut in advertising revenues and of limiting the development of commercial television. Booz, Allen has undertaken a series of European meetings (in London, Frankfurt, Paris and Madrid), bringing together television stations, advertising agencies and advertisers to discuss the danger presented by this legislation, and to propose a multi-client study on the future of commercial television in each country . . . . The results of the study will be presented to the governments concerned. Pressure groups will ensure contact with ministers involved. An information campaign will present the results of the study to the public at large.

The study then gives a summary of the forces in evidence in the Council of Europe.

The central hypothesis of this study is that the potential impact of the legislation is negative. Negative for advertisers and for advertising agencies (reduction in sales of existing product, reduction in the number of new products launched, difficulties in communicating with the segments of the market). Negative for the television stations (limited income from advertising, reduction in investment in technology and programmes, limited exports). Negative for consumers (limited choice of programmes, lowering of programme quality, the risk of longer advertising breaks, since commercials will have to be grouped together). Negative for 'culture and politics' (less local programming, more imports and easily interruptible programmes). As for the methodology of the study, *Stage I* establishes the relation between reduced advertising income, programme production and programme planning. *Stage II* demonstrates how the proposals reduce growth and export potential, both national and European. *Stage III* defines the impact of the proposals on industry and the economy in each country. *Stage IV* verifies the impact of the impoverishment of programme quality and reduction of consumer choice. Lastly, it evaluates the arguments against before arriving at its conclusions and recommendations. And to illustrate its scientific credibility, it is accompanied by various examples taken from a previous Booz, Allen study, the one which provided a statistical basis for the deregulation of British television in the 1990s.

The final exhortation: 'It is time to act. The commitment of advertisers, agencies and television stations to financing this study on a European scale will be proof of the importance of the danger for the audiovisual future.'

Above all, what these 'truth-operations' hint at is how lobbying has become a market and a profession. What yesterday still seemed inadmissible now becomes a natural function. Lobbying, a journalist of the specialist press affirms,

> is taking an important but delicate step . . . it begins the institutionalisation of influence groups. One can speak of a mini-cultural revolution: lobbying is no longer limited to the sombre colours of Parliament and similar edifices. It increasingly goes out onto the streets through operations which are directed at public opinion in order to have influence on political power . . . . One hopes that corporations will take the initiative in making a true technique of this 'lobbying mix' (the 'lobbying mix', with its five components – economics, law, politics, diplomacy and communication – is to lobbying what the 'marketing mix' and its four P's – product, price, promotion and place – is to marketing) . . . . The emergence of a true market should favour the creation of micro-agencies specialising in lobbying, extension of the lobbying sections within the public relations firms, but also means the rise of original alliances . . . . A time of exoneration is beginning. And with it, an urgent necessity emerges: the 'good lobbyist' code, with rules of the game which are accepted by all.[18]

10

THE SPIRIT OF ENTERPRISE
The limits of transparency

COMMUNICATION MINDED

'Everything communicates', as advertising practitioners and consultants endlessly repeat as we approach the third millennium, thereby wishing to demonstrate the elasticity of their imperious profession. Communication, from now on, levies its tax on every kind of project and activity. It has become *the* unifying concept.

The rhythm of mutation in the technical and scientific environment of the leading 'post-industrial' countries has led to the idea that the demand for communication has been provoked essentially by the massive arrival of new techniques of information and communication. An illusion and a tautology amply cultivated by inflation in promotional discourse about how to get out of the crisis, which has not hesitated to present the dissemination of new tools and networks as the most effective means to achieve the modernisation of the mode of growth and development. None the less, while these techniques clearly occupy a decisive place in the formulation of the demand for communication, it is equally obvious that they have nothing to do with its origins. To imagine otherwise is to become enclosed within sophistry, no more no less, and to ratify a new variant of technical determinism. The new demand for communication, and the new supply, have been generated in different places in consequence of multiple logics.

In the formation of these new professional markets, the enterprise and the workplace occupy an important position. According to the chief editor of the journal *Communication/CB News*, which was created in response to this new supply of expertise:

Everyone is unanimous on this point. Tomorrow, the chief executives coming directly from the area of communication will be numerous. Naturally, the taking of power by the 'dircom' [director of communication] will not occur systematically to the detriment of marketing. The latter is also as indispensable as management or production. But the marketing-minded enterprises of yesterday have become communication-minded. Communication, the same as marketing, is not so much a technique as a state of mind, an attitude, a preconceived idea, a principle of operation.[1]

The function of communication is in the process of taking its place within European enterprises just as it has done in the United States. There is a new entry in the company assets: what we can call the 'capital image' which comes under the control of the director of communication.

In 1988, the company Corporate carried out, for the first time in Europe, an enquiry into marketing and communication services among French, British, German, Dutch, Swiss, Belgian and Italian firms with a turnover of more than a billion francs. The objective was to take stock of the real structures, activities, budgets and preoccupations of these companies in relation to communication. To evaluate the way the company says who it is (as opposed to what it produces), that is, what it knows how to do and what it wants to do. Some results: in 80 per cent of the companies, communication is located at the highest level; in 56 per cent, the director of communication belongs to the board (as an executive, on the strategy committee, the board of management, and what in France is called the 'image committee'). This tendency is stronger in France (65 per cent) than in other countries. France is also where the highest salaries are found: 47 per cent of directors of communication earn more than 400,000Fr [approximately $65,000], 51 per cent earn between 240,000Fr [$38,700] and 400,000Fr. The European average is 24 per cent and 54 per cent respectively. In contrast, more than half the directors of communication in British firms don't even earn the lower figure. On the other hand, communication in France and Britain is more personalised than in Germany or Holland. Another consideration: how far the firm is mediatised. The principal objective is to guarantee a solid presence in the media. In short, the countries which resort most often to external services, Britain and France, are those in which advertising agencies and consultants are especially powerful and advanced and have been able to establish an organic relation with their clients.[2]

CAPITAL IMAGE

The integration of communication at the level of management precipitates the end of the piecemeal approach. The 'capital image' consists in the continual fusion of four elements: the financial image, the internal image, the brand image and the civic image. From communication fragmented into multiple messages, uncontrolled costs, discordant relations between compartmentalised offices (financial information, internal information, press, publicity, external or public relations), the company turns towards integrated communication, a declinable concept, the rationalisation of options and chosen media. Structures of financial communication, recruiting, sponsorship, lobbying, research and speech writing are installed alongside restructured traditional services.

But the regrouping of functions does not proceed without problems.

Although financial publicity continues in 79 per cent of cases in all countries to be in the hands of financial management, while in 70 per cent of cases recruitment is controlled by personnel directors, there is a very clear tendency towards the centralisation of functions, especially in France and Holland. In Germany and Britain the division of responsibilities is still pronounced, even though this does not seem to prejudice the coherence of communication activity.[3]

But on the horizon is the rise of the 'holistic' concept of communication control, with all its variants and nuances: 'corporate communication', 'total communication'. Communication as a vector of external cohesion and internal binding builds consensus, and thus contributes to the optimisation of investment and the global management of strategic options undertaken by the firm. Internally, it mobilises the human resources working in it, the forces of innovation, available intelligence. Its new vocation is to act in such a way that everyone becomes aware of giving 'added value' within the process and of having clients who have to be satisfied.

The Taylorian company with its pyramid structure is out of date. A new mode of organisation has appeared with 'corporations of the third kind'. The first kind was 'balkanised' by a division into 'territories' overseen by different powers, marked by a 'top' and a 'bottom' in diametrical opposition, which allowed no circulation of information. The 'new corporation' is constructed on another vision, that of the network in which information is no longer guarded but exchanged with third parties, to turn it into news which confers 'power'.

However, there is a world of difference between the project of integration of the four components of the capital image and its achievement, for there is a world of people working in the corporation who remember that the company's history can perhaps not be contained in the rose-coloured spectacles of the consensual concept of specialised communication.

Twists and turns of the 'consolidation of the internal image'. Dislocation between the 'desired image' and the 'actual image', or the 'perceived image'. Corporate warns that:

Corporations have certainly known how to set up numerous internal information circuits which in most cases favour direct contacts, even if they still consider the adherence of personnel to established objectives insufficient: only 29 per cent of firms consider their internal image to be a 'good enough' one, and 45 per cent think it needs significant improvement. One of the challenges of the years to come will be to create a true corporate culture and a strong sense of belonging in the midst of complex and varied groups.[4]

Despite its youth, the new catalogue of expert company communication services has already had numerable chances to deal with situations lacking consensus about social coexistence in the workplace. The orthopaedics of communication really seems rather weak when management – for there is always management – has to deal with a strike which has decided to pursue its claims to the very end. For social conflicts belonging to the 'first phase' continue to be found at the heart of the capital/labour relation even in the flexible corporation of the so-called 'third phase'!

All this only reflects the tensions running through the current process of rehabilitation of 'free enterprise'. For some this means acquiescence and the dilution of symbols of struggle, an end to the bosses' guilt complex, the desire for consensus based on a new concept of corporate rights (the reduction of taxes, fluidity of the labour market, simplification of law). For others it means the will and need for a new social contract, a new commitment, based on 'new economic citizenship', new rights for corporate workers, a general redefinition of the relation between the corporation and society. For the enterprise – this has been known since the first criticisms of Adam Smith – has no natural reason to bring its private interests in line with the collective interests of citizens, users, consumers and the national community.

Underlying the new debate about Fordist and Taylorian social regulation and exercise of authority in the workplace, society as a whole is posed the challenge of the composition and recomposition of the pyramid of social class, of categories and groups and social antagonisms. The centrality of the working class is gone, new social layers are in ascent, whose uncertain denomination reflects their groping sociological analysis: are they a new class of professionals, a new *petite bourgeoisie*, a 'third class', a technocracy? In any case, there is a transformation of the labour process through the increasing integration of this new class with intellectual labour, and above all new power relations. The appearance of what the sociologist Paul Beaud has felicitously called the 'society of connivance', which is characterised by the emergence of a new partner in social conflicts and negotiation: a 'median' class which is found in the strategic position of mediation.[5]

CRISIS COMMUNICATION

Since the late nineteenth century, the advertising industry has been encouraging the consumption of products and services. From hucksters selling snake oil from the back of horse-drawn wagons to corporate presidents promoting K-Cars, the goal has been to introduce, differentiate, and encourage consumption of products in a presumably competitive economic environment. Throughout, the fundamental purposes of advertising remained unchanged despite the sophisticated alterations in the methods, approaches, and slogans of advertising campaigns. In recent years, however, corporate advertisers have turned away from solely selling products, or even their corporate images. They have begun to advertise their point of view on social and political matters.[6]

This was the assertion, in 1981, of the American political scientist Robert G. Meadow. In 1978, the Supreme Court further expanded the boundaries of the First Amendment with a decision that corporations have a constitutional right to speak out on public issues through advertisements. Until this date, the prevailing concept in many state laws was that corporate money may be spent only on issues related to the corporation's business.

The enterprise was suddenly free. The 1960s had seen the deterioration of its capital image. An opinion poll carried out in the United States by Lou Harris in 1979 revealed that no more than 22 per cent of the American population had confidence in company directors, as opposed to 55 per cent at the start of the decade.

Those were years when corporations were effectively 'under siege'. To confirm this, it is enough to remember not the analysis of the besiegers but the statements made by public relations agencies – like Hill & Knowlton and Burson-Marsteller – who lent a hand to the besieged, thanks to which they saw their range of business much extended. The corporation, according to the highly respectable *Business Week* in January 1979,

is operating in a 'pressure-cooker' environment. It is under siege from consumerists, environmentalists, women's liberation advocates, the civil rights movement, and other activist groups. Their demands are being steadily translated into an unprecedented wave of intervention by federal and state governments into the affairs of business. Even without government interference, the activists are forcing changes in corporate operating policies that range from a halt in loans to South Africa to curtailment of infant milk-formula sales in less developed countries. The corporation also faces intensified competition in the marketplace, the growing threat of takeover by outsiders, and new challenges in employee relations.[7]

The corporation responds by becoming 'as much a political animal as an economic machine'. According to the president of Hill & Knowlton:

The corporation is being politicised and has assumed another dimension in our society that it did not have as recently as 10 years ago. . . . As a result, the corporation has become more conscious of using communications in all its diverse forms as a tool to accomplish its objectives, and it is articulating its positions more clearly and urgently to government agencies, legislators, shareholders, employees, customers, financial institutions, and other critical audiences.[8]

In this hostile environment a new product has appeared: crisis advertising. Its first field of application is the financial front, where the liberalisation of brokerage agency commission, and the deregulation of prices and exchange procedures, have created a proliferation of savage takeovers. Hill & Knowlton are on top of it. Another major public relations firm, in its time the third-largest in the world, namely Carl Byoir & Associates, carried its ardour to the point of producing for clients in the grip of takeover psychosis a list of twenty-three items enumerating the means of defence against attempts by rivals to take control. This was their 'Takeover Defence Checklist'. (In the Robert & Collins dictionary, 'takeover' is translated as 'seizure of power', associated with the following: dictatorship, army and political party.) Ironically, after providing its clients with an anti-takeover umbrella, Hill & Knowlton, which was founded in 1927, was taken over by J. Walter Thompson in 1980; in 1986, Carl Byoir too fell into the hands of the American agency; and then in 1987, the two public relations teams and their mother company were absorbed by the king of mortgage finance, Martin Sorrell, in the most bloody takeover in the history of advertising! (Since 1983, the three leading companies of the international public relations industry have all changed ownership. After Hill & Knowlton and Carl Byoir, it was the turn of Burson-Marsteller, also American and second-largest in the world, to be swallowed by another advertising giant, Young & Rubicam. Such is the degree of concentration in the industry that the two top companies between them pocket half the fees collected from the top fifteen PR firms.)

An investigation of 500 chief executives in eleven European countries by the Brussels team of the American management associations in 1978, showed that within the Community too, the major 'social challenge' confronting corporations on the eve of the 1980s was the question of information. Some 86 per cent of the directors interviewed indicated that over the preceding five years the development of an information strategy (both external and internal) had been top priority. Other social challenges were the 'physical working environment' (82 per cent); compliance with new social legislation (79 per cent); the participation of employees in decisions which affected them (77 per cent); the improvement of product safety (71 per cent); and the reduction of damaging environmental effects (69 per cent). These figures are an average. The scale of priorities varied according to the country. At 95 per cent, French and Italian executives considered information as the dominant challenge, against 88 per cent in the UK and 73 per cent in Germany.[9]

However, it was not until the second half of the 1980s when European companies – and the public at large – discovered the aggression of communication strategies in times of crisis, brought on by the outbreak of takeovers in every sector. For the French agencies it became a baptism of fire. 'It's a financial war, and a psychological war as well', explained the executive of Publicis responsible, at the start of 1988, for the media campaign accompanying the takeover launched by *condottiere* Carlo de Benedetti against the Société Générale de Belgique. When campaigns to sensitise and arouse public opinion – whose phraseology was rigorously codified for peace time – proved inadequate, the communiqués switched into a higher gear. To destabilise the adversary, the game of advertising allows every type of move, including those close to manipulation.

On occasion these strategies may be deflated quicker than they are blown up. That was exactly what happened in the case of the interminable takeover of the Société Générale de Belgique. The media *blitzkrieg* could not escape the ethos of the soap opera.

The Italian industrialist, gambling on a quick victory, based his strategy of conquest on particularly aggressive advertising. Profitable at first, it none the less rebounded against him when the affair turned into three months of trench warfare. Because beforehand he had mined the territory, looking for a compromise with adversaries previously presented as incapable. His adversaries undoubtedly wanted to make him pay for his media 'arrogance' (even if they knew they were condemned to reach an understanding with such an important minority shareholder). Conclusion: in some cases, there is everything to gain with a discrete strategy.[10]

Corporate's investigation also showed that in 1988 scarcely half of the European firms had set up plans for crisis advertising, and France was clearly backward in comparison to its competitors (France, 24 per cent; Britain, 42 per cent; Germany, 41 per cent; Holland, 50 per cent).

One should add that if, for the ordinary citizen, the new corporate logic of communication comes over primarily through the echo-chamber of the takeover bid, for the workers and employees of the company that changes hands it also means, above all, the attempt to smooth over the resultant asset-stripping and mass dismissals. These are things which, in most cases, the highly mediatised enterprise – bringer of modernisation – keeps carefully hidden.

RETHINKING THE SOCIAL

For transnational corporations the 1970s should have been years full of danger. They turned out, however, to be the epoch when, in order to protect their clients from new snags, international marketing specialists refined their assessment of 'political risk'. One example of this is BERI (Business Environment Risk Index). BERI provides a quarterly listing of fifteen economic, financial and political variables in forty-eight countries, using the services of 170 business and political specialists. Institutional stability, likelihood of nationalisation, trades union pressure, labour productivity, repatriation of profits, inflation rate, level of installation of telecommunications, and assorted other matters give a combined portrait of 'hostile environments'.[11]

In the construction of these problematic spaces, communication is not the least factor. On the contrary. This is clear from the virulent reactions of press and publicity executives who dismiss the demands of the Third World for a 'new world order of information and communication' without even considering a right to reply. The mobilisation of international corporate networks around these debates which dominated the 1970s does not disguise the size of the stakes at play on the two sides.

For the first time in their history, transnational corporations have been forced to think out a communications strategy to counteract networks set up by their adversaries. The best-known case, without doubt, is the Nestlé affair. The response of the other companies in the field was rapid and unanimous. In 1975, scarcely a year after publication of the first denunciations of its bludgeoning advertising policies, Nestlé managed to bring together a dozen other agro-food companies in the International Council of Infant Food Industries (ICIFI), which decided to issue its own code of conduct in the matter.

A global balance of the operation, offered eight years later by the firm's public relations director:

> The struggle in which we are engaged is of a political nature and on a political level, but it is not yet certain that the future will be one of economic, social, personal and political liberty. . . . Success in politics is not magical. Our enemies are not more intelligent than us and are not supermen. And having begun a political reflection, we should give ourselves some political objectives. . . . I feel it is essential that multinational firms under attack create a united group of talented and experienced professionals and, when needed, occasional consultants who, isolated from the everyday public relations of the firm, can concentrate their efforts on the political issues encountered by the multinationals. In the search for a receptive public and the elimination of a critical attitude, multinationals have

181

an invaluable weapon at their disposal: marketing and management personnel in the field.[12]

Speculating with politics, as this communications strategy strikingly demonstrates, consists not only in employing certain tools, but also in thinking in terms of social alliances:

We must either reactivate our traditional professional associations, or look beyond them for new allies among associations of peasants, workers and owners of small businesses, many of whom have been suspicious of multinational capital in the past for good reasons. We must affirm the common interests of all institutions which create wealth – large or small, private or governmental, national or multinational: in short, we must affirm the pluralism and the diversity of the human condition, an example of which is given by democracy as well as the free market of commerce and ideas. Multinational capitalism must never appear as the dominating rival to local interests or to national or tribal sentiments.[13]

To try and gain the trust of the countries of the South, Nestlé anticipated criticism by developing, here and there, products based on raw materials available *in situ*. In Nigeria, Nurtrand baby food is made with soya, maize and palm oil. In Sri Lanka, powdered milk is made from coconut. In Malaysia, they make their noodles not of wheat but of rice. In Ecuador and Singapore, they have two research centres working on products for the Third World – showcases which the Swiss firm never tires of publicising.

After reading this balance sheet, one understands better why the president of Hill & Knowlton proposed, back in the 1970s, that the term 'public relations' be substituted by 'public affairs'.

The balance from the point of view of the network of NGOs (Non-Government Organisations):

Nestlé has been forced to negotiate an agreement with pressure groups, committing itself to abide by most of the provisions of the WHO code in most countries. Other companies have changed some marketing practices, and more appear likely. Two UN agencies, WHO and UNICEF, have increased their stature and legitimacy somewhat through their efforts on this issue. . . . Health workers in scores of countries have changed practices in their own facilities. A wide variety of activities have been undertaken by the International Baby Food Action Network (IBFAN), its affiliate groups and other NGOs to publicise the problem and promote the solutions. The establishment of IBFAN was itself a positive step forward, marking a new initiative in the way NGOs organise internationally, and serving as a model for similar networks. . . . It is perhaps a glowing compliment to the effectiveness of IBFAN that a major [transnational] like Nestlé decided to copy some of IBFAN's informational and organisational strategies. As far back as 1980, Nestlé and ICIFI recognised the need to involve 'grassroots' organisations. . . . In late 1983, the company began to publish a monthly newsletter, *Nestlé News*, modelled on *IBFAN News*.[14]

The lesson seems to have produced results: at all events, the transnationals are more prudent, even if still a long way from fulfilling the codes of conduct demanded by international assemblies. An example of this new prudence: in April 1988, Coca-Cola offered 20,000 hectares of tropical rainforest which it owned in Belize, on the Caribbean coast of Central America, to the Massachusetts Society for the Protection of Birds. This unheard-of gift is actually the result of the failure of one of its most ambitious investment projects outside the United States. The Atlanta company had bought this land, in a country half the size of Switzerland and with a population of 160,000, an erstwhile British possession which became independent in 1981, in order to plant it with citrus fruit and install a processing plant. But the project was exposed and nature defence organisations were alerted. The Friends of the Earth led a movement to save the forest. The protests took off in Federal Germany, Britain and Sweden. The Greens threatened a European boycott of the American company. Coca-Cola, zealous of its image as today's young drink, was worried about the bad publicity.[15]

It must be said that seven years earlier Coca-Cola made the unhappy decision of turning a deaf ear to protests regarding political repression by the dictatorship against union militants in its Guatemala subsidiary. They had cause to rue it later. The company had to cede in the face of a boycott of its products organised by the International Union of Food and Allied Workers' Association in some thirty countries.

During the 1980s, another major front opened up for the professionals of crisis communication: the environment. Nuclear or chemical catastrophes, technological failures, pollution of rivers and seas, etc. – there is a long list of such accidents which specialists in strategic communication have classified as 'industrial crisis', 'major technological hazard' or 'emergency', and which they try to remedy through the new expertise of 'industrial or corporate crisis management'. Added to disasters of the 1970s like those of Seveso in Italy, the wreck of the supertanker Amoco-Cadiz off the coast of Brittany, or the nuclear accident at Three Mile Island, the following decade brought the explosion at the Union Carbide factory in Bhopal in India, the discharge of toxic chemicals into the Rhine at Basle by the firm of Sandoz, the wreck of the Exxon-Valdez, and many more.[16]

In the new theories of organisation through communication, the crisis is treated less and less as a series of isolated events and hot spots liable to destabilise the enterprise, and more as a permanent variable which must be taken into account even in times of 'normality'. 'Risk' is seen as one of the elements of industrial development. Crisis management, in fact, produces a new conception within enterprise culture. Remarks by an executive in charge of communication services at the Swiss firm of Sandoz after the catastrophe in Basle: 'We need to develop a "cybernetic perception of public relations". . . . To succeed in this, enterprises must consider their culture, their ethics of communication, and their choice of communicators in "times of peace".'[17] Making the best of the crises: in betting on communication to preserve its image-identity, the enterprise has discovered that crisis has its virtues. Beginning with those who are obliged 'to get rid of their backward sense of guilt', as the director of one public relations firm puts it. Communication as therapy – before, during and after the accident.

One preoccupation keeps returning: how to control the irrational within the enterprise and the unforseeable beyond it. But the distant horizon of this engineering of disturbances remains in every case the contemporary model of development and growth – and its propensity to ecological destruction – whose legitimation and purposes still lie behind every effort. In this cybernetic vision of the enterprise-system, everything comes up fresh, as if the ethics of the enterprise could be redefined solely on the basis of the principle of self-regulation by industrial actors.

THE LIMITS OF TRANSPARENCY

'You can have your car any color you want as long as it's black', promised Henry Ford, the father of Fordism. For a long time this phrase immortalised a management philosophy which left little room for the consumer. Those were times of 'product-driven' strategy. Then corporate strategy became 'market-driven'. During the 1980s, however, the decline of Fordism brought the emergence of a new concept: 'customer-driven', a strategy of 'deeply satisfying the customer'.

With the irresistible rise of external communication, and beyond the discovery by the corporation of the need for dialogue at local, national and international level, not to mention new movements with collective demands, there is a noticeable return to the consumer who now becomes the prime object of attention. No longer is the letter of complaint or hostile telephone call ignored. The satisfaction of the largest number is the condition of the company's survival in a situation where competition renders the client unfaithful and demanding. After-sales service, the design of user instructions, servicing of parts, suggestions boxes, the systematic reply to correspondence, are all aspects (among others) of a communications policy which looks after these relations.

Communication engenders communication. If relations with the consumer have become crucial for companies in general, it is vital for companies whose business is communication. Example: television channels in the context of the upset audiovisual market. In 1988 in France, 120,000 viewers made calls to the television stations each month, and 7,500 wrote letters. Correspondence to TF1 has tripled since 1983. Clearly, the sudden multiplication of commercial breaks with the privatisation of TF1 produced an influx of calls and letters. Since 1986, viewers have a new instrument for speaking to the television station: two-way videotext systems such as Teletel, which given the level of user-demand, produces income for the channel. In 1987, these communications represented for TF1 300,000 hours of connection on Minitel. And since nothing in the communication process is lost to use, various producers have themselves begun to elicit these teletext boxes where the viewer can express an opinion. Thus Antenne 2 has set up a box for every transmission. And a team of six to nine people reply via Minitel, thanks to a deferred electronic mail system. The growing integration of the user in programme production does the rest. As a co-ordinator of Antenne 2's teletext system explains, 'At the start of next season, we will increase the number of real-time teletext conversations with viewers and specialists on the subject [of the programme].' [18]

The consumers – for that is what they are – have already had time to assess the limits of interactive communication. Among the complaints:

Preoccupation with the image has come to prevail over pure information. The most characteristic case is that of the CGE (Compagnie Générale d'Électricité). This big industrial group in energy and communication, which never hesitated to spend $7m to project its image, announced last July in a short communiqué its entry into another big group, Générale Occidentale. The publication, at the beginning of April, of the 1987 results, was relatively discreet, whilst the image campaign, during the same period, continued strongly. . . . TF1 did not hesitate to call a quasi-confidential general meeting, which shareholders were not advised of. . . . The acme of a communications group! To know of it, they would had to have read the *Bulletin des annonces légales,* a periodical issued almost exclusively for companies and administrations. As the Bank of Suez, which at this moment was involved in a huge increase in capital and was making a fresh appeal to small shareholders, the COB (Commission des opérations de Bourse) – equivalent of the US Securities and Exchange Commission – reproached them with not providing sufficient detail about their consolidated accounts . . . while other banks, which were not appealing for savings, had published detailed accounts. [19]

The same type of statement in the United States: 'For too many companies, customer-driven is just another buzzword. . . . [It is possible] to collect horror stories of companies boasting of being customer-driven but putting management convenience first. The only way they're customer-driven is that they're driving customers away.'[20]

Paradoxes of modern communication: tumult rhymes with secret, overdose with scarcity, and transparency with opacity. Bitter reflections of directors of the French agro-food company Lesieur, which despite a massive injection of management-consultancy-communication fell to the German soap company Henkel and the American Colgate-Palmolive: 'The increased number of consultants produced a hidden power that was too important. On various occasions the general management was deprived of certain information which consultants had filtered out.'[21]

11

TOTAL COMMUNICATION
The crisis of public culture

TRANSFERENCE

In 1978 the Parisian press carried a display advert for a new product: a 'communication of general interest' in which the Eurocom group announced the birth of its new subsidiary Eleuthera. At the top in big letters: 'The society of communication is beginning.' And underneath: 'The society of production was yesterday. The society of consumption is today. But for how much longer? Tomorrow will see the apogee of the society of communication. A society where relations between people . . . become more and more complex. And therefore more and more important. It needs organising.'

With these premises established, then comes the programme/plan.

Advertising communication has demonstrated its capacities. Used today to develop commercial relations, it will be called on tomorrow to develop social, cultural and human relations. We have therefore created Eleuthera, the first communication agency of general interest . . . . To adapt the most sophisticated techniques of commercial advertising and place them at the service of relations between people. 'Social' communication – a redundant word? We hope so.

Ten years later, mission accomplished, the agency disappears and is reborn under another banner. In the poster campaign which launches it, 'communication agency of general interest' metamorphoses into 'total communications agency'.

Never has advertising literature been so lucky in its choice of words as here, in expressing the transfer of the norms and models of market communication to the ensemble of society, thereby defining the meaning given to the concept of 'communication': communication as a technique for the management and organisation of human relations.

This is the model of commercial relations as the gauge of social relations. To anyone who carefully reviews the Anglo-American classics of advertising, this was clear enough from the start. Only the successive

187

sublimations of various countries allergic to money and the market made it forgotten. But this peculiar notion of communication is at the very heart of the definition of 'the product'. A 'product' is 'anything that can be offered to a market for attention, acquisition, use or consumption'. 'Anything' includes 'physical objects, services, personalities, places, organisations and ideas'.[1]

DISINHIBITION

Cultural action, I think, is something in which we too are involved, and what is more, we adapt to people's needs, because we have the means to know them in depth. One could even say that true sociology is what we do and it is effective. For me, community and cultural workers are riding the slow train. They pretend to know people better than us, but in the end they don't use modern techniques, their universe is limited, they are afraid to express themselves, to utilise the media, now that these are much more means of mass communication than the theatre, for example. They defend themselves against us by labelling us as commercial, but this doesn't annoy me in the slightest, because our attitude is perfectly honest. We begin by listening to people and taking note of their wishes, which means that all the messages we send can only be accepted if they respond to an expectation, if they fill a gap or a wish. Therefore it cannot be said that there is manipulation. If people buy chewing gum, it's because they want to buy chewing gum. The community workers are bathed in a Christian anti-money ideology, but are completely ignorant of present-day society: we are within an ideology of profit, no more. To talk of anything else is a kind of dialectics which seems to me very complicated! [Laughter . . .][2]

This was the director of Eleuthera talking in 1979.

It has not taken ten years to readjust the scale of values to the norms of profit. Inflated fees for presenters and star journalists on television, public as well as private, in Italy or in France; the presumption of the fees paid to the strategists of advertising communication – as much as five or six times anything a university lecturer in the same discipline may hope to earn; the proliferation of the practice of advertorials – in flagrant violation of the ethical codes of journalism – compared to the real difficulty of talking about these new practices in public, debating them from the point of view of the democratic organisation of our society: these are only a few of the symptoms which demonstrate the new hierarchy and the precedence of a pecuniary ideology. Witness, in Britain, the way that in the last two or three years the media have been flooded with advertisements for credit facilities. King Money is the name of the game –

188

while the crisis in public service grows ever deeper, not only in terms of what public institutions represent but, above all, in the functions and professional practices of community service, especially in the fields of education and health. This switch is unquestionably the major cultural change of the 1980s.

Some have taken note of this new legitimacy of the market and decided on action. The times call for out-and-out pragmatism, and in large, late-capitalist countries a new type of commodity has made its appearance: the humanitarian product. Solidarity enters the marketplace. A huge onslaught of mailings, sponsors, hoardings and commercials has turned the collection of donations and grants into an operation of commercial dimensions. Purchase product X or Y and you participate in the struggle against hunger, cancer, unemployment, AIDS and other calamities. The 'réserve exceptionelle Band Aid' marketed by the wine merchants Nicolas (73,000 bottles of wine at 30Fr apiece, of which a quarter was donated to the humanitarian organisation) helped to finance hydraulic projects in Mali. Générale Sucrière – which had shed 1,000 jobs in three years – participated in the operation known as 'Community Restaurants for All' by giving meal-tickets to the unemployed. American Express offered New York meals-on-wheels 10 cents in the dollar for every meal eaten in a restaurant in the city using their credit card.

The rise of these methods of private philanthropy – directly proportional, it should emphatically be said, to the drying-up of public funds – suggests an appeal to a sense of guilt and bad conscience, but substitutes for the call of conscience, responsibility and citizenship. It seems to emphasise the urgent need for punctual action, but only delays the application of long-term solutions. Obviously it also entails a particular conception of information about our society and our two-speed planet.

Lastly, it also provides the advertising fraternity with an opportunity to produce a new popularising history of 'free enterprise'.

Together, we help. Thanks to you, when buying this packet, Danone gives 1Fr to *Médecins sans frontières* . . . the leading organisation for urgent medical aid in the world . . . . Because misery also exists in France, MSF has created *Solidarité France* . . . . At the beginning of the century, M. Carasso, founder of Danone, was deeply impressed by the illnesses that affect small children who live in unfavourable climatic and hygienic conditions. Convinced of the virtues of a milk-based product, yoghurt, and aware of the benefits of a balanced and healthy diet, M. Carasso decided to manufacture and market yoghurt. That is how Danone was born. Today, the link between Danone and *Médecins sans frontières* is the continuation of this dietary concern.

This is clearly a long way from the philosophy of enterprise and communication that animates those networks of thought and action set up by other, non-governmental organisations to counteract advertising strategies such as that employed by Nestlé, and the response organised by the agro-food lobby.

REVELATION

The end of closed-circuit communication? This is not the opinion of a young journalist on *Libération* who celebrated the twentieth anniversary of May 1968 in the columns of the famous daily in his own way.

> The old leaders and militants who are now converts to journalism and advertising swear with their hands on the hearts that those years vaccinated them against dogmatism and reiterative language: I am persuaded the opposite. A new reiterative language was born in those prehistoric years: the language of advertising and 'communication' . . . a confiscation of language to the benefit of a hierarchy jealous of its privileges.[3]

Everything considered, this could well be the most pertinent piece of analysis of the median class.

But for other components of society, the eruption of the problematics of communication means something else altogether. It has functioned to reveal the rigidity of the modes of organisation of the militants. A demystification of rituals. 'When you publish a pamphlet, people don't read it any more . . . . You have to tell stories which touch people in the first person, in terms of their own culture. And today their culture is audiovisual.' This was the explanation given by a hospital worker in Saint-Nazaire in February 1986, at a conference on video and the workers' movement. This meeting brought together a large number of independent video producers, who are increasingly invited to work for corporate employers. According to the organiser of the forum, the film-maker Jean-Pierre Thorn,

> Video, in questioning reality, breaks the rigid frame of the kind of writing which weighs only on the workers' movement. Today the politics of the image lie at the heart of the crisis being suffered by trade unionism. The old organisations still cannot tolerate images except as illustrations to their speeches. But this position has become untenable.

A new social contract, new consensual modes of organisation and command in the corporation, a new form of legitimation of the 'median class'; at the same time, previously unknown forms of social exclusion and segregation, and new forms of struggle and conflict both within and

190

outside the workplace: all this tends to make old militant practices and speech more anachronistic and hollow for both internal use and a captive public. The speech of an epoch when the idea of an undivided working class as the sole bearer of historical conscience was ascendant. A time of the ritual celebration of the alliance between the reprehensible *petite bourgeoisie* and the underclasses.

The 'need to communicate' has overtaken the whole social movement, beginning with the highly variegated texture of associative life where the term 'groups of citizens' has for many years included many domains of daily life (leisure, work and unemployment, health, solidarity, etc.), and now constituting a strong force of social intervention in the democratic direction of public matters. A common concern across all NGOs: 'It is no longer a question of directing oneself only to militants, but also to users, or better, the non-users, who have to be converted.'

The progressive dismantling of the welfare state – and in certain cases, the rationalisation of the financial management of social and cultural foundations – pushes the social movement, and the various components of civil society, to dilute their appeal for the traditional networks of initiates and the faithful, and to open out instead towards economic values and practices. This taking the market into consideration has produced a new relation with money, which in turn affects modes of organisation (transparency, professionalism, the conception of 'voluntary work', the role of salaried professionals within community groups) and the types of action undertaken. And also the modes of communication with the outside world. The need to preach a case to the large number of the unconverted has fomented the opening of a debate about the application of commercial methods of communication as a site of construction of social and financial credibility.

The search for subsidies, commissions and contracts thus involves diverse conceptions of the resources of the social movement, and above all, its aims. Opposed to the specialists in the creation of media events, who are carried along by the new ideology of enterprise – and who, in addition, make a good profit from providing services for community groups – are those afraid of losing their souls on the altar of the market and neo-liberal thought. Faced with the ascendant logic of enterprise, with its criteria of profitability and marketing techniques, they try to redefine the logic of the social movement, its criteria, its mobilisation around ideas, the invitation for dialogue and reflection. But mediatised culture has already so impregnated society with its own reflexes and mentality that it is hardly credible to conceive these two logics in uncontaminated face-to-face confrontation. The basic questions are these. What will be the mode of appropriation of the networks and existing methods of communication in the organisation of civil society? What will be the capacity of the social movement overall to invent

191

unknown communication practices more in harmony with the questions which it poses? Practices which function democratically, transparent, reaching for autonomy, with the power to propose collective projects for social change?[4] Questions which will not be resolved as long as 'communication' continues to be thought of as a panacea.

THE NEW ART OF GOVERNANCE

Very few states escape it. Ministers, public entities, national enterprises today all wield large advertising budgets.

'We have nearly a thousand advertising agencies,' confessed a Brazilian professional to a microphone of Radio France International in May 1988, 'and forty of them work for the government and soak up 60 per cent of the advertising spend.' In fact, the demand for communication through state advertising has little to do with geographical, political and economic differences. The government of France, neo-liberal or socialist, or of socialist Spain, or of one-party Mexico, the alternating Christian Democrat/Social Democrat governments of Venezuela, the neo-liberal government of Britain, they all have constant recourse to advertising to make their policies and achievements known to their citizens. During the 1980s, the state became the main competitor of the soap manufacturers and agro-food companies who are the leading advertisers.

According to the *Financial Times*, Margaret Thatcher's England takes first prize:

Her Majesty's Government this year has achieved what many a decade ago would have considered impossible: it has emerged as the UK's largest single advertiser, overtaking such established consumer goods companies as Unilever and Procter & Gamble. When Mrs Thatcher came to power in 1979, the Government spent a mere £31m on advertising, on things like road safety campaigns. But a decade which has seen record unemployment levels, the selling off of State assets, and the emergence of diseases such as AIDS, has pushed the Government into the forefront of the advertising world . . . it was perhaps hardly surprising that her government should try to use the techniques of persuasion to convince the public that her policies were right. Advertising expenditure by the Government has risen steadily since 1979 to a total £81.4m [in 1986] . . . this year [1987] will push that figure up to at least an estimated £125m – way ahead of any projected increase in advertising by Unilever.[5]

Virtually every big agency in London has benefited. J. Walter Thompson carries out recruitment campaigns for the Royal Air Force, Young & Rubicam for the Navy and the Royal Marines – continuing activity in addition to one-off operations like safety belts, conversion to metric or road safety. When costs began to spiral in 1979, a high government official thought it wise to comment: 'It's not big brother speaking. We're not propagandists in the worst sense of that word. We and our agencies are simply the instrument by which honest social aims, from energy conservation to safer road driving to prison officer recruitment find widespread expression through paid-for ads.'[6]

Referring back to its British and transnational experience, Saatchis gave a list in its 1985 report of the 'new advertisers' who had made a notable entry to the advertising scene during the previous ten years. Along with financial services (banks, insurance companies and other financial institutions) and retailers, it included 'governments in many countries [who] have begun to use advertising on an ever increasing scale to promote all kinds of social causes from road safety to the combat of drug abuse.'[7] Naturally such company reports never make any reference to the mounting criticism which occurs whenever such campaigns are initiated, since the increase in government advertising expenditure is often in direct proportion to the cuts in public spending imposed by the same governments. In Britain, for example, this became obvious in the case of the teacher recruitment campaign entrusted to Saatchis in 1989/ 90, when there was a public scandal concerning the number of children entering primary school, especially in London, who were bereft of teachers.

The French state came late to this form of social communication mediated by modern sales techniques. In 1982 the government of Quebec alone spent ten times as much as the French government in this area. It has been calculated that up to the beginning of the 1970s, for every franc spent on this type of social information in France, 100 were spent in Britain, Federal Germany, Sweden or Canada.[8] If the US is not included in the figures, this – as we have already noted – is because there the agencies have created their own body for carrying out campaigns of 'general concern'. This does not prevent various state offices contracting the services of public relations firms. For many years J. Walter Thompson has been the voice of the famous Marines, the elite corps in which the great pioneer of advertising himself carried arms a century ago.

The British government can boast the oldest tradition. The Empire Marketing Board, one of the first sponsors of the documentary film movement, was set up as early as 1926 to further the marketing of the produce of Empire through all available publicity media. The Central Office of Information, for many years the cornerstone of its social communications policy, dates from 1946. Its mission was to develop communication activities for administrative offices and public institutions, with the participation of experts or agencies, directed at the British Isles and abroad. The COI, which employs 1,000 people including 450 communications professionals, comes under the Chancellor of the Exchequer, the finance ministry which is in principle more neutral than the Cabinet Office.

For a long time, Jacobin France trusted in the institutional mechanisms of its public culture to communicate with the citizen. It took the French political administration thirty years longer than the British to approach the advertising agencies, and in 1976 set up the SID (Service d'information et de documentation). This body, charged with providing specialised information on the civil service and an information service aimed at the public and general users, is close to the political power of the Prime Minister. Responsible for all ministerial campaigns, but excluding the semi-public and nationalised sector, it co-ordinates and organises requirements, and ensures respect for the principle of public competition, putting contracts out to tender by at least four different agencies. Lastly, it supervises the development of campaigns and sets standards of efficiency by means of 'post-tests' carried out afterwards.

The installation of a socialist government in 1981 in no way modified the principle of the need for these campaigns of general concern. On the contrary, official advertising budgets took off with campaigns to encourage reading, the creative use of free time, and on women's rights. The tendency of the state to trust in the advertising sector was reinforced. In 1982, the sum given over to these campaigns went up to $25m (160mFr) – including taxes – as against $9.5m (62mFr) in 1979. To evaluate these figures they should be adjusted, to take account of the rebates allowed on tariffs for campaigns classified as of general concern (in television, government pays only a quarter of the commercial rate). The adjusted figure for the state advertising spend is pretty close to that of the two or three largest private advertisers: L'Oréal, Colgate-Palmolive or Unilever. Of the twenty-six operations, 60 per cent were given to the state-controlled Havas group, and none to the Americans. The teams which had worked most with the preceding regime were virtually discarded, while the (unpaid) originator of François Mitterrand's campaign slogan, 'La Force tranquille' ('The Quiet Force'), carried off the campaigns for solidarity with the unemployed and energy saving.

Nevertheless, on their accession to government, some Socialist Party workers expressed serious reservations about the virtues of using advertising. An enquiry among the socialist ministers at the time of the first international colloquium on social persuasion (held in Paris in December 1981, six months after the presidential electoral victory), indicated clearly the disarray of the leftists faced with these new techniques of governance. Testimonies were recorded like 'When the left was in opposition it had other fish to fry and thought about the question very little', or 'Till today, the left has only gone in for militant communication, or at best, political marketing', or again, 'To say that a social communication is politically neutral is idealistic'. These reflections give some indication that the matter was left very much up in the air.[9]

The use of these 'techniques of social persuasion' during the first years of the socialist government were far from generally accepted on the left no less than on the right. In addition to the inevitable partisan accusations reproaching the powers that be with transforming their communications policy into propaganda through opinion polls, more fundamental questions were also raised about the new way in which democracy was functioning. 'One may ask', remarked Bernard Miège in May 1982, 'if one cannot see in public communications the reinforcement of a process of public opinion management, all the more dangerous if you consider that it takes the place of democratic discussion.'[10]

A very similar question was formulated by a journalist on *La Vie française* a few months later:

> A legitimate sender of messages, the government, if it resorts to advertising, falls willingly into triviality: it modifies its language, disguises it and thus approximates to other types of communication – more accessible to the mass of those it addresses – even identifying itself with them. To what end? To be better understood, of course, but also, to seduce and convince. Because if, in commercial advertising, seduction induces purchase, in matters of public concern, where it deals with ideas, it induces conviction. Acting in this manner, and with these techniques, the government doubles up its forces: it conserves the value of its public power, to which it adds the seductive capacity of 'commercial' practices. Thus, by virtue of this outrageous behaviour, we approach the conditions of manipulation . . . . The normal relation which operates between government decision and communication is no longer respected. In many ways, it seems as if communication is itself converted into an act of government, and in some cases, takes the place of decision . . . . Advertising is sometimes a medium for avoiding real changes in administrative practice which are needed to effect a genuine improvement in communication between the administration and the public.[11]

The irony in all this is that the admiration of the socialist left in France for communication through social advertising, much like its submission to the logic of the media between 1981 and 1986, is of no help to it in elections, and in March 1986, it was forced to hand over the reins of government to a right-wing coalition.

The development of a positive attitude towards advertising by the French socialists is in line with the majority of European socialist parties that came to power in the 1980s, and contrasts with their attitude in the 1970s. The situation in Britain, where the Labour Party remained in opposition, was different. According to a report in *Campaign* in July

1990, 'Labour's attitude to advertising has never been better than ambivalent. At worst it has been downright hostile.' But now Labour 'has been forced to re-evaluate its attitude, having previously mistrusted advertising's manipulative strength and resented the industry's general support for the Tory cause'; and there is 'less fear within the industry that a Labour administration will weigh it down with legislative chains'. Indeed, the Advertising Association has already held talks with Labour 'in an attempt to influence policy'.[12] Perhaps one should recall that the Labour Party's *Green Paper on Advertising* of 1972 was among the few policy documents produced by European socialists which made the American advertising industry sit up and take notice.

THE CRISIS OF PUBLIC CULTURE

Not all the theorists of marketing show much affection for these state advertising strategies which try to alter the relations between the administration and the administered. Is there not a problem in the administration's debility, its incapacity for fresh thinking about the issue? There is. And a fascination with the prowess of advertising and adpeople? This too. But there is also much more to it.

Presenting itself as a technique for the decentralisation of information, as a means of opening out towards the mass of the population, public communication is well suited to the centralisation of the state. This is what Jacques Lendrevie believes:

Advertising is a very accomplished form of centralised information. It is centralised itself. A campaign is a set of instructions from A to Z which can be decided on and controlled by a single person or a very small team, at the highest level and with maximum guarantees. It is a spokesperson which you alone manipulate and which promises to deliver you a considerable, practically guaranteed audience for a chosen message, supposedly such that the message sent will be the message received (though the latter, in reality, is quite another matter). Advertising is a communication which is believed – at the highest level – to be capable of complete control. Generally, ministerial departments worry only too little about problems of information and day-to-day communication between services and their users. Advertising campaigns, however, are directed or at least strictly controlled by the administrators. But then who is speaking? The politicians or the civil servants?[13]

This is an explanation unafraid to get to the bottom of the matter. A rare event with the rise of the mentality of advertising. Notice that these remarks date back to 1980.

In effect, the state and its administrative logic, in order to face up to a loss of legitimacy, have looked for alternatives among the procedures employed in the private sector. To arrest the crisis of the state – which is evidently not terminal – it has resorted to 'management' (which offers the state a method of rationalising the way it is run) and to marketing (which engages the public in an altered relationship). In the slide from citizen to customer can be seen the evolution of the relation of the state apparatus to civil society, and of conceptions of the intervention of public power in the private life of the administered.

'Where is public management going?' asked the organisers of a 1980 colloquium jointly set up by the University of Paris-Dauphine and the Centre d'Enseignement Supérieur des Affaires, which is connected to the HEC (École des Hautes Études Commerciales). 'Where is private management going?' answered Romain Laufer. By this he wanted to point to the structural and not incidental character of the introduction of management techniques, in this case those of advertising, into state management, and the impossibility of an answer without rehearsing the traditional dichotomy between the cultures of the public and the private sectors. Thinking out loud about his own doubts, Laufer suggested the following hypothesis: 'In the big private sector companies, let's say that parallel with the introduction of managerial logic in administration, they experienced the evolution of their management towards forms approaching those of the public sector, whilst administrative and political logics were progressively introduced in their midst.'[14]

The legitimacy crisis of the state, which is none other than a crisis in the limits between the public and private sectors, is a question of the shock and mix of cultures which grew ever deeper during the 1980s.

The royal route chosen by the centralised state, the practice of public communication, has radiated out through the whole of the body politic. Practice and know-how, how to apply the rules of enterprise to create the 'extra' which turns something into an event: the knowledge of communication reaches regional and local government too. Any important municipality aspires to having its own 'communication' plan aimed at integrating the local population in the common project. And above all – in the context of decentralisation – to achieve new triumphs in such a highly competitive situation by attracting companies to the locality. From now on, the notion of management forms part of the daily Ten Commandments of the municipality, which discovers that it too is a product, a provider of services and the bearer of a market.

'Today', says a local mayor, 'all elected representatives communicate. Because everything is communication! Dustbins on the pavement, a council truck, these things are municipal media. The mayor who can't explain the reason for electing him runs the risk that his initiatives, however praiseworthy, will become the subject of daily complaint!'[15] But if, in the language of management, 'the art of communicating is the democratic participation of people in the life of the city', then the art of politics is still to be sewn up. 'Everything you see in a community is communication. To forget it, not be prepared to issue messages, means running useless electoral risks.' Image shock. The weight of the vote.

Even when the old practices of Jacobin institutions and their culture of secrecy have been rendered obsolete, the new strategies of public communication are still able to erect new screens.

REJECTION OF POLITICS?

More than three decades after the American networks, French society has discovered the 'must' of political marketing: commercials. The audiovisual law of 30 September 1986 itself, passed by a right-wing majority and dealing with freedom of communication, removed the obstacles to the privatisation of the premier public service channel and authorised political advertising on the small screen outside the official period of electoral campaigning. The law of 13 December 1985, passed by a socialist majority, established the precedent by allowing transmission of advertising with a political character.

The numerous hearings held by the CNCL (Commission nationale de la communication audiovisuelle) to investigate forms of control over this new kind of political advertising, revealed the differences between partisans and opponents.[16]

In favour – the majority of the right, the extreme right, and advertising consultants: 'This form of advertising reflects among politicians a will to modernise and integrate in the communications society'. A political communications consultant adds: 'It is urgent to readjust political discourse to what has become habitual in media consumption. The more it responds to the needs of spectacle, which is one of the needs of society today, the more the rest will become free.'

Against – the Socialist Party, the Communist Party, the Social Democratic centre, political scientists and a few advertising experts. 'We fear a degradation of debate and discussion, and consequently, the discrediting of political life, as well as the aggravation of the financial inequalities between political parties.' The director of the department of Havas-Conseil specialising in institutional advertising adds: 'There is a professional lobby which defends its empire, a pressure group: adpeople, left or right, who are pushing hard to enlarge their market without considering the consequences: making politics and power on television into a circus.'

The country's citizens have said 'No!' plainly and massively. This is clearly conveyed in a Harris poll for *Stratégies* in May 1987 which was the first sounding of national opinion on the subject of political commercials. Two out of every three people questioned (whatever the sex, age, profession or political tendency) were quite opposed or completely opposed to them. Among right-wing voters, between 52 and 56 per cent were against the position held by their leaders. The disapproval of left-wing voters was even higher: 86 per cent of communist voters and 71 per cent of socialists were hostile. Sympathisers of the extreme right stayed in line: with 48 per cent in favour and 41 per cent against, they were the only exception to general disapproval. 'Don't knows' were no more than 14 per cent. This is more or less the same proportion as abstainers in presidential elections.[17] Why this hostile majority? In the first place, fear of disadvantage and a loss of identity in the case of small groups; fear also, of the trivialisation of politics; and lastly, the suspicion that such commercials are anyway useless.

The most decided are the youth: 84 per cent of under-25s do not believe in the influence of commercials on politics, which, they maintain, remains the domain of conviction, not seduction. Meanwhile one of the arguments of those in favour is precisely that it can seduce young people, by moulding into the audiovisual forms they are supposed to love, especially advertising.

Who believes the future can be foretold? In 1988, the law was reversed, and France reverted to the situation which exists in Britain, where political advertising on television has never been considered acceptable, and a system of party political broadcasts operates instead.

12

THE WEAPONS OF CRITICISM AND THE CRITICISM OF WEAPONS

A new subjectivity?

NOT FROM INFORMATION ALONE. . .

Advertising is no longer what it was, and nor is criticism. The list of critical writings on advertising is not very long. Since the end of the 1970s, the room they occupy on the shelves of libraries and bookshops has even shrunk, like old leather. But there has been an avalanche of textbooks, manuals and instructional literature for professionals in advertising, marketing and management, whose function is not exactly to distance themselves from their subject.

The great epoch of critical investigation was in the 1960s and early 1970s (with a chronology, appearance and mode of expression corresponding of course to the specific circumstances of each country). This was the epoch when structuralism triumphed and discovered the symbolic. Structural anthropology at that time taught that symbolic interchange is the fundamental structure of all culture, while linguistics proposed to construct a science of signs, a 'veritable science of culture inspired by semiology', in the words of a leading light of =0the time, Roland Barthes, author of *Mythologies*.[1]

In placing the accent on the symbolic, the structural approach revealed a quality in the activity of advertising which had been largely ignored: the dreamlike. Previous critics – more particularly, those inspired by the consumer movements – had considered advertising as an instrument of promotion endowed with a single positive dimension, its functionality: factually objective information, informative communication with nothing mendacious, dishonest or fake. An idealisation. The aspect of spectacle escaped them, the dimension of artifice which tries to arouse the spectator's pleasure in advertisements through humour or aestheticism.

In those days students demonstrated on the streets and on campus against so-called consumer society. Conservative functionalism and its 'closed discourse' were stigmatised and their analysis of the 'manifest content' of the products of mass culture swept away by the tide of lectures in ideology which decoded signification and ran its meaning to ground.

The demystification of the discourse of advertising and its idea of modernity were accompanied by the rise of new forms of social consciousness of sexism, racism and other kinds of social exclusion.

This heated moment of theoretical and social argument about advertising and the marketing environment of the media also sees the emergence of a certain ambivalence. Instruments fine-tuned by anthropology and structural linguistics also enable the advertising industry to carry out a professional revolution, and to achieve legitimacy in societies still reluctant to marry culture and business. It emerges, as one writer puts it, that what Claude Lévi-Strauss calls 'primitive thought' (la pensée sauvage)*, is not peculiar to 'primitive' societies, but that

> trademarks in contemporary society function a little like totemic systems or pagan polytheism. This anthropological vision absolves advertising: there is nothing new under the sun . . . . It allows a reconciliation with industrial culture . . . . Philosophically it implies a sort of idealism of the sign. Since man is a symbolic being, constituted through and through by the symbol, one can take this as far as considering that 'everything is a sign' and the referent is no more than its 'projected shadow'.[2]

Linguists and semiologists made an essential contribution to the clarification of the phenomena of coding and decoding in advertising discourse. Lexical analysis and les sémio-tests made their appearance in the big French agencies at the beginning of the 1970s. It was only in the 1980s that the leading Anglo-Saxon companies began to appropriate these 'sciences of interpretation'.[3]

THE REFERENT

In 1976, at an opportune moment, an isolated study came out which chronicled this referent that had been silenced by the idealism of the sign: *Captains of Consciousness* by Stuart Ewen.[4] It is still today one of the very few historical studies on the formation of the apparatus of advertising. The author demonstrates the appearance of new doctrine, consumptionism, in the same period of the 1920s, which sees the establishment in America of the mode of organisation, the system of control of production and the labour process, known as Taylorism. The captains of industry were able to worry a little less exclusively about production problems and turned their attention to those of the consumption of the goods which they put on the market. The transformation of the captain of industry into a manager was born out of crisis. Pressuring the

---

* The eponymous book title is translated as *The Savage Mind*. [Translator's note.]

consumer by means of marketing became indispensable in order to launch into new mass-production methods and at the same time strangle the social conflicts which accompanied mass production. Ewen demonstrates with precision the mechanism which allowed consumption to be presented as the natural expression of democracy. He situates the role of advertising in the construction of the target 'family', the masterpiece of this 'modern architecture of daily life' which combines roles for the New Woman, the Father, and the Youth.

In 1971, in a pioneering but once again isolated study, the German philosopher Wolfgang Haug began to forge the concept of 'commodity aesthetics': to situate the advertising apparatus in relation to the construction of identity. This was another way of bringing out that the referent really exists. He writes:

> The efficiency principle of commodity aesthetics is practised by every half-way decent salesperson; the Archimedean Point of all his promises lies in the buyer, not in the product. 'The wish is father to the thought.' This also holds true for the consumer. Commodities are moulded according to this wish – primarily in their shape and exterior. They are already elaborated into complex pictures on the package and transformed into 'images'. Image is not only to be understood as 'iconic', but more in terms of the word 'Imago', as in 'imaginary'. Commodity aesthetics organises imaginary spaces around the commodity. They contain the inklings of the identity that is shown as mediated through the use of the commodity in question. These inklings offer the addressee the promise that after purchase, they will reflect in his new self-representation, and, in this way, they will solve the problem of identity.
>
> The imaginary spaces around the product are intended to become spaces in our imagination that will be filled through aesthetic-symbolic activity . . . . A pair of pants, a cigarette, a drink are now 'more' than just pants, cigarettes and drinks. Their consumption induces an imagination of identity. In this regard commodity aesthetics will model needs and the way in which we experience their gratification, thus dramatically influencing everyday culture.[5]

Haug thus tries to overcome the limits of the analysis of the two Marxist economists, the Pauls Baran and Sweezy, in their *Monopoly Capitalism* of 1966. Here the two authors demonstrate how 'monopoly rather than competition rules contemporary capitalism'. They insist on the role of 'the management of demand by the oligopolies which dominate monopoly capitalism'. According to them, the process of demand management begins and ends with the market for the commodity – first as 'test markets', and, when product and package production have been suitably designed and executed, as mass-advertising marketing.[6]

In 1977, the Canadian Dallas Smythe came up with one of the first analyses of the organic link between advertising and the way the media function. He also distances himself from the analysis of Baran and Sweezy, whom he charges with being too indebted to theories of psychological manipulation. At the same time, he asks about the blindspot which, he thinks, affected the materialist approach to the media. He explains:

What do advertisers buy with their advertising expenditures? As hard-nosed businessmen they are not paying for advertising for nothing, nor from altruism. I suggest that what they buy are the services of audiences with predictable specifications who will pay attention in predictable numbers and at particular times to particular means of communication (TV, radio, newspapers, magazines, billboards, and third-class mail). As collectivities these audiences are commodities. As commodities they are dealt with in markets by producers and buyers (the latter being advertisers). Such markets establish prices in the familiar mode of monopoly capitalism. Both these markets and the audience commodities traded in are specialised. The audience commodities bear the specifications known in the business as 'the demographics'. The specifications for the audience commodities include age, sex, income level, family composition, urban or rural location, ethnic character, ownership of home, automobile, credit card status, social class and, in the case of hobby and fan magazines, a dedication to photography, do-it-yourself crafts, foreign travel, kinky sex, etc.

How are advertisers assured that they are getting what they pay for when they buy audiences? A sub-industry sector of the consciousness industry checks to determine. The socio-economic characteristics of the delivered audience/readership *and* its size are the business of A. C. Nielsen and a host of competitors who specialise in the rapid assessment of the delivered audience commodity. The behaviour of the members of the audience product under the impact of advertising and the editorial 'content' is the object of market research by a large number of independent market research agencies as well as by similar staffs located in advertising agencies, the advertising corporation =!and in media enterprises.[7]

Dallas Smythe certainly privileges economic logic in his analysis, to the detriment of the cultural logics which equally constitute the mode in which the television apparatus constructs the social relationship with its audiences. But there is no denying that the polemic launched by this investigator came at an opportune moment. Through its radicalism, it attacks the holes in the idealism of the sign. In a general way, Smythe calls into question a dominant tendency in the approach taken by left criticism of the media and advertising in particular; namely, the instrumental vision of advertising and the overall mode of communication which, while it distinguishes between good and bad advertising, good and bad use of 'advertising techniques', is unable to capture the essence of technical-commercial logic.

It was precisely this instrumental vision which started to spring leaks at the end of the 1970s, in a Europe where the notion of public service as the organisational principle of the audiovisual media is radically called into question on the one hand by market forces, and on the other, by progressive movements in various countries struggling to create free radio and television.[8]

Through the refutation of the instrumental vision of advertising and the media emerges progressively an epistemological break in relation to manipulative concepts of power. For a long time the term 'poisoning' or 'manipulation' had been the critical point of reference. Student slogans and denunciations by leftist parties, not to mention the religious establishment and various theories, all embodied this way of seeing and analysing the social operation of the advertising apparatus. The conception is already found, in the 1930s, among the welfare state economists, who distinguish between the good and bad use of advertising; between constructive advertising and the other, aggressive kind; between informative advertising and the advertising of persuasion and manipulation; and who do not hesitate to propose that the state should eliminate the evils of competitive advertising, conserving only the constructive aspects.[9] It is also found in those years in the analyses of mass-behaviour theories by progressive thinkers like Tchakotine.[10] Nearer to us in time, it is taken up in the charges made by Vance Packard against the 'hidden persuaders', whom, he says, the consumer is unable to resist.[11] It is found in Baran and Sweezy. It infiltrates, finally, the analysis of the advertising's strong power of conviction by the liberal economist John Kenneth Galbraith, who believes that if this skilful form of mass persuasion which accompanies the adjustment of demand had been lacking, growing abundance would easily have decreased people's interest in acquiring more and more goods.[12]

Interrogation of the theory of manipulation produces other hypotheses. For one thing, it makes it possible to ask about the substantial mutations going on in the mode of capital accumulation. It leads to questions about the unprecedented nature of what Michel Foucault, referring back to Jeremy Bentham, calls 'the network of disciplinary mechanisms running through society'. At one extreme, the 'discipline blockade', 'the enclosed institution, established on the edges of society, turned inwards towards negative functions', in other words, the prison, school, factory, barracks and hospital which all share a common form of organisation. At the other, the 'discipline-mechanism' itself, a functional system of subtle coercion designed to 'improve the exercise of power by making it lighter, more rapid, more effective' – in short, a flexible system of regulation, a mode of organising space and time and insuring the positive reproduction of disciplined behaviour in society at large.[13]

For another thing, the decline of the idea of manipulation leads back ever more urgently to the question, long neglected, even ignored, by the structuralist approach and its passive conception of the receiver: what the devil do consumers do with what they obtain, absorb, and pay for? How do they use these things? To formulate these questions also opens up the topic of popular culture, distinct from the conservative sociological tradition which has confused it with what is known as mass culture. It is the merit of Michel de Certeau to have begun to situate these problems theoretically. Challenging Pavlovian constructs of the subject, he insists on the need to consider the numerous ruses daily employed by consumers to subvert the networks of ordinary commodities and established order through the way they put things to use. The basis of a true anthropology of use inspired those who remain dissatisfied with or indifferent to three theories of social reproduction which omit to consider the active role of the user of the social and cultural apparatus. A return to the daily 'micro-procedures' which the philosopher Henri Lefebvre, fellow-traveller of Surrealism, Situationism and heterodox Marxism already spoke of in the 1950s. Only the 'critique of everyday life' seemed to him adequate for an understanding of how the modernity of the marketplace could painlessly install itself on the horizon of human happiness.[14]

Before the 1970s were over there was another important change in critical approaches to advertising. Basically its origin was in the growing awareness of major world imbalances. For the first time, the international dimension of advertising was raised and debated in the representative bodies of the nation states, and in the context of a radical questioning of the power relations between the major industrialised countries and the nations of the so-called Third World. The most fruitful commentaries were unquestionably those of people who had spoken least: for example, the discussions which took place about the marketing strategies of the transnational agro-food and pharmaceutical companies, which resulted in 'codes of conduct'. In grappling with the question of advertising as a transnational system, criticism stripped bare a whole model of development and growth. Just as in other situations and other movements, denunciations began to be made by people worried about the survival of a planet threatened by a model of hyper-consumerism of commodities and resources.[15]

New forms of collective struggle began to produce a response to transnational consumption patterns. The first action network, IBFAN (International Baby Food Action Network) with 100 groups in 64 countries, provided a role model for other similar networks: Health

Action International (HAI) with 120 activist locations; Pesticide Action Network (PAN) with 300 groups and individuals; Action Groups to Halt Advertising and Sponsoring of Tobacco (AGHAST), run by IOCU (International Organisation of Consumer Unions), the main link between international pressure groups. Their motto: 'Think globally – Act locally'. All of them combined local campaigning with national and international efforts via meetings, information exchanges and pressure campaigns on advertising regulatory bodies. Above all, these actions gave birth to new historical subjects and ways of co-operation and exchange between North and South, a new kind of internationalism.

Nevertheless, the innovatory character of these collective actions cannot hide the weakness – within traditional social organisations under late capitalism, whether parties or unions – of the analysis of these models of hyper-consumerism which profit a fifth of humanity, and without which this increasingly complex apparatus of global communication and marketing would not make sense. This failure became so glaring in the course of the 1980s that in the course of confrontations within the European Community, those poorly thought-out criticisms of unfair advertising were of little weight in the face of the lobbying carried out by the advertisers, agencies and media tripartite, who rapidly understood the global nature of the stakes involved in the rise of the 'communication society'.

THE NEW CONQUEST OF SPACE

During the 1980s, the space occupied by advertising worldwide expanded considerably. The processes of deregulation and privatisation of the systems of information and communication have opened up access to screens and targets which only yesterday, in the name of public service and interest, or the protection of vulnerable categories of the population, were kept closed. Advertising has suddenly become an essential actor in the financial deals of the new hyper-competitive audiovisual landscape; an unavoidable presence in the high spheres where the forms to be taken by the regime of television in the immediate future are discussed and decided; and lastly, a paragon of the so-called modernity of the media. Advertising is less and less content to channel funds and control the appearance of commercials on the screen, and has increasingly become a major protagonist in the new regime of television. It provides more than ever before the model of media organisation.

Advertising has achieved greater social legitimacy. The new primacy of the market, the ideas of enterprise and 'company spirit', has much to do with this. The 1980s have been consecrated to the hegemony of the corporation and its values, and their role in restructuring our societies, as well as the parallel decline of the welfare state and the welfare economy.

The vanguard of capitalism no longer dances to the rhythm of Taylorism and Fordism, even when ample sectors of the active population worldwide – women and men – are still subject in their daily life to these vertical forms of organisation and production, in the workplace and on the part of authority. The system of production has to appropriate the information, experience and know-how of those it puts to work. If social contradictions arise, better not to confront them face on, but negotiate and exploit them to make them productive. The slogan of this vanguard consists from now on in the flexible management of complex industrial structures. The search for integration is found at every level, from the integration of workers in the same firm, through the construction of 'company spirit', to the integration of consumption, distribution and production. All of which requires the creation of a 'new mentality'.

The massive call to communication as a technique for the management of social relations contributes to forging this new 'corporate identity'. Confined for a long time to the edges of 'national identity', the notion of 'identity' is appropriated by experts in corporate communication and the sociology of organisations, who are not shy about conceptual transference. Turning to the notion of national identity in the work of the historian Fernand Braudel, a corporate communication specialist wrote in 1988:

> In a passage where 'corporation' can be substituted for 'nation', Braudel explains: 'a nation can only exist at the cost of continual self-searching, transforming itself in line with its logical evolution, opposing others unfailingly, identifying with the best and most essential in itself, and in consequence recognising itself in a brand-name image, passwords known to initiates (be they an elite or the mass of the population, which isn't always the case). To recognise itself in a thousand aptitudes, beliefs, ways of speech, alibis, the vast oceanic unconscious, obscure ideological confluences, myths, ghosts . . . . Moreover, every national identity implies, necessarily, a certain national unity, it is like a reflection, a transference.'[16]

From the concept elaborated by the historian to talk about communication as a technique for managing social contradiction is no more than a step, which systems theory is happy to take.

But the expansion of advertising space also takes place through a new mapping of historical and geopolitical spheres. The transnationalisation of economies and cultures does not operate today solely under the banner of American power. With the appearance of protagonists from other territories, other histories and other cultures have made their début. And not only 'other ways of doing business', but also other forms of resistance. Accustomed to conceive the international model of the valorisation of capital in terms of the most advanced country – did Marx not write that 'the most industrialised country presents the others with the image of their future'? – we forgot the 'added value' of these other capitalisms, secondary in world terms but in movement towards transnationalisation. This is as true for the First World as for the Third World. This new aspect is even more contradictory, since in these other territories, innumerable intellectuals, mobilised during the 1960s and 1970s, no longer believe in the possibility of realising the political utopias which would abolish the huge world imbalances, and they have channelled their knowledge and expertise into 'administrative research'.

The new geopolitical division of the world, which has brought the collapse of 'actually existing socialisms' and the end of the cold war, only adds further complexity to the panorama of power relations involved in the construction of a planetary space. Faced with the multiple entice-ments to which these societies awakening to liberty are now subjected, a crucial question arises: what shape will be taken by the investigation of a social model beyond what the Hungarian video-maker Istvan Javor calls 'economic totalitarianism', and what Vaclav Havel simply calls 'the materialism of the Western consumer societies'? Contrary to what is too-often thought in the Europe of the Community, steeped in its prosperity and the idea that it possesses the key to democracy, this crucial question concerns the citizens of every country at the moment when the 'advertis-ing paradigm' tries to impose itself at all points of the compass as the dominant mode of communication between individuals and commu-nities.

These new challenges are so important that the old diplomacy and international geopolitics monopolised by the state and its political actors tend to give way to the new actors of the geo-economy. It is not for nothing that certain Mexican commentators have seen in the project for a single market from the Arctic to Yucatán a new version of the Monroe Doctrine. In other words, a continuation by economic means of the old project of political annexation of Latin America, for which they have suffered so many brutal interventions by gunboat diplomacy since the end of the nineteenth century.[17] These regional global spaces are henceforth macro-territorial units where the process of de-territorialisa-tion and re-territorialisation of national and local spaces is partly played out.

THE MUTATION OF PUBLIC SPACE

With the rise in force of the norms of privatisation and the market, a new cycle has begun in the modes of social regulation.

At the beginning of the 1970s, the German philosopher Jürgen Habermas signalled the manner in which the democracies of the big industrialised countries were being transformed into what he called 'societies of generalised public relations'.[18] A theme which he developed more fully in his major work on the appearance and decline of public space, or the public sphere, as a constitutive element of bourgeois society.[19] Here he demonstrated how one of the most fundamental aspects of the bourgeois revolutions in England and France lay in the sanctioning of the subjection of political power to the principle of publicity. In general terms this means: political decisions are henceforth adopted by bodies whose functions are explicit for everyone (constitutional) and according to procedures that are also known and relatively transparent (laws voted by parliament); publicity presupposes for its realisation the legal sanctioning of the sites of debate on collective interests (in the realm of the state, parliament; beyond it, in clubs, a free press, café society and other sites of social gatherings), as well as the institution of mechanisms capable of providing the citizenry with information and explanation of the options (advertised debates, posters, official bulletins, etc.). Political choices are elaborated under the eyes of all, according to a contradictory procedure in which confrontation of opinions leads to decision-making.

According to Habermas, the invasion of the public sphere by the techniques of advertising – which becomes necessary from the economic point of view – has taken liberal democracy from one form of publicity to another: from a form that appeals to the public use of Reason (*Aufklärung*) and reflection by its receivers, and which signifies the demystification of political domination, to one that resorts to emotion, manipulation, logics of irrational bent. This latter form of publicity is satisfied with the accumulation of behavioural responses determined by passive assent, which ask nothing more of the citizen–consumer than consenting behaviour. Without being committed to Habermas's concept of manipulation – strongly influenced by work carried out in the 1960s – which leaves little room for action by civil society, one can only adopt the central questions which the German philosopher addresses. Questions about the modifications to which political struggle is subjected with the appearance of these new forms of publicity, with their return to secrecy and opacity, contemporaneous with the emergence of experts in advertising communication; and the fragmentation of perception on the part of media-users, increasingly disconnected from a global vision of collective concerns.

Habermas's principal merit is to have anticipated questions which became pressing with the passage of the 1980s and the crisis of the welfare state, a form of state which still seemed eternal at the time that he began his interrogation of the concept of the 'public sphere'.

With the legitimacy crisis of the state and of public service, marketing (which like the sophistical philosophy of old chose empiricism as its method, rhetoric as its means and pragmatism as its aim) has aligned the practices of actors in the public sphere with those of the private sector. As Romain Laufer and Catherine Paradeise commented in 1982:

> From now on, the activities of administration, politics, and enterprise follow the same paths as management and marketing: the divisions within and between each of these sectors which liberal discourse kept separate have been scrambled. The fixed relations of exclusion and subordination have been destroyed by practice. The distinctions between the market and the firm, between governor and governed, citizen and the body politic; equally between the activity of the entrepreneur, the politician and the administrator, who all require information about different publics in order to define their products; who all employ the weapon of seduction through advertising; who all, in short, concern themselves with the same form of management of their 'fabrications' and 'sales', and also =of their image.[20]

The new public space will be more and more driven by 'images'. Not only the images carried by the electronic entertainment media, where fiction and advertising, advertising and actuality increasingly interpenetrate, but also the images which construct 'corporate visual identity'. Design, logo, symbol, packaging, in short everything which constitutes the 'communicating dimension' of the product, or better, which transforms the product into a means of communication. The visual supply is a function of the acceleration of the process of renewed stimulation of sales and the internationalisation accruing to the packaging of the product. A study issued in 1989 by the French Ministry for Research and Technology even states that 'graphics and design will be the differentiating factor on the increasingly competitive international market in the next few decades'. We can add that high-profile strategies and mediatisation stimulate corporate production of films and videos about the corporation itself for use both internally and by the general public.

This ascendant legitimacy of the image – and the image as a growing source of legitimacy – overthrows the paradigms to which political scientists as much as sociologists have been habituated. For anyone looking for new paths of research on the evolution of public space, the hypotheses proposed by Fredric Jameson on 'Postmodernism and the market' are especially pertinent.

> In the tendential identification of the commodity with its image (or brand-name or logo), another, more intimate symbiosis between the market and the media is effectuated, in which boundaries are washed over (in ways profoundly characteristic of the postmodern) and an indifferentiation of levels gradually takes the place of an older separation between thing and concept (or indeed economics and

culture, base and superstructure). For one thing, the products sold on the market become the very content of the media image, so that, as it were, the same referent seems to maintain in both domains. This is very different from a more primitive situation in which to a series of informational signals (news reports, *feuilletons*, articles) a rider is appended touting an unrelated commercial product. . . . I think a profound modification of the public sphere needs to be theorized, the emergence of a new realm of image reality which is both fictional (narrative) and factual . . . and which now – like the former classical 'sphere of culture' – becomes semi-autonomous and floats above reality, with this fundamental historical difference that in the classical period reality persists independently of that sentimental and romantic 'cultural sphere', whereas today it seems to have lost that separate mode of existence, culture impacting back on it in ways that make any independent and as it were non- or extra-cultural form of reality problematical (in a kind of Heisenberg principle of mass culture which intervenes between your eye and the thing itself), so that finally the theorists unite their voices in the new doxa that the 'referent' no longer exists.[21]

USER-CUM-CONSUMER IN THEORY AND PRACTICE

'Advertising is the shortest route from producer to consumer', wrote the founder of J. Walter Thompson in 1909. A small problem remains: in spite of the years and the human and financial resources which have been invested in research, the consumer is still a black box and the *bête noire* of the producer.

Maximum technique, minimum efficiency. The more exposure, the less the consumer remembers. To the great displeasure of professionals in commercial persuasion, advertising misses the target. The great majority of messages get lost, are not decoded, not remembered, or are interpreted according to some other code. Advertising is reduced to promoting itself.

This observation is so current within the profession that the theorists of 'less government' within the business have converted it – a little perversely – into an argument for the deregulation of the sector, that is, the end of rules governing the volume of advertising. In 1976, as the confrontation between the US advertising industry and the federal authorities intensified, one analyst commented: 'Will it be impossible for advertising to remain adequately productive under the new imperatives [of increasing, though more restrictive regulation]? Well, right now 85% of the advertising messages don't persuade because they are not seen or heard. Another 5% to 10%, although registering, are not believed.'[22]

Again it would help to know what is being spoken of and what is being measured. Nothing is less clear when you scrutinise the different ways in which the research financed by the industry has defined and treated the question of the 'effects of advertising' in the domain of the firm, the economy and society. The debates which permeated the strategies of privatisation and deregulation of television in the 1980s hardly moved beyond these two poles: on the one side, the opponents of privatisation – or more precisely, the caricature of their position by the partisans of deregulation – argued that advertising is wasteful and a drain on resources; it leads to monopoly and eliminates price competition; it raises barriers to market entry and cancels out or reduces competition between firms; it raises costs and prices and results in excess profits; it produces false differentiation by magnifying small or imaginary differences; the information it provides is largely misleading. By contrast, the partisans argue that advertising provides consumers with information on goods and services to enable them to make a choice between the many alternatives; it encourages economic growth, investment and jobs; it maintains and enhances competition; it allows increasing efficiencies of scale (and hence lower prices); it increases, maintains or stabilises demand and thus reduces market risk; it provides incentives to raise living standards. More recently, a new argument has been added: advertising is conducive to a flow of national programming and thus allows an escape from dependency on foreign production.

The most lucid among the few economists of advertising recognise that there is still little hard evidence. According to a report produced for the ITV Association in Britain:

> To say that the function of advertising is communication is to verge on the tautological: the question that has to be addressed is what are the effects advertising produces which make the supplier of consumer goods and services willing to spend money on it. And at the level of the firm – or of the brand – the question is easily enough answered: it is, typically, ultimately to create, maintain or increase sales, for existing, modified or new products or services, in a competitive environment. At this level there is not a great deal of academic research available – academics can only rarely secure access to all the detailed information, most of it commercially confidential, necessary for proper analysis . . . . No awards are offered for papers reporting instances where advertising failed to work, and nobody in a position to write such a paper would risk his career by doing so. At the level of the *market* . . . with the application to the question of the disciplines of applied economics, and more particularly with the refinement of statistical and econometric methodology, it became progressively clearer that advertising, whatever it might do for brand shares within a market, could rarely be shown to have any substantial effect on the market as a whole . . . . Findings of this nature,

it might be noted, were not universally accepted by the advertising industry, the less economically sophisticated participants in which have often tended to argue that advertising in some way increases the flow of goods and services and therefore leads, among other benefits, to increased employment and other socially desirable outcomes.[23]

Things get a little clearer. The laws of profitability in the advertising industry remain to be discovered. Whether in relation to the firm or the economy, it is impossible to isolate the impact of advertising. The old witticism, which advertisers repeatedly quote at their agencies, remains vigilant: as William H. Lever, founder of Lever Brothers, put it, 'Half the money I spend on advertising is wasted. The trouble is, I don't know which half.'

The trouble is that all uncertainties become dogmatisms when it comes to constructing a discourse of legitimation to justify an audiovisual policy whose stakes are more important than knowing whether this or that campaign succeeds in selling more tubes of toothpaste!

One thing remains certain: the 1980s have seen an intensification of the concern to understand the black box of the consumer. More and more energy, intelligence and scientific studies have been mobilised by commercial and industrial interests to sound out the process of consumption. In order to try and answer the most elementary question: why, for example, prime-time television has become the Grand Central Station of advertising, instead of the movie theatre with its captive audience, where at times you can hear a pin drop? For the agencies, not to try and find the answer is to remain bound by tariffs determined by audience ratings. And above all, it means a failure adequately to adapt to the new forms of television consumption produced by zapping. Always supposing this is an obstacle which could be avoided!

For very different reasons, the problems which face the receiver are also a tangle. There are those who refuse to submit, with their eyes closed, to the logic of privatisation, and continue asking awkward questions about the social model and relations implied by the dynamic which integrates production, distribution and consumption within the culture industries. There is a great temptation to divide up the field of investigation and isolate the act of consumption from the new apparatus of production. Nothing could be more illusory. As the millennium draws to a close, an intellectual quest becomes clear: how to confirm that the referent still exists, and on the other hand, also understand the ruses employed by users and appreciate their capacity to subvert the programme. Only cynicism or ingenuousness permits the direct confrontation of the two – alternatives which in reality can only be complementary.

Power is not what it used to be, either. But it is still there. And being there, so too are the power relations between individuals, groups, peoples, nations, economies and cultures. What is radically altered with the prodigious rise of this industry of social mediation or engineering of assent are the modes in which power is exercised and the nature of authority. That said, however, it is vital to remember that for millions upon millions of individuals living on this planet, vertical authority, the omnipresence of the repression and manipulation of information – in a word, the dictatorial mode of power – continues to confine their daily lives.

In the current state of reality and the mental landscape, the theoretical panorama oscillates between two postures. The first consists in leaving certain things hanging in the air, trusting in the creative spontaneity of the 'disinterested and casual consciousness of the autonomous individual', and, in the end, adherence to the neo-liberal idea of the absolute sovereignty of the consumer, which ironically, is also a Romantic notion.[24] From here it is only a step to new dogmas and received ideas about the death of ideology, the liquefaction of structures, the evaporation of the logic of social compliance, the invalidation of the very idea of society, whose legitimation is the task of the new median class. It is not a matter, therefore, of questioning the new structuring logics at work in our society, since one way or another they define the reach of the cultural hegemony of the bearers of knowledge and know-how of modernisation.

The second theoretical position consists in disinvesting both the old determinist schemes of structuralism, which conceive the consumer–receiver as a passive subject with no more power than the target at which the arrow flies, and the relativism of ego and behaviourist psychology. To try and find another way of speaking, at one and the same time, of individual liberty and social determination. This is the same as proposing that the effects of advertising on society are not to be found where they are most expected.

For the truth is, many debates on the 'effects of advertising' on society are affected by a serious flaw. They remain too close to the individual advertisement or consumer, while our society is immersed in advertising as the dominant mode of communication. A mode of communication which, whether one wishes it or not, structures choice by establishing a scale of priorities and social preferences in the use which society makes of collective resources – not to mention the individual, as both consumer and citizen.

For the epistemological break of the 1980s to bring about a return to ideas of use and the user and to produce new critical theories, it needs to be let off the leash. The user or consumer must not be left alone in front of the screen, negotiating the meaning of the message in all its multiple mediations. The democratic imperative within mediated and mediatised society must still be allowed to engage with forms of collective expression and organisation of resistance. In place of the slogan 'Less government, more market', intoned by the partisans of professional self-regulation and the metabolism of market regulation, it is vital to speak of 'Less government, more civil society'. That is, more participation by social organisations, more regulation by networks of citizen solidarity over the networks of social control produced by the 'communication society'.

THE NEW TOTALITY

Global, globalisation, total, holistic: under the heterogeneous forms of its social presence, the network of applications of commercial techniques to human relations never ceases to claim the single-mindedness of its project. Instruments and expertise bring a cybernetic vision of society into play. Whence arises a paradox: the more these models of organisation conquer new territory, the more they make us forget that we still occupy a place within history: living, working, amusing ourselves, desiring, seducing and being seduced by our desires, in societies criss-crossed by diverse and multiple interests. Likewise the more they try to divert us from looking inwards. The locus of production of a new rationality of social control, new forms of the exercise of power, new modes of social integration, this industry of mediation is also a privileged site for the formulation of a vulgarised postmodern discourse about the end of the social domain, the inconstancy of the social, the loss of meaning, the renunciation of the rational basis of all values. For advertising leaves truth and falsehood behind.

One person's certainty is another's doubt. The flourishing vigour of 'totalisation' in the advertising industry contrasts with the agony of this concept in the social sciences of late capitalist society. The loss of credibility this concept has suffered signals the end of pretensions to the construction of global theories, and is the fruit of a process of re-examination no less contradictory. The bitter taste of totalitarian horrors; scepticism of discourses which emphasise systems and the spirit of systematisation; defiance in the face of the abstract 'macro-subjects' of Power, State, Society; a preference for individual identity and new intersubjective relations, which try to replace the need to know every-thing with the desire to understand what is happening to the self, the group, the environment. This much is certain. But there is also a huge step backwards towards positivism and philosophies of individual con-sciousness, a return to the illusion that individual emancipation liberates us from history, and from everybody else too. (As Bertrand Russell once said, 'I'm a solipsist, and I can't understand why everyone else isn't as well.')

On the one hand, a communications network, and a concept and vision of the planet as a world market, where you have to think globally and act both globally and locally. On the other hand, fragmentation, by token of

215

local and individual action and agitation, whose meaning tends to decrease to the same rhythm as the old objects of study wither; and the progress of the new forms to replace them, both individual and collective.

A NEW TYPE OF SUBJECTIVITY

In their report of 1985, entitled 'Proposals for Education in the Future', under the direction of the sociologist Pierre Bourdieu, the professors of the Collège de France wrote as follows:

> Among the functions attributable to culture, one of the most important is without doubt the role of self-defence against all forms of ideological pressure, religious and political: this instrument of free thought, like the martial arts in other terrains, allows today's citizens to protect themselves against abuses of symbolic power directed against them, be they advertising, propaganda or political or religious fanaticism.[25]

An affirmation that can only be shared by those for whom the idea of critical consciousness still retains some meaning. But if advertising is no more than a category among the various abuses of symbolic power, does this identify the new forms of social regulation correctly? To take up the simile of the martial arts, is this indeed the correct terrain of combat (given that one has decided that combat is necessary)?

The moment has arrived to ask not what culture can do in the face of the abuses of advertising and marketing, so much as what advertising and marketing have done to culture. At the risk of becoming ineffectual, no analysis, no intervention can elude the question of the hegemony exercised by the pragmatics of marketing over the modern mode of communication. Just as no protagonist of audiovisual production can afford to ignore the implications of the industrial and commoditised mode of production and diffusion for the status of the work, of creation, and the author. Because like it or not, commoditised space has become so pervasive that it becomes impossible to continue thinking of culture as a reserved and uncontaminated terrain. This space has surely become a domain which regulates human relations, as well as the locus on to which conflicts between social projects have been displaced. One cannot explain the process of privatisation of public space – nor its reconstruction – without taking into account the fact of unequal exchange between mercantile reason and public reason, mass culture and 'high culture', mass culture and popular cultures, globalised industrial cultural production and individual cultures. Beyond this incessant and daily process of appropriation and re-appropriation, outside these relations of competition and conflict between culture and economy, it is scarcely possible to imagine the reconstruction of the instruments of free thought, which allows the citizenry to protect itself from these abuses of symbolic power.

Because the capitalisation of culture is also the capitalisation of the most existential levels of subjectivity in the consciousness of the citizen-consumer, who is increasingly influenced by the specialised activities of the professionals and their techniques and devices. The commoditisation of culture is, above all, the production of new kinds of subjectivity. It is precisely because of this qualitative leap in the management of subjectivity that cultural struggles and the stakes involved regain their strategic importance.

This is just what Felix Guattari has described so well – one of the few psychoanalysts to have grasped this new condition. Namely, how and why late capitalism, or 'integrated world capitalism', has increasingly devolved the foci of power from the productive structures of goods and services to those of the sign and subjectivity – mediated, for sure, by the mediatised apparatus of communication:

It is no longer possible to imagine opposing all this only from outside, through traditional political and union activity. Similarly, it becomes imperative to confront its effects amidst daily life in the home, the neighbourhood, the workplace, cultural life and even personal morality. We may note, simply, that one of the main symptoms through which these effects are manifest consists in the infantilisation of human conduct (which must not be confused with 'becoming childish'). Capitalist 'subjectivity', as it is mediated by professionals of every type and size, is manufactured in a form which pre-empts the existence of any intrusion of events likely to annoy or disturb it. Every singularity must be avoided, must be subjected to its devices, its professionals and specialised frames of reference. Thus it goes so far as to try and direct whatever belongs to the method of discovery and invention of the infant, of art or of love, as well as whatever relates to anxiety, pain, death, the feeling of being alone in the cosmos . . . . By appealing to consensual sentiments attached to concepts of race, nation, professionalism, sports, the idealised media star and concupiscence, it becomes intoxicated and anaesthetises itself, in a feeling of pseudo-eternity. It is in the ensemble of these 'fronts', intricate and heterogeneous, that new political and social practices must organise themselves, jointly with new aesthetic practices and new analytic forms, able to work at 'resingularisation', or individual and collective re-appropriation of subjectivity. In effect, 'capitalistic' subjectivity is by no means assured of winning, as it has been over the last decade. Not only could the present financial and economic crisis result in important reformulations of the social status quo and the 'mass-mediatised' imaginary which it supports,

217

but some of the themes sustained by neo-liberalism, such as flexibility in the workplace =and deregulation . . . could perfectly well rebound against it.[26]

One must still be bold enough to declare that the noisy space of desire and dreams with which the networks of the world market try to seduce us in their search for the calculable and predictable individual, is clearly not the secret utopia of the Subjects of the City of the World. The International of the management of consensual sentiment is not, in all certainty, the cosmopolitanism of cultural difference.

The democratic marketplace so beloved by the heralds of this new 'human right of commercial free expression' is in no way the same as the democracy of the defenders of human rights, the rights of the citizen and of nations. Between them there lies the immense abyss with which the new and inegalitarian rationality has bisected a planet that is pierced by social exclusions.

NOTES

1 THE GEOSTRATEGY OF THE NETWORKS

1 'A raider on the prowl', *Newsweek*, 30 November 1987.
2 *Acquisitions Monthly*, cited in *International Herald Tribune*, 25 March 1988, p. 36.
3 'Ten men who shaped advertising', *Advertising Age*, 7 December 1964, p. 6.
4 D. Johnston in *1986 Annual Report JWT Group*, New York, 1987, pp. 4–5.
5 S. Alter, 'J. Walter takeover', *Advertising Age*, 15 June 1987, p. 1.
6 ibid., p. 68.
7 McCann-Erickson Worldwide, *The Story Behind the Names on the Doors*, New York, 1987. The history of the agency is reconstructed from this document and the annual reports of its activities.
8 For the trajectory of the Saatchi brothers, see P. Kleinman, *The Saatchi & Saatchi Story*, Weidenfeld & Nicolson, London, 1987.
9 F. McEwan, 'For the first time an element of fear', *Financial Times*, 29 October 1987, Part II (Section iv).
10 W. Burger, 'The message merchants', *Newsweek*, 21 March 1988, p. 32.
11 M. Jones, 'How British idealism could win over reluctant US clients', *Campaign*, January 1987, p. 13.
12 C. Soula, 'La pub sans frontières de frères Saatchi', *Libération*, 25 March 1987, p. 13.
13 Saatchi & Saatchi, *Annual Report Year Ending September 30, 1986*, London, p.4. Figures for preference shares are 41 per cent, pension funds; 35 per cent, unit trusts, insurance and investment companies; 15 per cent, individuals; 9 per cent, other holders.
14 F. McEwan, 'Voting with their feet', *Financial Times*, 29 October, 1987, p. 21.
15 ibid.
16 'Viewpoint editorial', *Advertising Age*, 3 April 1989, p.16.
17 *Le Monde*, 1 July 1987, p.24.
18 M. Bleustein-Blanchet, 'A l'heure de l'Europe, où en est la publicité française?', *Le Monde*, 17 January 1979, p. 36.
19 *Le Figaro* (Supplement 'Économie'), 2 February 1989, p. xii.
20 *Sunday Times*, 7 May 1989, p. D-13.
21 *Le Nouvel Economiste*, 24 March 1989, p. 69.
22 'Thompson tightens organization', *Advertising Age*, 7 December 1964, p. 202.
23 C. Pfaff, ' "New Economics" in France may kill fixed commission', *Advertising Age Europe*, 23 October 1978, p. E1.

24 'An advertising age roundup. Big issue for '88: compensation', *Advertising Age*, 23 November 1987, p. 1.
25 ibid.
26 L. Kaplan, 'Pub: combien tu veux Doudou dis donc?', *L'Événement du jeudi*, 28 July–8 August 1988.
27 'Intervista a Alex Kroll', *Strategia*, 16–31 May 1988.
28 *Financial Times*, 4 May 1989, p. 12.
29 *Financial Times Survey*, 27 April 1989, p. 34.
30 *Advertising Age*, 6 February 1978.
31 See the dossier on advertising in the Soviet Union published by *Advertising Age*, 12 March 1979.
32 'Editorial: marketing's new frontier', *Advertising Age*, 26 February 1990, p. 30.
33 'Graduates. Finding tomorrow's winners today', *Marketing Week*, 28 March 1986, pp. 30–2. For an historical perspective, see J. Tunstall, *The Advertising Man in London Advertising Agencies*, London: Chapman and Hall, 1964.
34 C. Blachas, 'Editorial: pression sur les commerciaux', *Communication & Business*, 25 April 1988, p. 6.
35 Ph. Rombaut, 'Business Generation', *Le Vif/L'Express*, 9–15 January 1987, p. 8.
36 'TV's megamoguls leave their mark', *Variety*, 20 January 1988, p. 188.

2 CULTURE SHOCK

1 T. Dillon, *Never Boil an Alarm Clock*, New York, BBDO, 1968.
2 For examples of these other ways of looking at popular culture, see E. Hobsbawm and T. Ranger (eds), *The Invention of Tradition*, New York, Columbia University Press, 1983, and P. Burke, *Popular Culture in Early Modern Europe*, New York, New York University Press, 1978.
3 D. J. Boorstin, 'The rhetoric of democracy', *Advertising Age International*, 15 January 1979.
4 K. Lynch, 'Adplomacy faux-pas can ruin sales', *Advertising Age International*, 15 January 1979.
5 'German marketing blends US know-how', *Advertising Age/Europe*, 12 November 1979.
6 C. Endicott, 'Ad growth mirrors rise in world living standard', *Advertising Age*, 30 April 1980, p. 138.
7 OECD, *Recent Trends in International Direct Investment*, Committee on International Investment and Multinational Enterprises, Paris, 1980.
8 United Nations, 'Changes in the pattern of FDI: an update', *The CTC Reporter*, no. 23, New York, 1987, p. 4.
9 N. Dinçbudak, *Les Réseaux transactionnels et l'avenir des systèmes financiers*, IDATE, Montpellier, 1988.
10 *Advertising Age*, 29 October 1971.
11 'Editorial viewpoint', *Advertising Age*, 21 March 1977, p. 24b.
12 D. Cudaback, 'US creativity no longer sets pace for Europe', *Advertising Age*, 21 March 1977, p. 24a.
13 *Advertising Age*, 16 July 1979.
14 L. Wentz, 'Europe opens wallet: Saatchi', *Advertising Age*, 4 July 1988, p. 26.
15 Advertising Association-EAT, *The European Advertising & Media Forecast*, London, NTC Publications, vol. 3, no. 3, December 1988. See also Starch-Inra-Hooper/IAA, *World Advertising Expenditures Report*, 1988.
16 G. Lagneau, *Les Institutions publicitaires, fonction et genèse*, Paris, 1982

(Doctoral thesis for the Université René Descartes), p. viii. See also H. M. Solomon 'Public Welfare, Science and Propaganda', in *Seventeenth Century France, The Innovations of Theophraste Renaudot*, Princeton University Press, 1972.

17 'Marcel Bleustein-Blanchet on the future of advertising in Europe', *Advertising Age International*, 30 May 1977, p. 59.

18 C. Endicott, 'Ad growth mirrors rise in world living standard', *Advertising Age*, 30 April 1980, p. 138.

19 J. Stratte, 'French ad traits', *Advertising Age*, 27 March 1978.

20 *Communication & Business*, 25 April 1988, p. 55.

21 Remarks by the director of the agency Le Goues et Associés. [Author's note.]

22 R. Gavioli, *Grands Prix. I film premiati in trent'anni di festival del cinema pubblicitario*, SIPRA, Turin, 1984.

23 R. Gavioli, op. cit., p. 35.

24 R. Lima Martensen, 'O ensino da propaganda no Brasil', in *O Estado de São Paulo* (Suplemento do centenario), 20 December 1975, p. 4.

25 *Wall Street Journal*, 27 February 1975.

26 J. J. Boddewyn, *Use of Foreign Language and Materials in Advertising*, New York, IAA, 1978.

27 D. Cudaback, 'French language law beginning to worry foreign marketers', *Advertising Age*, 21 March 1977.

28 *Barriers to Entry in the Korean Advertising Industry*, American Chamber of Commerce in Korea, Seoul, December 1984.

29 T. McCann, *An American Company: The Tragedy of United Fruit*, Crown, New York, 1976.

30 J. Meyers, 'BJK & E avoided Contra scandal', *Advertising Age*, 11 May 1987, p. 48.

3 THE LIMITS OF THE GLOBAL SCENARIO

1 See especially T. Levitt, *The Marketing Imagination*, The Free Press/ Macmillan, 1983.

2 J. Perris, *What's Going On in the Media? A Scenario of Opportunities*, Saatchi & Saatchi Compton Worldwide, Media Department, London, 1987.

3 Saatchi & Saatchi Annual Report 1984.

4 G. Levin, 'Shops shape up for foreign growth', *Advertising Age*, 6 March 1989, p. 4.

5 Saatchi & Saatchi Annual Report 1985.

6 ibid.

7 T. Levitt, 'Innovation in Marketing', quoted in Saatchi & Saatchi Annual Report 1984.

8 Y. Wind and S. Douglas, 'The myth of globalization', in *The Journal of Consumer Marketing*, 1986, no. 2. See also, B. C. Blanche, 'Le marketing global: paradoxe, fantasme mondialiste ou incontournable objectif pour demain?', *Revue française de marketing*, August–October 1987.

9 *Advertising Age*, 6 April 1987.

10 E. Nelson, 'Challenge of the new young', *Focus*, June 1986, p. 39.

11 Dentsu Annual Report, 1989.

12 'Bajo la mirada de Ogilvy', Interview with F. Correa, *Publicidad y Mercadeo*, Caracas, February 1988, pp. 28–30.

13 On the redeployment of international accounts, see K. Cote and S. Milmo, 'Managing mega accounts', *Focus*, April 1987.

14 K. Cote, 'Pepsi's satellite challenge', *Focus*, October 1986, p. 23.
15 T. Syfred, 'Pan-European problems for satellite advertisers', *Marketing Week*, 6 February 1987, p. 46.
16 M. Waterson, 'Surprise findings of new comparative ad study', *Focus*, June 1986, p. 47.
17 Advertising Association-EAT, *The European Advertising & Media Forecast*, London, NTC Publications, vol. 3, no. 3, December 1988. See also A. Mattelart, M. Palmer 'L'Europe de la publicité. La critique des sources', *Médias Pouvoirs*, Jan–March 1991; A. Mattelart, M. Palmer, 'Advertising in Europe: Promises, pressures and pitfalls', *Media, Culture and Society*, July 1991.
18 K. Ohmae, *Triad Power*, New York, Free Press, 1985.
19 J. R. Goodyear, 'The future development of international research . . . The multi-lingual, multi-national, multi-variable', Seminar on International Marketing Research (Englefield Green, UK, 16–18 November 1988), ESOMAR (European Society for Opinion and Marketing Research).
20 R. Barthes, *Mythologies*, Paris, Seuil, 1957, pp. 44, 165. Another reference from around the same time is H. Lefebvre, *Critique de la vie quotidienne*, Paris, L'Arche, 1958.
21 J. Baudrillard, 'La morale des objets', *Communications*, 1969, no. 13.
22 *Business International*, 6 August 1978.
23 D. Perrot, 'Réflexions pour une lecture de la domination à partir des objets', *Encrages* (Université Paris-VIII), no. 1, 1979.
24 A. Chetley, *The Baby Killer Scandal*, War on Want, London, 1979.
25 See A. Mattelart, *Transnationals and the Third World, The Struggle for Culture*, trans. D. Buxton, South Hadley (Mass.), Bergin & Garvey, 1983.
26 E. Guinsberg, *Publicidad: manipulación para la reproducción*, Universidad Metropolitana (Universidad Xochimilco), Plaza y Valdés, Mexico, 1987. See also V. Bernal Sahagún, *Anatomia de la publicidad en México*, Nuestro Tiempo, Mexico, 1977 (2nd edn).
27 F. Rello *et al.*, *La industria agroalimentaria*, Mexico, 1980, unpublished. See also the dossier 'Transnationales et agriculture en Amérique Latine' (under the direction of G. Arroyo), *Amérique Latine*, no. 1, January–February 1980.
28 F. Rello *et al.*, ibid.

4 MEDIA WORLDS

1 'The business of media', *Business Today*, December 1987, p. 73.
2 ibid.
3 *Broadcasting*, 9 December 1974.
4 'R.D.: the national book on an international level', *Advertising Age International*, 9 April 1979, p. S-2.
5 ibid.
6 On the internationalisation of the American media see: A. Mattelart, *Multinational Corporations and the Control of Culture*, trans. M. Chanan, Hassocks (Sussex), Harvester Press, 1979. On national/international tension, see A. and M. Mattelart, *De l'usage des médias en temps de crise*, Paris, A. Moreau, 1979 (especially the chapter on 'La culture intérieure').
7 M. Bird, 'Ideas for hire', *International ADMAP*, Summer 1984, p. 63.
8 M. E. Chamard, '*Marie Claire* et *Elle* magazines globetrotters', *Libération*, 24–25 September 1988.

9 I. L. Frias and R. Bedoya, 'Conversación con Carlos Monsivais', *Diálogos*, Lima, January 1988.
10 W. Rukeyser, in *Advertising Age*, 14 December 1987, p. S-4.
11 R. Bechtos, 'Asian edition looks like a strong entry: WSJ', *Advertising Age*, 13 September 1976, p. 61.
12 S. Milmo, 'Global view pulls in readers', *Focus*, March 1986, p. 45.
13 R. Bechtos, 'Asian edition looks like a strong entry: WSJ', op.cit.
14 J. M. Wilson, 'The global film: will it play in Uruguay?', *The New York Times*, 26 November 1978. On the problematic of the global film, see C. Michalet, *Le Drôle de drame du cinéma mondial*, La Découverte, Paris, 1987. See also T. Guback, *The International Film Industry*, Indiana University Press, Bloomington, 1969.
15 J. Valenti, 'Technology is no big, bad wolf to the savvy Yank movie-makers', *Variety*, 20 January 1988, p. 10.
16 See A. S. Vieux, 'Le nouvel âge d'Hollywood', *Le Monde des affaires*, 21 May 1988.
17 *The Independent on Sunday*, 18 March 1990.
18 P. Wintour, 'Labour unveils plan to save film industry', *Guardian*, 31 May 90, p. 13.
19 A. S. Vieux, op. cit.
20 Market share following calculations by Bipe (Bureau d'informations et de prévisions économiques) in a limited circulation study on *Le marché des programmes audiovisuels international*, August 1987.
21 P. Besas, 'Crossovers vie for megabuck tortilla', *Variety*, 23 March 1988, p. 43.
22 *Variety*, 23 March 1988, p. 69.
23 Interview by C. Humblot, *Le Monde radio-télévision*, 10–11 September 1988.
24 H. Behar, 'Un entretien avec David Puttnam', *Le Monde*, 30 September 1987.
25 'Coke's high-priced bid for entertainment', *Business Week*, 1 February 1982.
26 A. Woodrow, 'La création française: crise ou reprise', *Le Monde radio-télévision*, 14–15 November 1987, pp. 16–17.
27 *Variety*, 15 October 1986, p. 61.
28 M. Adelson, 'Global markets looming as bigger slice of TV pie', *Variety*, 20 January 1988, p. 186.
29 P. Besas, 'Crossovers vie for megabuck tortilla', *Variety*, 23 March 1988.
30 ibid.
31 'Entrevista con Miguel Alemán Velasco, director general de Televisa', *Cine-Video*, Madrid, March 1988.
32 E. Guider, 'Sky, Super Channel', *Variety*, 20 January 1988, p. 128.
33 D. Britt, 'Stereotypes fade as the barriers fall', *USA Today*, 19 March 1988, p. 7.
34 K. Rotmyer, 'A Spanish accent is very "in" these days in Madison Avenue', *Wall Street Journal*, 24 January 1975, p. 25.
35 D. Lestrade, 'La disco hispanique', *Libération*, 28 April 1988.

5 THE VANGUARD OF DEREGULATION

1 P. Musso, 'Communication: domination ou régulation', *Société française*, Jan-March 1988.
2 L. Morrow, 'Feeling proud again', *Time*, 7 January 1985.
3 For a history of deregulation see J. Tunstall, *Communications Deregulation, The Unleashing of America's Communications Industry*, Basil Blackwell, 1986; and D. Schiller, *Telematics and Government*, Ablex, Northwood, NJ, 1982.

4 J. R. Meyer, *The Economics of Competition in the Transportation Industries*, 1959.
5 For a view of deregulation by some of its leading militants, see M. L. Weidenbaum, 'The benefits of deregulation', *Policy Review*, Washington, Heritage Foundation, Summer 1987.
6 'Is deregulation working?', *Business Week*, 22 December 1986, p. 2.
7 E. B. Weiss, 'What's ahead for admen, starting third 100 years', *Advertising Age*, 19 April 1976, p. 125. See also D. Tuerck (ed.), *The Political Economy of Advertising*, American Enterprise Institute for Public Policy, Washington, 1978; D. A. Worcester, *Welfare Gains from Advertising*, American Enterprise Institute for Public Policy, Washington, 1978.
8 For a general view, see D. Kunkel, 'From a raised eyebrow to a turned back: the FCC and children's product-related programing', *Journal of Communication*, Autumn 1988, vol. 38, no. 4.
9 E. J. Markey, 'Pendulum swinging back from blind deregulation toward protecting public', *Variety*, 20 January 1988, p. 181.
10 B. Guillou, *Le management des enterprises américaines de communication face à la déréglementation*, SPES-DGT, Paris, 1986, internal document.
11 'Bajo el signo de Leo. Entrevista', *Publicidad y Mercadeo*, Caracas, Venezuela, March 1988, p. 43.
12 R. MacDonald, 'Start worrying tomorrow', *Television Business International*, April 1988, p. 56.
13 ibid.
14 N. Dinçbudak, *Les réseaux transactionnels et l'avenir des systèmes financiers*, op. cit.
15 'Bank says: save on costs with swaps', *TV World*, December 1987, pp. 25-6.
16 P. K. Susz, 'El cine en la encrucijada', Corto Circuito no. 1, 1987, p. 13.
17 J. Beting, 'O setimo mercado', *O Globo*, 27 May 1982.
18 *Variety*, 23 March 1988, p. 45.
19 Interview with Augusto Marzagão, vice-president of Protele (Televisa) and European director, June 1988.
20 *Televisa*, Cenit Publicidad, Mexico, undated.
21 C. Monsivais, 'Le Mexique comme pays neuf', *Libération*, 30-1 July 1988.

6 THE NEW FRONTIER OF THE OLD CONTINENT

1 V. P. Buell, *The British Approach to Improving Advertising Standards: a Comparison with the United States Experience*, Business Publications Services, Amherst (Mass.), 1977.
2 'New rules laid for TV sponsors', *The Guardian*, 21 March 1990.
3 See G. Murdock *et al.*, *Mass Communication and the Advertising Industry*, Paris, UNESCO, 1985; on the history of the advertising industry in Britain, T. R. Nevett, *Advertising in Britain: A History*, London, Heinemann, 1982; R. Williams, 'Advertising: magic system', in *Problems in Materialism and Culture*, London, Verso, 1980 (originally published in *New Left Review*, 1960, no. 4); on the history of advertising in the United States, S. Fox, *The Mirror Makers*, New York, William Morrow & Co., 1984; for an analysis of the professional discourse on advertising, E. Clark, *The Want Makers*, London, Hodder & Stoughton, 1988; M. Schudson, *Advertising, The Uneasy Persuasion*, New York, Basic Books, 1984.
4 'Publitalia shook dozy ad mkt.', *Variety*, 23 April 1986, p. 128.

5 *The European Advertising & Media Forecast*, Advertising Association-EAT, op. cit.; *Television Business International*, April 1988, p. 63.

6 *Variety*, 23 April 1986.

7 ibid., p. 148.

8 'JWT jumped on private TV wagon early for clients', *Variety*, 23 April 1986, p. 148.

9 V. Damico, 'E necessaria una riforma per l'intero sistema radiotelevisivo', *La Pubblicitá*, no. 5, 1988.

10 'Le vittorie concentrate su due sole reti', *Electronic Mass Media Age*, 25 May 1988.

11 P. Rossetti, 'Ve le diamo noi l'America', *Paese Sera*, 3 June 1988.

12 J.-F. Lacan, 'Le comportement des téléspectateurs devant la publicité', *Le Monde*, 22 March 1988, p. 17. For a depth study, see G. Bertrand, C. de Gournay, P. A. Mercier, *Fragments d'un récit cathodique. Une approche empirique du zapping*, CNET/Réseaux, Paris, November 1988.

13 See the dossier 'Télé: la pub prend le pouvoir', *Télérama*, 17 February 1988.

14 According to estimates found in *Advertising Age*, 28 March 1988, p. 33. On the history of the advertising boom in Italy and Spain, see A. Pilati, *Il nuovo sistema dei media*, Comunitá, Milan, 1987; E. Bustamente and R. Zallo (under the direction of), *Las industrias culturales en España*, Akal, Madrid, 1988.

15 See Commission of the European Community, *Television Without Frontiers: Green Paper on the Establishment of the Common Market for Broadcasting, Especially by Satellite and Cable*, Brussels, June 1984, sixth part. Also EEC, 'La politique audiovisuelle de la Communauté. Proposition de directive du Conseil concernant l'activité de radiodiffusion', *Bulletin des Communautés européennes*, Supplement 5/86. For the point of view of the advertising industry, see R. Rijkens and G. E. Miracle, *European Regulation of Advertising: Supranational Regulation of Advertising in the EEC*, Elsevier, Amsterdam, 1986.

16 *Journal officiel des Communautés européennes*, 27 April 1988.

17 See H. Ingberg, *Offre publique audiovisuelle-OPA*, Union des partis socialistes de la Communauté européenne (document), Brussels, 1988.

18 P.-A. Gay, 'La conférence européenne de Stockholm sur l'audiovisuel', *Le Monde*, 25 November 1988.

19 *Le Monde*, 6 April 1989, p. 14.

20 R. Rijkens, 'Europe admen must defend their industry', *Advertising Age International*, 12 February 1979, p. S-4. See also A. Mattelart, M. Palmer, 'La formation de l'espace publicitaire européen: la liberté d'expression commerciale en quête de légitimité', *Réseaux*, no. 42, July–August 1990.

21 S. Downer, 'Central Americans urged to defend ad system', *Advertising Age International*, 11 June 1979, p. S-1.

22 P. H. Power, 'UNESCO has begun a very serious attack on the advertising concept', *Advertising Age*, 22 December 1980. See also C. Roach, 'The US position on the new world information and communication order', *Journal of Communication*, Autumn 1987, vol. 37, no. 4.

23 J. J. Boddewyn, *Foreign Languages, Materials, Trade and Investment in Advertising: Regulation and Self-Regulation in 46 Countries*, New York, IAA, 1985. On the stakes in these debates, see: K. P. Sauvant, *International Transactions in Services: The Politics of Transborder Data Flows*, Westview Press, Boulder, 1986. On the position of the US government and the American business milieu, see the *Annual Report of the President of the United States on the Trade Agreements Program*, 1983 (presented to Congress in April

1984); J. D. Aronson and P. F. Cowhey, *Trade in Services, A Case for Open Markets*, American Enterprise Institute, Washington DC, 1984.
24 *Advertising Age Europe*, 26 March 1979, p. E.20.
25 World Federation of Advertisers, Report and Review, Brussels, 1988 and 1989.
26 P. de Win (WFA's president), 'Editorial', *WFA Report*, November-December 1989.

7 CHANGING ROLES

1 'Lorimar scores on TV and Wall Street', *Business Week*, 22 October 1984, p. 76.
2 D. Kilburn, 'Dentsu looks inward', *Advertising Age*, 20 April 1987, p. 63.
3 F. Segers, 'SogoVision fronts for NHK programs', *Variety*, 23 April 1986, p. 219.
4 'Polémiques autour d'Havas', *Le Monde*, 1 April 1987, p. 15.
5 J.-M. Dru, 'La fin ne justifie pas les moyens', *Le Monde*, 1 April 1987.
6 T. Bannister in C. Soula, 'Lendemain de pub pour les Saatchi', *Libération*, 15 September 1987, p. 15.
7 J. W. Spalding, '1928: radio becomes a mass advertising medium', *American Broadcasting, A Source Book in the History of Radio and Television*, under the direction of L. Lichty and M. Topping, Hastings House, New York, 1975, p. 228.
8 'How advertising and advertising agencies started and grew in the US: a brief history', *Advertising Age*, 7 December 1964.
9 D. MacDonald, 'The history of JWT: its battle to climb back to number one', *Campaign*, 29 March 1985.
10 M. and A. Mattelart, *The Carnival of Images, Brazilian Television Fiction*, trans. D. Buxton, New York, Bergin & Garvey, 1990.
11 'Genesis of the "Soaps"', *Advertising Age*, 20 August 1987, p. 140.
12 M. Adelson, 'Global markets looming as bigger slice of TV pie', op. cit.
13 J. Dempsey, 'Barter biz boom heads for shakeout', *Variety*, 1 April 1987, p. 70.
14 ibid.
15 K. Cote, 'The barter option for Europe', *Focus*, June 1987, p. 13.
16 A. Woodrow, 'Espaces publicitaires contre programmes clés en main', *Le Monde*, 18 November 1987, p. 18.
17 Huitièmes assises nationales du mécénat d'entreprise, ADMICAL (Association pour le développement du mécénat industriel et commercial), Paris, 21 June 1988. On patronage, see 'Dossier sur le financement privé de la culture', *Politiques culturelles*, Notes d'information du Conseil de l'Europe, nos 5-6, 1987; J. Myerscough (under the direction of), *Funding the Arts in Europe*, Policy Studies Institute, London, 1984. See also Conseil de l'Europe, *Comment financer la culture? Méthodes et moyens dans cinq pays*, Strasbourg, 1984; and J. de Chalendar and G. de Brébisson, *Le Mécénat en Europe*, La Documentation française, Paris, 1987.
18 D. Hawkes, *The Identification of Commercial Messages and Sponsorship*, Seminar on the Future of Television Advertising in Europe, organised by EAT, September 1987.
19 J. Michaela, 'Brazilian creatives mix avant-garde, sentiment', *Advertising Age*, 13 April 1987, pp. 64-6.
20 ibid.
21 Conselho nacional de auto-regulamentaçao publicitaria-CONAR, *Codigo brasileiro de auto-regulamentaçao publicitaria*, São Paulo, June 1983.

22 D. Aragao and A. Beuttenmuller, 'As novelas estao em crise, mas faturam como nunca', *Jornal do Brasil*, 15 June 1980.
23 See J. Méndez, *El País*, 1 May 1989.
24 'Le projet "Top Sellers" ', BBDO-CLM Agency, Paris, 1984.
25 ibid.
26 ibid.
27 ibid.
28 See C. Mercer, 'A poverty of desire, pleasure and popular politics', in *Formations of Pleasure*, ed. Jameson *et al.*, London, Routledge, 1983.
29 *La production des films publicitaires en France en 1988*, Syndicat des producteurs de films publicitaires, Paris, 1989.
30 'Interview with C. Palouzie', *Le Cinéma publicitaire en Belgique, Revue belge du cinéma*, hors série, 1987. See also F. Méredieu, *Le film publicitaire*, H. Veyrier, Paris, 1987, p.114.
31 G. Bartulli, 'Sogni di celluloide', *Communicare*, Milan, June 1987.
32 ibid.
33 'Peter Ustinov: ce que je pense de la pub', interview by R. Champseix, *Communication & Business*, 25 April 1988, p. 55.
34 Investigation by R. Champseix, *Communication/CB News*, Cannes Special, 20 June 1988.
35 Comments of Stan Dragoti in J. Pendleton, 'Hollywood buys the advertising concepts', *Advertising Age*, 9 November 1988, p. 158.
36 H. Gauville, 'Goude, la French correction de Marseille', *Libération*, 18–19 June 1988, p. 31.

8 AUDIENCE MEASUREMENT

1 Asa Briggs, *The BBC: The First Fifty Years*, Oxford University Press, 1985, pp. 149–51.
2 S. Ewen, *The Captains of Consciousness, Advertising and the Social Roots of the Consumer Culture*, McGraw-Hill, New York, 1976, p. 54.
3 Cited in Ewen, *The Captains of Consciousness*, op. cit., p. 22.
4 'How advertising and advertising agencies started and grew in the US: A brief history', op. cit., p. 8.
5 ibid.
6 ibid.
7 D. Cohen, *J. B. Watson: The Founder of Behaviourism*, Routledge & Kegan Paul, London, 1979.
8 On the relationship with social sciences and university research, see F. Skelly, 'The impact of advertising on the social sciences', *Advertising Age*, 21 November 1973.
9 'The Advertising Council: an American phenomenon', *Advertising Age*, 21 November 1973.
10 Saatchi & Saatchi, *Annual Report Year Ending September 30*, London, 1980, p. 8.
11 'And now, a word from the sponsors: we're watching', *Business Week*, 5 August 1985.
12 For the analysis of Nielsen and AGB, see *This is Dun & Bradstreet*, The Dun & Bradstreet Corporation, New York 1985; *AGB Research plc Annual Report 1985/1986*, London.
13 See 'Research business report, special report', *Advertising Age*, 11 June 1990.
14 J. Honomichl, 'Dawn of the computer age', *Advertising Age*, 20 August 1987.

15 C. Wilson, 'Peoplemeter fight hits France', *Advertising Age*, 25 January 1988, p. 66.
16 'Television in the peoplemeter age', *Broadcasting*, 7 September 1987.
17 See T. Kelsey, 'The earth moves for the ratings industry', *The Independent on Sunday*, 18 February 1990.
18 M. and A. Mattelart, *The Carnival of Images*, op. cit.
19 'Matrimonio a la fuerza' and 'Rating electronico', *Producto*, no. 54, Caracas, 1988.
20 L. Bogart, 'Mass advertising: the message, not the measure', *Harvard Business Review*, September–October 1976.
21 See the dossier on audience measurement published by *Dossiers de l'audiovisuel*, no. 22, INA-La Documentation française, Paris, 1988.

9 THINK TANKS

1 C. Dussart, *Le Marketing de la troisième vague*, Quebec, Chicoutimi, 1985.
2 K. Weik, cited in T. Peters and R. Watermann, *In Search of Excellence*, Warner Books, 1982, p. 101.
3 Saatchi & Saatchi, *Annual Report Year Ending September 30*, London, 1984, pp. 10–11.
4 B. Cathelat, *Styles de vie*, Éditions d'Organisation, Paris, 1986.
5 M. Herpin, 'Socio-styles', *Revue française de sociologie*, 1986, no. 2.
6 Quoted in 'La recherche sur les audiences des médias audiovisuels', *Technologie, culture et communication, Rapport Mattelart-Stourdzé*, La Documentation française, Paris, 1982, vol. 1. (Translated as *Technology, Culture and Communication, A Report to the French Minister of Research and Industry*, North-Holland, 1985).
7 F. Madrières, 'Pour une meilleure stratégie de communication: portrait robot ou roman photos', *La Communication publicitaire. Recherche et réalité*, Paris, IREP, 1986, pp. 9–10.
8 N. Herpin, 'Socio-styles', *Revue française de sociologie*, 1986, no. 2.
9 E. Neveu, 'Des "classes sociales" aux "sociaux styles". Misère de la sociologie branchée', *Arguments*, no. 9, 1987.
10 Quoted in J. Saville, '*Marxism Today*: An Anatomy', in *The Retreat of the Intellectuals, Socialist Register 1990*, eds Milliband and Panitch, London, Merlin, 1990, p. 37.
11 ibid.
12 A. Michalowska, 'Voilà les euro-styles de vie', *Marketing Mix*, April 1989, p. 31.
13 See A. and M. Mattelart, *Penser les médias*, La Découverte, Paris, 1986, published in English as *Arguments in Media Theory*, trans. J. Cohen and M. Urquidi, University of Minnesota Press, Minneapolis, Minnesota, 1991.
14 F. Madrières, op. cit., pp. 12–13.
15 P. Queen, quoted in M. Gershman, 'The twilight of advertising', *Management Review*, June 1988.
16 E. Fouquier, 'Les aventures de récepteur: petite théorie de l'expérience de réception', *Télévision et publicité. Réflexion sur la communication*, Paris, IREP, 1987.
17 See M. de Certeau, *The Practice of Everyday Life*, trans. S. Kendall, Berkeley, University of California Press, 1983.
18 G. Forestier, 'Le lobbying s'exhibe', *Communication/CB News*, 3 October 1988, p. 47.

10 THE SPIRIT OF ENTERPRISE

1 C. Blachas, 'Edito: communication-minded', *Communication/CB News*, 3 October 1988, p. 6.
2 Corporate, *'L'État de la communication Corporate des entreprises en Europe*, Paris, 1988.
3 ibid.
4 ibid.
5 P. Beaud, *La société de connivence*, Aubier-Montaigne, Paris, 1984.
6 R. G. Meadow, 'The political dimensions of nonproduct advertising', *Journal of Communication*, Summer 1981, p. 69.
7 'Special report: The corporate image, PR to the rescue', *Business Week*, 22 January 1979, p. 47.
8 ibid.
9 J. Humble and M. A. Johnson, *Corporate Social Responsibility, The Attitude of European Business Leaders*, Management Centre Europe, Brussels, 1978.
10 G. Goubert, 'Un échec de communication', *Communication & Business*, 25 April 1988, p. 47.
11 S. J. Paliwoda, *International Marketing*, Heinemann, London, 1986.
12 R. D. Pagan, 'Porter la lutte sur le terrain des détracteurs du capitalisme multinational', *Vers un développement solidaire*, Geneva, May 1983.
13 ibid.
14 A. Chetley, 'The power to change: lessons from the baby campaign', *IFDA Dossier*, no. 52, March-April 1986.
15 E. Coron, 'Coca-Cola fait roter les amis de la nature', *Libération*, 12 April 1988.
16 E. Fasel, in P. Lagadec, *États d'urgence: défaillances technologiques et déstabilisation sociale*, Paris, Seuil, 1988, p. 133. See also from the same author: *Major Technological Hazards, An Assessment of Industrial Disasters*, Pergamon, 1982; P. Shrivastava, *Bhopal, Anatomy of a Crisis*, Cambridge (Mass.), Ballinger, 1987.
17 C. Tortel, 'Des images anti-crise', *Le Monde*, 30 April 1988, Business Section ('Affaires'), p. 29.
18 N. Bellaiche, 'Les télés considèrent-elles les téléspectateurs comme des clients?', *Communication & Business*, 25 April 1988, p. 39.
19 D. Gallois, 'L'incommunication financière', *Le Monde des affaires*, 30 April 1988, p. 14.
20 J. Solomon, 'Customer is king', *Wall Street Journal (Europe)*, 18 July 1989, p. 1.
21 D. Pourquery, 'Lesieur éclaté', *Le Monde des affaires*, 5 March 1988, p. 4.

11 TOTAL COMMUNICATION

1 P. Kotler, *Marketing Management: Analysis, Planning and Control*, Prentice-Hall, New York, 1980, p. 351.
2 C. Quénard, 'La vraie action culturelle, c'est nous', *Autrement*, no. 18, April 1979, p. 179.
3 M. Assayas, 'Ces aînés n'ont rien à transmettre', *Libération*, 8 January 1988, p. 36.
4 See C. Bert, *Associations et communication. Nouvelles valeurs, nouvelles pratiques*, University de Haute-Bretagne, département sciences de l'information, Rennes, 1988.

5 D. Churchill, 'Government is big spender', *Financial Times*, 29 October 1987.
6 'Government advertising escalating in Britain', *Advertising Age/Europe*, 25 June 1979, p. 14.
7 Saatchi & Saatchi, *Annual Report Year Ending September 30*, 1985, p. 18.
8 M. Le Net, *Livre blanc sur la communication sociale adressé à M. le Premier Ministre*, Paris, ICOS, 1983.
9 Remarks quoted in the *Livre blanc*, op. cit.
10 B. Miège, 'Le pouvoir et les systèmes d'information: s'interroger sur les enjeux fondamentaux', *Actes du troisième congrès de la SFIC* (Société Française des Sciences de l'Information et Communication), May 1982.
11 J. Martine, 'Gouvernement et communication', *La Vie française*, 23 August 1982.
12 *Campaign*, 13 July 1990, pp. 21, 47.
13 J. Lendrevie, *L'Administration et les campagnes de persuasion par les mass media*, Paris, 1980, mimeographed document presented to the colloquium on 'Where is public management going?' (*Où va la gestion publique?*), Paris, 28–30 May 1980.
14 R. Laufer, *Commentaire sur la communication de J. Lendrevie*, at the colloquium mentioned above.
15 Y. Mourousi, 'Entretien avec A. Trampoglieri', Supplement to *Le Monde* ('Mairies 1986, Communiquez!'), 16 October 1986.
16 CNCL, Study under the direction of J. Baudrier, Paris, June 1987. Substantial extracts were published in *Dossiers de l'audiovisuel*, no. 17, January–February 1988 ('Télévision/Spectacle/Politique').
17 G. Bonnet, 'Pub politique à la TV', *Stratégies*, May 1987.

12 THE WEAPONS OF CRITICISM

1 In this connection see J. Williamson, *Decoding Advertisements, Ideology and Meaning in Advertising*, London, Marion Boyars, 1978.
2 R. Lellouche, 'Publicité, aliénation, éthique: quelques réflexions philosophiques sur les médias, la télévision et la publicité', *Télévision et Publicité*, Paris, IREP, 1987, p. 121.
3 See B. Whalen, 'Semiotics: an art or powerful marketing research tool', *Marketing News*, 13 May 1983. See also K. Christian Schröder, 'Marketing and semiotics: critical reflections on a marriage of paradigms', *Journal of Pragmatics*, 1989, no. 4.
4 S. Ewen, *Captains of Consciousness*, op. cit.
5 W. Haug, *Commodity Aesthetics, Ideology & Culture*, New York, International General Editions, 1987, p. 168. See also the same author's *Critique of Commodity Aesthetics*, Cambridge (England), Polity Press, 1986.
6 P. Baran and P. Sweezy, *Monopoly Capitalism, An Essay on the American Economic and Social Order*, New York, Monthly Review Press, 1966.
7 D. W. Smythe, 'Communications: blindspot of Western Marxism', *Canadian Journal of Political and Social Theory*, Autumn 1977, pp. 4–5.
8 See A. Mattelart and J. M. Piemme, *Télévision: enjeux sans frontières*, Presses Universitaires de Grenoble, 1980.
9 See especially A. Pigou, *Economics of Welfare*, London, 1938 (4th edn).
10 S. Tchakotine, *Le viol de foules par la propagande politique*, Paris, NRF-Gallimard, 1952 (original French edn 1939). Translated in English as *The Rape of the Masses*, New York, Alliance Book Co., 1940.
11 V. Packard, *The Hidden Persuaders*, Harmondsworth, Penguin, 1957.

12 J. K. Galbraith, *The New Industrial State*, Boston, Houghton Mifflin, 1967.
13 M. Foucault, *Discipline and Punish, The Birth of Prison*, trans. A. Sheridan, London, Penguin, 1977, p. 209.
14 M. de Certeau, *The Practice of Everyday Life*, op. cit.; H. Lefebvre, *Everyday Life in the Modern World*, trans. Rabinovitch, New Brunswick, N. J., Transaction Books, 1984.
15 By way of example, see the works already cited by V. Bernal Sahagun and E. Guinsberg. More recently, see J. G. Sinclair, *Images Incorporated: Advertising as Industry and Ideology*, London, Croom Helm, 1987.
16 P. Schwebig, *Les communications de l'entreprise, au delà de l'image*, Paris, McGraw-Hill, 1988, pp. 29-30.
17 On the USA-Canada free trade agreement as global communication project see: M. Raboy and P. A. Bruck (eds), *Communication Against and For Democracy*, Montreal, Black Rose Books, 1989; V. Mosco, *The Pay-Per Society*, Toronto, Garamond Press, 1989.
18 J. Habermas, 'The public sphere', *Communication and Class Stuggle*, A. Mattelart and S. Siegelaub (eds), New York, International General, 1979, vol. I.
19 J. Habermas, *L'Espace public*, Paris, Payot, 1978.
20 R. Laufer and C. Paradeise, *Le prince bureaucrate, Machiavel au pays du marketing*, Paris, Flammarion, 1982, p. 150.
21 F. Jameson, 'Postmodernism and the market', in *The Retreat of the Intellectuals*, R. Miliband and L. Panitch (eds), op. cit., pp. 107, 109.
22 E. B. Weiss, 'What's ahead for admen, starting third 100 years', op. cit., p. 125.
23 H. Henry, *Towards a Better Understanding of the Economics of Television Advertising, A Report for the ITV Association*, London, 1988, pp. 10-11.
24 G. Lipovetsky, *L'Ère du vide, Essai sur l'individualisme contemporain*, Paris, Gallimard, 1983.
25 *Proposition pour l'enseignement de l'avenir, Rapport des professeurs du Collège de France*, Paris, Minuit, 1985.
26 F. Guattari, 'Les nouveaux mondes du capitalisme', *Libération*, 22 December 1987, p. 5.

INDEX

INDEX

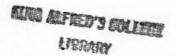